With Justice for Some

With Justice for Some

Victims' Rights in Criminal Trials

GEORGE P. FLETCHER

ADDISON-WESLEY PUBLISHING COMPANY
Reading, Massachusetts   Menlo Park, California   New York
Don Mills, Ontario   Wokingham, England   Amsterdam   Bonn
Sydney   Singapore   Tokyo   Madrid   San Juan
Paris   Seoul   Milan   Mexico City   Taipei

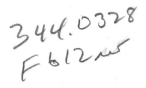

Many of the designations used by manufacturers and sellers to distinguish their products are claimed as trademarks. Where those designations appear in this book and Addison-Wesley was aware of a trademark claim, the designations have been printed in initial capital letters.

LIBRARY OF CONGRESS CATALOGING-IN-PUBLICATION DATA

Fletcher, George P.
    With justice for some : victims' rights in criminal trials / George P. Fletcher.
        p.   cm.
    Includes index.
    ISBN 0-201-62254-8
    1. Victims of crimes—Legal status, laws, etc.—United States.   2. Criminal procedure—United States.   3. Afro-Americans—Crimes against—United States.   4. Jews—Crimes against—United States.   5. Women—Crimes against—United States.   6. Gays—Crimes against—United States.   I. Title.
    KF9763.F58   1995
    344.73'03288—dc20
    [347.3043288]   94-32263
                                                                                                    CIP

Jacket design by Lawrence Ratzkin
Text design by Karen Savary
Set in 11-point Calisto by Pagesetters, Inc., Brattleboro, VT

1 2 3 4 5 6 7 8 9 10-MA-98979695
First printing, December 1994

For Daniela
"O wise young judge how I do honor thee!"

CONTENTS

With Justice for Some

The New Political Trial

THEY TAKE TO THE STREETS. YOUNG BLACK MEN SET FLAMES TO stores, hurl stones, and overturn cars at the corner of Florence and Normandy. The country watches the melee on television. Days later we know Los Angeles has suffered over 50 deaths and a billion dollars worth of property damage—the worst urban riot in America this century. Normally docile and retiring Hasidic men leave their houses of prayer and march stormily over the Brooklyn Bridge, chanting, "No justice, no peace." Another group, another time, another place: Thousands of gay men mass on Castro Street and march to City Hall. They burn eight police cars, smash the doors to the City Hall, and leave a record of gay consciousness in memory of Harvey Milk.

These are citizens telling us that they hurt. By expressing their pain in the streets, they are creating a new form of American political trial. When a million Communist subjects take to the streets in Leipzig, they have a political goal in mind: The regime must go. Blacks and Hispanics in Los Angeles, Jews in New York, gays in San Francisco—they have no specific objective for change. They mourn the denial of justice. The system is corrupt, but how should it change? Frustrated, embittered, without a political program beyond the demand for justice, they riot. In a free society, with abundant

1

modes of communication, the streets have become the primary vehicle for expressing their rage.

They are left raw by a jury verdict, a legal decision. But they were not on trial. Nor was anyone with whom they identify. It was not the prosecution of an African-American that sparked the burning of Los Angeles. It was not the conviction of a Jew or of a homosexual that led to their people's pain. Yet they think they are on trial, they feel that they are being judged, and this is new. A novel form of political trial has crystallized in the political life of the United States.

The anguish of the victims is expressed in the language of blood. Rhetorical questions inform the outrage: If Rodney King bleeds, does it not match the wounding of a white man? Is Jewish blood not as red as Gentile blood? Is there a double standard for shooting point-blank into the head of a gay man? Shylock spoke for all despised groups when he asked, "If you prick us, do we not bleed?"[1] Hasidic Jews found their protest echoed in the biblical passage they had just read in synagogue. As a jury of their neighbors turned its back on a brother, observant Jews heard from the pulpit: "What hast thou done? The voice of thy brother's blood crieth unto Me from the ground."[2]

In the new political trial, the victim is the focus of attention. We have come to think of these courtroom dramas by the names of the person shot or beaten. The name Rodney King will resonate in the history of American race relations long after the four police officers who bloodied him on March 3, 1991, are forgotten. The image of Yankel Rosenbaum lying on the hood of a car, bleeding to death, spitting in the face of his identified assassin, will remain in Jewish consciousness. And the 1979 prosecution of Harvey Milk's killer will be remembered as an event that signaled a new gay consciousness in America. Nor will we soon forget the other victims in these stories and the passions they ignited. Little Gavin Cato, lying under a station wagon at the corner of President Street and Utica Avenue, will long be associated with the Brooklyn insurgence and riot that began on the night of the accident, August 19, 1991. And Reginald

Denny, the white driver pulled from his truck on the night after the first Rodney King verdict, generated his own "case" and his own set of controversies about racial justice in the United States.

In the old form of political trial, the state sought to persecute a criminal defendant for its immediate goals. The show trials of the Communist regime, the sentencing of Julius and Ethel Rosenberg in response to the Korean War, the prosecution of the Chicago 8 (later down to 7) after the riots at the 1968 Democratic convention—these were all trials in which the state sought its objective by selecting some individuals to stand for an opposition it wanted to eliminate. By striking at a few, the embattled government hoped to exorcise the many. The political leaders of the state make the identification. They pick Nikolai Bukharin, they single out the Rosenbergs, they find the supposed leaders of the riot and make an example of them.

In the new political trial, the identification occurs on the side of the victim and comes not from the state but from the people. No official told the gays of San Francisco to identify with Harvey Milk after an angry Dan White walked into city hall and shot him as well as Mayor George Moscone. No one told the Jews of Crown Heights: This is one of you lying and dying on the hood of the car. No one told the blacks of Los Angeles: Watch the 81-second video tape and cry, for that is you lying beneath the torrent of baton blows. In the old political trial, the goals were set at the top. In the new form they spring from the roots, from the mean concrete of our urban culture.

Feminists have generated their own brand of political trial. They too have taken to the streets in an effort "to take back the night." Their targets have been the law of rape and the plight of women battered in the home. Rape trials, particularly of celebrity defendants like Mike Tyson and William Kennedy Smith, trigger the self-identification of women as a new political class. The trial of Mike Tyson became a drama larger than a case of intercourse at the borderline of consent. The victim, Desiree Washington, came center stage. Her dignity and the dignity of every woman became the issue. She became the vanguard of the "no means no" movement. A woman should be able to go willingly to a man's hotel room and then say no: I am not here for sex. Women's sexual favors cannot be taken for granted.

The feminist revolt against the abuse of women is reshaping the law, not only of consent in rape cases but of self-defense in cases of domestic violence. The law now intrudes into sexual and marital relationships that once were thought not to be the law's business. Trials that raise these questions become the testing ground for the committed woman's sense of self. She is on trial when the rape victim asserts that she said no and meant it. She is in the dock when her sister strikes back against torture in the home and is then prosecuted for murder. These, too, are part of the movement from the bottom up. They contribute to the shape of the new political trial.

Oddly, there is no single word in our language to refer to this group—gays, blacks, Jews, and women—who have too long suffered a legal system indifferent to their dignity and their rights. They are not all "ethnic groups." They are not all "minorities." Yet they have in common their disempowerment, their neglected voices, their disadvantaged position in American society. They as well as other prominent groups—Native Americans, Asian-Americans, Hispanics—have never sent one of their kind to the White House. Though they number some of the most talented people in the United States, not one of them has been seen fit to be president or vice president. At various times in our history, they have all experienced social and institutional exclusion. They are Americans in the shadows.

They seek their dignity in the heat of controversy. They fight back in the courts. When the frustration becomes intense, they take to the streets. I take to the pen.

This is an angry book. I am angry at my fellow lawyers for not being willing, in the aftermath of the first Rodney King verdict on April 29, 1992, to rethink the foundations of our legal system. Lawyers love to blame imaginary targets. A defense lawyer walks into criminal court and argues on the implicit assumption: "Someone in this room is guilty, and it is not my client." As a profession we blame the 12 men and women on the jury in Simi Valley for their biased verdict. We accuse the predominantly black and Hispanic jury that acquitted Lemrick Nelson, the youth charged with stabbing Yankel Rosenbaum. We fault the experts who generated a case for mitigating and partially excusing Dan White's killing of George Moscone and Harvey Milk. The system is just fine. It is particular individuals who go awry.

The jurors in these cases find their lives in ruin. In good faith they listen to the arguments and follow the judge's instructions as well as they can understand the arcane language of the law. Yet the jurors who mitigated the crime of Dan White, the suburbanites from Simi Valley who acquitted the four Los Angeles police officers, the people of color in Brooklyn who said they had a reasonable doubt about Lemrick Nelson's guilt—their lives are affected forever. They suffer incessant media attention; they internalize the public's hostility toward their verdicts. No wonder that the tendency in the new political trials is to keep the identity of the jurors secret and, as in the second Rodney King trial, to whisk them away by helicopter as soon as they reach a verdict. The jurors are but the messengers of a defective legal system. We may not like the verdicts they bring back, but they are not to blame.

Perceiving the defects of the system is not so easy. In the aftermath of the Los Angeles riots the American Bar Association quickly assembled a blue-ribbon task force to recommend changes in our system of criminal justice.[3] Their proposals are pap: Don't transfer cases to communities with low numbers of minority residents. Send more pro bono lawyers in to represent ghetto residents. But these ideas tinker at the edges of a legal system rent by structural defects. The superficiality of the ABA report, the thinking of the best and the brightest in the legal profession, testifies to the gravity of the problem.

Most lawyers are by nature conservative. They revere the past. They master the law as it is and have an investment in keeping it that way. They know virtually nothing about the philosophical foundations of their system, and they are parochial about alternatives tried successfully in other legal systems. If something works abroad, it is suspect; it is not the way things are done here.

It is time that we start thinking about foundational issues: about our attitudes toward fair trials and criminal punishment, about what we can fairly expect of jury verdicts, about the proper role of victims in criminal trials. We are accustomed to say that the People prosecute crime. But who are the People in a multicultural society? The starting point for radical thinking is the recognition that we face a new phenomenon in American criminal justice. The victims of discrimination are now organized. Blacks, Jews, gays, women—they will no longer tolerate second-class status. They seek vindication for past grievances in the trials that take place today. The violence and protest, the anger and contempt—all are the products of a legal system that has yet to grasp the forces of the new political trial.

In this book I ask for a justification for institutions and practices we take for granted. I consider alternatives tried in Western Europe and even in the former Communist countries of Eastern Europe. I question whether the American system is the best in the world. In the end I propose solutions, ten specific solutions listed in the last chapter. They range from changing the role of the victim in the criminal trial and restructuring the jury to altering the impact of experts on the moral issues of criminal responsibility.

A single thread ties together the ten solutions. It is the thread that ties the victim to others in relationships of trust and respect. It is the thread that comes undone when a violent crime occurs. Then, when the social fabric rips, the victim is alone. The minimal task of the criminal trial, I argue, is to stand by victims, to restore their dignity, to find a way for them to think of themselves, once again, as men and women equal to all others. Convicting and punishing the guilty is our way of expressing solidarity with those who have fallen prey to the pervasive violence of American life. When we fail to act, when we let the guilty go untouched, we betray the trust that enables people to live together in peaceful interdependence. When a crime is left unsanctioned, the government—and all of us responsible for the government—become complicitous in the evil. The victim's blood is on our hands.

Solidarity with victims represents a new way of thinking about criminal punishment. Thus an alternative way emerges in the centuries-old debate between those who advocate deterrence of future offenders and those who yearn for retribution by making the punishment fit past crimes. Each of these traditional views has something to offer, but none adequately accounts for punishment in a time when deterrence seems not to work and the promise of abstract retribution rings hollow. The imperative of punishing the guilty springs not from our personal duties to high ideals but from our relationships with the humbled victims in our midst.

The argument begins slowly. I invite the reader to join me in a study of specific cases, big cases, the high-profile events of the newspapers. As the lawyer in the common law tradition works with precedents, I start with case histories grouped around four classes of victims—gays, blacks, Jews, and women. On the whole, these are cases of failure, cases where the system has failed to hear the victim. In each of these trial tales, a lesson for reform emerges from the day-to-day details of sparring in court. The voice of the neglected has something to teach us about seeking justice for all.

CHAPTER ONE

Gays

"Let the bullets that rip through my brain smash
through every closet door in the nation."
—*Harvey Milk in a tape-recorded last will and testament.*[1]

IMAGINE A VIDEOTAPE PEELING OFF THESE STAGES OF IMPEND-
ing violence: An intense-looking 32-year-old white male arrives by
car at the main door to city hall on Polk Street where a metal
detector confronts all who seek entrance. As the young man steps
out of the car, the driver moves on and the visitor walks around to the
McAllister Street side of the building. He opens a window near
ground level and steps over the sill and into the building. Someone
calls out to him to stop and identify himself. A brief conversation
ensues and the young man, an insider who can pass scrutiny, continues on his way.

Within a minute or two, he arrives at the largest office in the
building, the mayor's office, and after about ten minutes the mayor
invites him in. The two men enter a private sitting room behind the
main office. Then: a brief conversation, a drink, and four gun shots,
the last two almost point-blank to the head of the dying mayor. The
gunman steps into the hall. There is one live cartridge left in his .38
revolver. He reloads from the ten extra rounds he has in his pocket
and proceeds directly to the other side of the building, room 237. He

puts a key into the door and, as he enters, a young woman approaches him and tells him that a supervisor, an elected official, wants to talk to him. He says he'll be back in a few minutes. He finds another supervisor in his office and invites him to step into an office across the hall. They close the door. A very brief conversation precedes another round of gunfire, this time five shots at close range. A second man falls dead. The killer finds the keys to the car that brought him to the building and flees the scene. An hour later, as the city begins to grieve, the assassin calls his wife from a church. Together they walk to a police station and he turns himself in and confesses his crime.

The scene at San Francisco City Hall on November 27, 1978, could not have been clearer had it been on videotape. If ever there was a scenario of killing in cold blood, that imaginary video would capture it. We need not know names. We need not know that the two victims were leading figures in San Francisco politics, Mayor George Moscone and Supervisor Harvey Milk. Here we see a man bent on killing. He avoids detection of his concealed weapon by entering city hall by way of a ground-floor window. He shoots the mayor without apparent provocation, without any apparent need to defend himself. There is no evidence of a struggle, no sign that the mayor was armed. The killer methodically reloads his gun and walks directly to the site of the second killing. He is no madman inclined to shoot everyone in sight, for he abstains from aggression against Diane Feinstein's assistant, who stops him in the hall, and goes for his second target, Harvey Milk. There follow five more shots, after he takes care to usher his victim to a private place. This is a scenario of murder, and we need not know much more about the killer to be convinced that he should pay the full legal penalty for spilling the blood of two human beings.

Six months later the People of California prosecute Daniel James White for first degree murder, a charge that carries a potential sentence of death in the San Quentin gas chamber. The People* are

---

* When capitalized, "People" refers to the prosecution; when not capitalized, "people" has its usual meaning.

convinced that he is guilty, and even liberals like Supervisor Carol Ruth Silver, ordinarily sympathetic to the plight of the criminally accused, want to "throw the book" at Dan White. Imagining the sequence of events at city hall on the morning of November 27 is the only case one needs to establish guilt.

Yet crime—even the obvious crime of Dan White—troubles us. We want to know why it happened. The search begins for a motive, an engine of action that can explain why a man might kill two distinguished citizens of his city. The background circumstances start to become relevant. We look for a context that will enable us to integrate the horror of violence into a world we can better understand.

Mindless violence haunted San Francisco that month. The 900 cult suicides in Jonestown, Guyana had dominated the news for a week as residents mourned the death of those Bay Area followers of Jim Jones. Death by violence, even violence to self, invites more of the same. If 900 could die out of their faith in a guru gone mad, two more deaths were not beyond imagining. The world came unhinged in those days before and after Thanksgiving 1978, and murder came within the grasp of Dan White's mind.

The killer had reasons for striking out violently. Dan White too was a supervisor, one of the 12 elected in November 1977 under a new plan that enabled districts within the city to elect their own supervisors. The new system of direct and local representation brought new voices to the Board of Supervisors. White, with no credentials other than having served both as a city police officer and fire fighter, won a seat in District 8, a lower-middle-class blue-collar neighborhood. Gordon Lau represented the Chinese neighborhood. Carol Ruth Silver came from the Mission district after having won the support of gays, women, and Hispanics. And Harvey Milk joined the Board from District 5, the Castro, the neighborhood of mostly gay men and lesbians, many newcomers to San Francisco, now linked in the public mind with the City itself.

Dan White took a dissenting position in board politics. San Franciscans were ahead of the nation in adopting an ordinance that prohibited discrimination against homosexuals in employment. Harvey Milk celebrated the ordinance as an invitation to gay men and women to come out of the closet without fear. White was the only member of the Board opposed to the measure. He tried, in addition, to stop the annual Gay Day parade on grounds of public indecency and nudity. From one point of view, he stood for "family values." As Carol Ruth Silver recalls, he was a kind of Dan Quayle ahead of his time. In the view of other supervisors, he was homophobic, a reactionary, a man clearly out of sync with the new beat driving San Francisco.

The dissonance of politics took its toll on Dan White. He felt alone on many issues. His salary of less than $10,000 hardly compensated him for the long hours he put in at city hall. The scuttlebutt was that Dan and his wife could not make ends meet. She was pregnant and had to give up her teaching job. Their fast-food stand on Pier 39 was not doing well. As the bills piled up, Dan did what many people do under frustrating circumstances: He decided to resign. On Friday, November 10, he submitted his resignation in writing to Mayor Moscone.

After pondering his decision over the weekend and hearing from his supporters in District 8, White changed his mind. He went to Moscone and told him that he wanted to withdraw his resignation. We do not know for sure what Moscone said in reply, but White heard a promise of support and a commitment to reappoint him as the supervisor of District 8. Yet on November 20 the mayor wrote him a letter denying he had promised to reappoint him. White began to feel betrayed. He tried to rally the residents of his district. He sought signatures on a petition and received a few thousand gestures of support (the press reported a lower number). One poll showed that 75% of the district voters had favorable feelings toward him. Yet Harvey Milk intervened and urged the mayor, for political reasons, not to make the reappointment. On some issues, such as the location of drug rehabilitation centers, the Board was split six votes to five, with the conservatives holding the edge. Milk urged the appointment of a liberal, which would change the balance of power.

Dan tried the law. He brought a suit to enjoin the mayor from reappointing anyone else to his seat. His legal argument rested on a technicality: He should have submitted his letter not to the mayor but to the clerk of the Board. On Friday, November 24, the day after Thanksgiving, he had a hearing in his suit for an injunction. Failing to get the relief he expected, he returned home alone, obviously dejected. His wife had left to attend a wedding in the Midwest. On Sunday evening, November 26, after two days of brooding at home with his son Charlie, White heard from a journalist that he would not be reappointed. His wife had returned, but he slept on the couch, for fear, he said, of disturbing her. After she left the next morning, he got up, shaved, dressed in a business suit, and set forth, with his aide driving, to encounter the hostile powers in city hall. He decided to take his .38 special and ten extra cartridges with him.

When we add the personal animosity that White felt for Moscone and Milk, the murders become comprehensible. We can fit the killings into a mold of anger-plus-revenge that rings familiar to us. Understanding the wellsprings of the action seems hardly to lessen the crime. Yet when those wellsprings are interpreted as mental illness, the defense gains a foothold. They can parlay an understanding of the actor's motivation into a case for mitigating the crime from murder to manslaughter and thereby eliminate the risk of the death penalty. It was the success of this defense that outraged the gay community and made the Dan White case the first in our series of new political trials.

For the gays of San Francisco, the slaying of Harvey Milk was much worse than an ordinary killing. Harvey Milk was gay pride personified. He ran for office as a committed homosexual. He celebrated his victory as an expression *of* gay power, won *by* the gay vote, and *for* gay interests—as well as for the interests of all threatened minorities and the public at large. There was almost something prophetic in the way this Jewish transplant from Long Island spoke of gays as the emblem of all minorities. If gays lost their rights, who knew who would be next? "Look what happened in Germany," Harvey would say from time to time.[2]

When State Senator John Briggs sought, in an electoral initiative dubbed Proposition 6, to ban homosexual teachers from the state's schools, Harvey Milk led the uphill fight against the myth that gay men are more inclined than heterosexual men to abuse children. In the end, Ronald Reagan, Jimmy Carter, and even Dan White came out against the initiative as a threat to civil liberties. When in early November 1978, the California public voted down the initiative by an overwhelming majority, Harvey Milk was at the height of his political power, and Dan White at the nadir of his.

There is no evidence that Dan White killed Harvey Milk *because* Milk was gay. There were many votes on the Board for gay rights, including those of Carol Ruth Silver and Gordon Lau. Yet White chose Milk and not the others. True, Milk had opposed his reappointment. And Milk was the supervisor most clearly identified with the gay cause. But this does not make the killing an expression of homophobia. Whatever the subtleties of White's motives, the gay community felt the killing to be an attack on the gains they had made in their struggle for public acceptance. It was worse, in their minds, than killing the mayor, however decent a man he was. The slaying of Harvey Milk not only extinguished a life: it claimed symbolic victims in the culture at large.

Thus the trial of Dan White loomed in the minds of the gay community as an opportunity for self-vindication. These dissidents from mainstream life, these men and women who knew that the dominant society regarded them as deviant, now took refuge in the processes of indictment and prosecution. They sought comfort in the possibility that the system might work. Justice would be done. Dan White would get what he deserved. The jury would convict him of a double murder, and if he was not sentenced to death, as permitted under California law, he would receive at least a life sentence.

That is not the way things turned out. After an 11 day trial in May 1979, the jury convicted White not of murder but of the lesser crime of manslaughter. Under California's new determinate sentencing law, he could receive no more than four years of jail time on each of two counts of manslaughter. His sentence was in fact seven years and eight months. With time off for good behavior, he could be out of jail in less than five years.

The mitigation of Dan White's condemnation set off delayed shock waves. San Francisco had reacted to the killings of November 27 with a show of peaceful solidarity. Gay and straight, black and white, men and women, all marched shoulder to shoulder in a candlelight parade of mourning. Market Street overflowed with grieving, from the Castro to city hall. There was no anger, only sorrow. Yet on May 21, 1979, the night of the verdict, the disappointment doubled. Feeling betrayed by a system they thought might work, about 5,000 gay men gathered to release their rage in the city's face. They began breaking windows, overturning police cars, and setting them ablaze. This night of violence came to be known as the White Night. There was no turning back. Gay men would no longer tolerate being treated as less than full and equal citizens.

There was no doubt in their minds that the "gay" factor had made a difference. Killing a gay man was somehow all right. As the police sometimes turned a blind eye after gay bashers did their dirty work, the court and jury had seemingly turned their backs on the memory of Harvey Milk. As Jim Elliot, a labor organizer and friend of Harvey's, summed it up: If Dan White had merely killed George Moscone, he would surely have been guilty of murder "and been in San Quentin the rest of his life."[3] But killing a gay man somehow made the entire episode less than egregious. In Elliot's words: "But sad to say, I think there are a lot of people in this world that still think that if you kill a gay, you're doing a service to society."[4]

Though White's defense lawyer, Douglas R. Schmidt, never explicitly attacked the dignity of homosexuals, he played on the theme from the outset. In his opening statement to the jury, he skipped over Moscone as victim and concentrated on Harvey Milk: "Dan White came from a vastly different lifestyle than Harvey Milk. Harvey Milk was a homosexual leader and politician. . . ."[5]

Schmidt went on to say that as a supervisor White sought to defend the "traditional values of family and home."[6] He could have

developed White's political and moral profile by contrasting it with-
Moscone's liberalism. Yet contrasting White's lifestyle with that of
an Italian-American populist mayor would have had little rhetorical
value. The choice was clear: Harvey Milk should be the point of
reference. The implication was that gay men rejected the traditional
values that many, if not all the jurors shared. Of course, this tactic
might have backfired if the jury had included one or two gay men or
lesbians. But, in ways that we have yet to explore, Schmidt had
managed to keep gays off the jury. The jurors were sympathetic to a
covert attack on "the gay lifestyle." And if they thought ill of those
outside the mainstream of "family and home," they might well have
had subconsciously shared the anti-gay sentiments sensed by Jim
Elliot in the labor circles he knew well.

However anti-gay sentiments might have affected the course of
the Dan White trial, the official line of the law is that all homicide
victims are of equal dignity. There is no way that Schmidt could have
argued openly that Milk's blood was less red than that of the jurors.
There is no way to institutionalize second-class citizenship in the
law. The path of argument must seek a legitimate home. And pur-
poseful discrimination against gay victims is not legitimate.

The law has its ways of deflecting the public's passion to blame
murderers for their crimes. In the Dan White case, the particular
technique was to channel the debate into a finely tuned analysis of
White's mental health. If some kind of argument about mental
illness could carry the jury, White would have a chance for the
lighter crime of manslaughter rather than the charge of first-degree
murder. How and why these arguments about mental illness became
relevant in California, and how expert psychiatrists acquired power
to influence the jury, is the story I now tell.

Blaming and Understanding

The outbreak of violence in front of San Francisco City Hall on May
11, 1979, expressed, in one boiling moment of passion, a dispute that
had long been simmering. The fight was not just about gays and their

rights but about a broader issue: Whether common people can trust their own instincts about when and why criminals deserve punishment. The gays said in effect: We trust our own judgment. We know whom to blame for killing one of ours. We can see in our mind's eye the sequence of events leading up to the killing of Milk and Moscone, and if there was ever a heinous and despicable killing, this is it.

For too long, the professional legal culture had been skeptical of its powers of moral condemnation. Judges and lay juries became more and more reluctant to blame the obvious evils that came before them. With the rise of a self-confident psychiatric profession in the last 50 years, judges and commentators on the law began to think that they no longer had the tools or the wit to understand why people commit violent crimes. What happened on the surface of things, what one could imagine taking place in a violent crime, was not what "really" happened. For to know and understand the truth of what happened, one needs to consider the inner life of the suspect. One must turn to his mental state, her mental condition, his psychological history. The wisdom of the times became understanding crime not as an expression of evil but as the acting out of mental illness.

Psychiatrists became the recognized experts of the mind. Crime, it seems, has something to do with a mind gone awry. Rational people, normal people, do not commit crimes. And so we cannot judge, evaluate, and punish crime without expertise about deviant minds. The result: a gradual shift of power over crime and punishment from public institutions to private psychiatrists. This unwitting "privatization" of our collective moral judgment meant that paid psychiatric experts were becoming the key players in our trials of guilt and innocence. In the trial of Dan White, as we shall see, the vast majority of the testimony came from a half-dozen paid experts who examined the defendant and opined about his inner life.

The danger in this trend toward private expertise is captured in the French aphorism, *Tout comprendre, c'est tout pardonner*. The more you understand why someone commits a crime, the less likely you are to blame him. The more you locate Dan White's deeds in the context of his psychological history, the more you lose the passion to stigmatize his acts as evil and punish him as an expression of our collective disapproval. In the 1950s and 1960s the leading voices of criminal law sought, as far as possible, to deemphasize blaming and to bring psychiatric expertise into the courtroom. In this transformation, crime became "deviant behavior," and punishment became "treatment." The function of trial was no longer to seek the facts and condemn evil, but to understand the mind of the suspect.

The bias in favor of the psychiatric understanding of crime exploded in the Dan White case. The night of violence, the protest against the conviction for manslaughter and the light sentence, reasserted the common man's capacity to condemn crime as an evil assault on human dignity. The gays who sought justice for Harvey Milk had no interest in the inner workings of the killer's mind. White acted in cold blood. He executed a double killing of two men at the heart of community life. His criminality lay bare on the facts known to everybody.

It is no accident that the confrontation between blaming the criminal and understanding the criminal came to the fore in a homicide case. Over the centuries, the law of homicide has evolved into a finely tuned system for gauging the evil of the killing. Homicide is unique in many ways. The sin and crime of taking life represent a secular harm with religious overtones. Virtually all other crimes against persons or against property may be countered by the victim's consent. Theft, with consent, is just another business deal. Rape, with consent, is a harmless, perhaps loving act of voluntary intercourse. But consent has no role to play in justifying the taking of human life. The assumption is that our lives are not ours to trade or relinquish. Henrik Ibsen brought his wit to this cultural assumption in *Peer Gynt*: Our lives belong to the Buttonmoulder, and only He can determine when our time has come.

Homicide typically occurs in the context of ongoing human relationships. Criminologists report that in the United States roughly one-quarter of all homicides come by the hand of strangers.[7] The typical case resembles Dan White's slaying of Harvey Milk and

George Moscone. The killings derive from disputes in the family, between lovers, on the job, and from disciplinary actions or turf battles in underworld relationships. The resort to the gun or the knife springs from the interaction between victim and slayer.

As the common law took shape, it began to distinguish among three levels of criminal homicide, each level reflecting a different degree of input on the side of the victim. The victim has maximum input in cases of his aggression against a defender. If the defender had retreated to the point at which his back was "against the wall" and he had no further means of evasion, his slaying in self-defense was excused—wrongful and unlawful but exempt from ordinary criminal punishment. It was called *se defendendo*, and at least until some time in the 19th century the slayer suffered the forfeiture of his property as a sanction. Because he was not to blame for his act of self-preservation, however, his life was spared.

For the first few centuries after the Norman Conquest, the defenses to homicide were based on *se defendendo* plus another possible excuse called "inevitable accident." If neither of these grounds for excusable homicide was present, the defendant was guilty of murder and was subject to execution. It is worth noting, however, that if the slayer was a raving lunatic (under the power of the moon—"luna-tic"), if he behaved like a "wild beast," he fell outside the power of the courts and directly under the jurisdiction of the Crown, which could deal with him in a way to protect public safety.

By the end of the 16th century, the common law had worked a second major refinement in the levels of culpability for homicide. If the victim and the slayer inflicted blows on each other, or if the victim had openly committed adultery with the slayer's spouse, the killing was regarded as provoked and was punishable as manslaughter rather than as murder. These are cases in which the victim contributes partially to her own demise. He participates in a fight; she commits adultery with the slayer's husband. These are cases of killing, it was said, without "malice aforethought." The punishment for manslaughter was less severe than the gallows. Before the rise of the modern prison system in the 19th century, branding the thumb was a frequent sanction.

The highest level of homicide, called murder, materialized in malice aforethought—malice, for short. There could be no malice if there was an inevitable accident or necessity of self-preservation. More importantly, there was no malice if the killing was provoked. Thus if the killing was intentional (and not in self-defense), the question of murder turned entirely on the presence or absence of provocation. In the second half of the 18th century, Blackstone could sum up the entire law of homicide in one neat principle: Killing another human being "amounts to murder unless where *justified* . . . , *excused* on the ground of accident or self-preservation; or *alleviated* into manslaughter. . . ."[8] The first category covered executions and a later version of killing in self-defense, the second category encompassed homicide by accident and *se defendendo*, and the third category focused on the inquiry whether the killing was provoked and therefore without malice.

The refined perception of how killers interact with their victims distinguishes homicide from other crimes. In other areas of criminal law, where victims contribute to their own misfortune, we resist tempering the crime by laying some of the blame on the contributing victim. There is no mitigation for auto theft if the owner carelessly leaves the keys in his car, no defense to a charge of mugging that the tourist went walking in the park at night. There is no legal mitigation for rape if the victim engages in a sexually provocative come-on. Yet there is mitigation for homicide on the basis of the victim's actions toward the killer.

This distinctive feature of homicide lends itself to differing interpretations. One line of thought is that homicide is alleviated or mitigated on the basis of the victim's actual contribution to his or her own death. If the victim does part of the deed, a lesser responsibility falls on the actor who pulls the trigger or thrusts the knife. The other line of interpretation shifts the focus from the actual interaction between the parties to the internal experience of the killer. His subjective perception and reaction to the provocation become the pivotal points of judgment. The argument is that if the killer experiences excitement, a flush of passion, a momentary loss of control, he or she is less to blame for the act of killing.

This turning inward, this shift in focus toward the inner life of the killer, was but the first step in the historical process that peaked in the manslaughter verdict for Dan White. Other refinements of the law reinforced the idea that the inner life of the defendant should determine the degree of his crime and the severity of his punishment. For example, the threat of capital punishment has always loomed in the background of murder trials. A conviction for murder would expose the defendant to the death penalty; a conviction for manslaughter would spare his life. In 1794 Pennsylvania introduced a refinement that quickly spread to the rest of the country. If the killing was "deliberate or premeditated," it could still be called murder in the second degree but be exempt from the death penalty. The new form, or grade, of murder became murder in the first degree, with malice plus premeditation *or* deliberation. In California's revision of this definition, the requirement for "murder one" becomes tightened. In the Dan White case, the prosecution had the burden of proving beyond a reasonable doubt that the killing was "willful, deliberate, *and* premeditated."[9]

The language of these "mental states" fogs the lens of anyone who tries to perceive clearly whether a murder warrants more serious or less serious punishment. No one quite knows what the terms "malice aforethought" and "premeditation" mean. So lawyers invent turgid phrases in an attempt to capture the elusive distinctions among levels of homicide. The common law finds "malice" when "the circumstances attending the killing show an abandoned and malignant heart."[10] This language appears to us today, in the flush of our scientific advances, as too quaint for the serious undertaking of courtroom judgment. We are inclined now toward a sociological construction of evil. Malice, California lawyers began to say in the 1950s, consists in bad motives, such as a "base, anti-social motive" or, with a little more condemnatory verve, in whether a motive "reflects a wanton disregard for human life."[11] Thus one phrase replaces another, and juries are left pondering what they should be deciding when they retire to deliberate guilt or innocence.

The underlying question in evaluating a homicide is actually very simple. To what extent was the killer acting from within rather than under the pressure of external circumstances? To what extent was he or she self-actuating or autonomous in choosing to take the life of another human being? The more self-actuating the killer's actions, the more he or she is to blame and the more severe the punishment deserved. If the victim threatened the life of the slayer, then, of course, the killing is minimally autonomous. The killer, with his back to the wall, has no choice but to kill. Accordingly, common law courts concluded that this was an excused killing that should be sanctioned at most by the forfeiture of property. An accidental killing, without fault, was equally beyond the control of the actor and was therefore treated in the same way.

One notch up the scale of self-actuation, the courts had to evaluate whether the victim had provoked the homicidal attack. If provoked, the killing was merely manslaughter and was punished less severely. And if there was no provocation, the killing was said to be with "malice aforethought." The states of "pre-meditation" and "deliberation" added a point on the scale higher than malice by underscoring thinking and reflection prior to the action.

The picture that comes into focus is this: The most culpable form of homicide is the one that reflects planning, thinking, and calculated action. The least culpable form is the one that occurs with minimal input of the killer's personality: the killing occurs spontaneously, under the heat of passion, under the pressure of circumstances, triggered by external factors. Dan White's killing bore many of the signs of a calculated, planned killing. He took his gun and ten extra shells with him on the morning of November 27. He sometimes carried a gun for self-protection, but he had not done so during the preceding month. He entered the building surreptitiously. He shot Moscone four times, twice at point-blank range. He reloaded the gun. He directly and unhesitatingly found the second person he regarded as having wronged him and shot him five times. It is not surprising, then, that Assistant District Attorney Thomas F. Norman would have regarded this as the clearest case of murder he had prosecuted in over 20 years.[12]

Yet the gradual attachment of the courts to the inner psychological self would deprive these signs of Dan White's calculation and planning of their incriminating power. The trend began in the effort to reform the insanity defense to be more hospitable to the supposed wisdom of psychiatrists about human behavior. A few words of the ensuing history are in order.

Prior to the mid-19th century, lunatics—like witches—were thought to be a special class of people. In the 18th century, they were compared to brutes and "wild beasts" and treated generally as incapable of evil. The turning point in the evolution of the defense was M'Naghten's case, which was not an appellate case in the traditional sense, but rather a speech by Chief Justice Tindal to the House of Lords in 1843.[13] The legislative branch was appalled by the acquittal of Daniel M'Naghten after he killed a bystander in an attempt to assassinate Prime Minister Robert Peel. The legislators had called the chief justice to testify about the proper understanding of the insanity defense, and in his speech he set forth the famous test requiring knowledge of "the difference between right and wrong" that became the standard approach to insanity in English and U.S. courts.

The M'Naghten test linked individual responsibility to the actor's cognitive understanding of "the nature and quality of the act he was doing" and "if he did know it, [whether] he did not know he was doing what was wrong."[14] The question is not whether the actor knows the difference between right and wrong in the abstract, but whether he understands that the particular act of killing is wrong. But this is hardly enough to establish insanity; if it were, any sociopath, any person who was totally out of touch with the morality of his time, would be exempt from punishment. An additional component in the test is whether this defect in understanding derives from "a defect of reason, [or] a disease of the mind."[15] Thus enter the modern idea of mental illness and the profession charged with knowing about diseases of the mind—the alienists, now called psychiatrists.

In the period after the Second World War, when the mental health professions came into increasing prominence, judges, academics, and doctors relentlessly criticized the M'Naghten test for having too constricted a view of the way in which mental illness might affect an unbalanced individual's capacity to commit a crime. The supposed defect in the M'Naghten test is that it focuses exclusively on cognition—on what the actor believed—rather than on his capacity for self-control. One way to broaden the inquiry was to include some control-related corollary in the definition of insanity, such as the "irresistible impulse" test.[16] Anyone compelled by an impulse could be excused. An elegant, radical reformulation of the question burst upon the legal scene when federal appellate judge David Bazelon posed the test for insanity as whether the act was "the product of a mental disease or defect."[17] In a more modest and more influential program of reform, the American Law Institute proposed rewriting state statutes by substituting the concept of "appreciation" for "knowledge" in the M'Naghten test and, in addition, to excuse those persons who did appreciate the wrongfulness of their actions but "could not conform [their] conduct to the requirements of law."[18]

The subtle notion of appreciation invited psychiatrists to reflect on the way the accused's mental condition rendered him unbalanced, deprived him of normal affect, and prevented him from understanding violence as ordinary people do. The additional clause on conforming "conduct to the requirements of law" permitted the experts to testify on the way in which the accused's mental condition undermined his volition and drove him to commit his crime. The California courts took a slightly different tack in expanding the M'Naghten rule to make psychiatrists feel comfortable testifying about whether the accused was legally capable of committing the crime. In 1967, the courts added the word "understanding" to the traditional rule so that the jury could find the defendant insane if he was "incapable of knowing or understanding the nature and quality of his act" or "incapable of knowing or understanding that his act was wrong."[19] It should have been easy for any psychiatrist to direct his testimony to the accused's affect and his "understanding" that he was doing the wrong thing. By 1978, however, even this latitude seemed insufficiently broad, and the state supreme court adopted the more accommodating test of the American Law Institute.[20]

With regard to expert testimony on the degree of an offender's guilt—whether for murder or manslaughter—California became the most receptive state. As early as 1949, the state supreme court held that psychiatric testimony was admissible to show that a prisoner charged with assaulting a guard with malice did not have the "malice" necessary for conviction.[21] Opposition to the death penalty played a covert role in the decision, for had the defendant been found guilty he might have died in the gas chamber. Once embarked on this path of hospitality toward mental health experts, however, the courts could not halt the trend. By 1966, the judges had developed the extra-statutory defense of diminished capacity, which permitted the defendant in every murder prosecution, backed up by paid psychiatrists, to seek a conviction for manslaughter.

In the course of this development, the courts invested new meaning in the concept of malice. At common law, as I have noted, malice was synonymous with a killing that was neither excused, justified, nor mitigated on grounds of provocation. It was a negative concept, established by the absence of a good reason to think that the killing was less than fully heinous. Now, in the burgeoning culture of postwar California, malice became an affirmative concept, full of rich, judgmental ideas. Note this portion of the definition of malice that the court gave the jury in the Dan White case:

MALICE AFORETHOUGHT—DEFINED[22]

Malice is implied when the killing results from an act involving a high degree of probability that it will result in death, which act is done *for a base, antisocial purpose* and with a *wanton disregard for human life* by which is meant *an awareness of a duty imposed by law not to commit such acts* followed by the commission of the forbidden act despite that awareness. . . . The mental state constituting malice aforethought does not necessarily require any ill will or hatred of the person killed.

Aforethought does not imply deliberation or lapse of considerable time. It only means that the required mental state must precede rather than follow the act.[23]

There is almost nothing in this definition that appeals to common sense. Malice here is not the same thing as malice in real life. "Aforethought" here does not mean beforehand. The message is clear. Malice is a term of art, a lexicon for insiders. To wade through the technical terms, you need a guide and the guide is the expert who testifies at trial about whether the defendant had malice or not.

The rise of diminished capacity in California—the defense that reduces murder to manslaughter—dovetails with the best-intentioned efforts toward criminal law reform. In 1958 the American Law Institute, in its enormously influential Model Penal Code, adopted a similar approach to distinguishing the two grades of homicide. Though the Code's purpose is to abolish the concept of malice, it retains a version of provocation that rests squarely on the killer's experience of being disturbed. It is no longer critical that there be some objective threat from the victim or even from a third party. Provocation becomes an inner distortion. It is now called "extreme mental or emotional disturbance."[24] The only qualification on the kind of disturbance that will mitigate a criminal homicide is that there be "a reasonable explanation or excuse."[25] With five psychiatrists testifying on his behalf, Dan White could presumably have generated "a reasonable explanation" for his killing two men.

Opening the door to psychiatric testimony on malice and provocation concealed a paradox in the interface between law and psychiatry. The entire structure of the criminal law assumes that normal individuals can control themselves and choose whether to violate the law. Not all psychiatrists share this assumption. Many nurture a professional bias in favor of scientific determinism. Without much philosophical rigor, they believe that a person's background and education (and perhaps genes) determine his actions.

A good example of this bias surfaces in the testimony offered in People v. Dan White. The defense called psychiatrist Dr. Jerry Jones as one of its five mental health experts. On cross-examination, the prosecutor Thomas Norman probed Jones's views about the nature of the choices White made in the course of taking his gun, proceeding to city hall, entering through the window, and finally pulling the trigger nine times. Jones's determinist philosophy came to the fore. He insisted: "A person cannot make choices. It's not possible to make choices. . . ."[26] Norman let these remarks pass, but they came up again in this illuminating passage:

Q. Was he at that time capable, just prior to the shooting, of making a decision: Shall I shoot him or shall I not? . . . I am asking you if he was capable?

A. I thought we already decided you can't not make a decision.

Q. You did. . . . [I]s it true at this time?

A. You can't not act. So he was capable of acting, behaving, and he was behaving.

Q. He made a choice, didn't he?

A. Okay. I said you can't not make a decision. Yes. Yes.[27]

No passage could more clearly reveal the enormous philosophical gap between the medical craft of healing and the legal craft of assessing guilt. Jones's view is that whatever we are doing, we are "deciding." If White takes the gun, by definition he "decides" to take it; if he does not take it, he "decides" not to take it. This is the point of his double negative: "You can't not act." This subtle linguistic move renders the notion of decision ubiquitous and therefore irrelevant. Prosecutor Norman uses the term "decision" as a basis for imposing moral and legal responsibility; if White decided and chose to shoot Moscone and Milk, he was responsible for his actions. Jones uses the same terms as though they were the inevitable concomitants of being alive. Deciding, choosing, acting—these bear no connotations of self-actuation, and thus they are compatible with a view that all conduct is determined by physical factors.

At the same time, however, the cunning of language entraps Dr. Jones—not as a philosopher of the human mind but as a normal human subject. As he says in his first answer of the exchange, "I thought we already decided. . . ." This use of "deciding" is intended clearly to impose responsibility. If the witness and the prosecutor had already "decided" something, the prosecutor should accept that "decision" as a basis for further questioning. He has an obligation of consistency based on his prior decisions. But if "decisions" were something that happened willy-nilly, not choices but just transient sensations of the mind, no obligation of logical consistency would follow from having made a decision in the past.

Junk Food and Junk Science

Power corrupts, and the ability to influence the course of criminal trials is power. Passing judgment—definitive and official judgment—on another human being's conduct could beguile a man or a woman into thinking that he or she actually possesses the wisdom for this awesome task. As psychiatric influence waxed over the determination of guilt, the medically, but not legally, trained experts began opining on the legal issues that distinguish murder from manslaughter and first-degree murder from second-degree murder. In California homicide trials of the 1960s and 1970s, it was common to hear psychiatrists talking about legal categories of guilt as though they were aggressive oracles of the law rather than patient students of human deviance.

The transcript of the Dan White trial provides one of the most convincing examples of this distortion of the expert's role. Reading the testimonies of the defense's experts moves one both to smile at their presumption and to feel sorrow that the law has come to this. Here is defense counsel Douglas Schmidt eliciting what he wanted to hear from his first witness, Dr. Jerry Jones:

Q. Did you form an opinion as to Dan White's capacity to hold malice aforethought in his mind on November 27, 1978, and if so, what is that opinion?

A. I felt that he had the capacity . . . to intend to kill, but that doesn't take much, you know, to try to kill somebody, it's not a high-falutin' mental state. I think he had the capacity to do something for a base, anti-social purpose. I think that he had the capacity to know that there was a duty imposed on him not to do that, but I don't think he had the capacity to hold that notion in his mind while he was acting; so that I think that the depression, plus the . . . tremendous emotion at the moment, with the depression, reduced his capacity for conforming conduct. . . .[28]

This is not a psychiatrist speaking in his professional role; the entire vocabulary is borrowed from the law. These are the same technical terms that appear in the instruction, quoted above, that defines malice aforethought. Lawyers barely understand these terms. The best account that anyone could give of arcane expressions like "base anti-social purpose" or "an awareness of a duty imposed by law not to commit such acts" would be historical and functional. We could try to explain where this language came from and the task it performs in seeking a moral difference between bad homicide (manslaughter) and really bad homicide (murder). To represent to the jury that this language has scientific content verges on self-deception and duplicity. For psychiatrists to express themselves on concepts that lie beyond their scientific expertise demeans their profession.

The bite of Dan White's defense lay in these psychiatric protestations of his diminished responsibility. Douglas Schmidt coaxed one witness after another to repeat the liturgy about their "professional opinion" that, if believed, would garner a lower verdict and lesser punishment for the man who killed Harvey Milk and George Moscone. The jargon of the law comes through clearly in the assessments of Dr. George F. Solomon and Dr. Donald Lunde as well as the psychologist Richard P. Delman. On cross-examination, the

prosecutor Thomas Norman did his best to coax the experts toward
admitting that White's rational plan of execution reflected premeditation, deliberation, and the capacity to make choices.

When it came time for the prosecution to mount a refutation of
the defense line-up, there was an expert, Dr. Roland Levy, willing to
formulate an equally blunt conclusion in favor of condemning Dan
White:

> **Q.** Doctor, did you feel that the Defendant was precluded by
> anything that including mental disease or disorder, from
> whatever source, from forming that quality of thought which
> we understand in our law as malice?
> **A.** Well, in terms of the capacity to form malice I found
> nothing that would indicate a lack of such capacity.[29]

All these professional opinions, those for the defense and those
for the prosecution, are based on visits the experts made to Dan
White. The psychiatrists came three or four times and White was
willing to talk to them each for eight to ten hours. The defense of Dan
White took shape in these private moments in the jail cell in which the
interviewing mental health professionals gathered impressions about
whether they could describe the killings on November 27 by using the
legal categories of intent, malice, premeditation, and deliberation.

Of all the experts who spent time with Dan White, the most
sensible and circumspect on the legal issues was Dr. Martin Blinder.
He would not give the defense a straight reply on the ultimate
question whether the defendant had acted with malice. The most he
was willing to say after outlining the pressures that affected White's
behavior was that "his capacity to harbor malice would be significantly affected by these three powerful pressures upon him."[30] (The
three pressures are discussed below.) Yet of all the mental health
professionals who testified, Blinder and his diagnosis of White's
condition drew the most criticism and even ridicule. All the other
experts focused on White's moodiness, which, they claimed,
reached the point of clinical depression. The signs of this depression
were loss of sleep, weight gain, and loss of sexual interest. Blinder's

analysis went far beyond these symptoms, which are rather common in modern corporate life. He coined the famous argument that White killed because he had been eating too much junk food.

The first of the three pressures bearing down on White, therefore, was his diet. We do not know exactly what he had eaten in the week prior to the shooting, but his sister testified that about ten days before the shooting she had brought him "two packages of chocolate cup-cakes, eight candy bars and a six-pack of Coke."[31] This is hardly a precise accounting of a week's eating habits. Blinder in fact knew very little about White's consumption on the days prior to the shooting. His testimony is devoted to scientific studies of the way others eat:

> [T]here is a substantial body of evidence that in susceptible
> individuals large quantities of what we call junk food, high
> sugar content food with lots of preservatives, can precipitate
> anti-social and even violent behavior.[32]

This hand contains so many wild cards that it could trump any more sensible view of human behavior. First, who are the "suscepti-ble individuals"? How do we know whether White was one of them? Second, how much is a "large quantity" of junk food? How many Twinkies and doughnuts do you have to eat before you enter this altered state? Third, what is the force of the verb "can precipitate"? What this means, I take it, is that sometimes (we do not know how often) an extreme diet produces behavioral changes.

Blinder tried to pitch these generalities to Dan White's specific circumstances by eliciting two other "powerful pressures." One was White's physical exhaustion and the other: "by the day of the shoot-ing all of these pressures on him seemed to reside within, or be personified by Mayor Moscone and then Supervisor Milk."[33] From this rather superficial analysis of White's situation, Blinder con-cludes:

> [I]f it were not for all the tremendous pressures on him the
> weeks prior to the shooting, and perhaps if it were not for the

ingestion of this aggravating factor, this junk food, with all three factors, did not impinge upon him at the same time, I would suspect that these homicides would not have taken place.[34]

The testimony of the other expert witnesses is aptly described as junk law, for they testified about concepts they understood neither historically nor functionally. They could only try to intuit the meaning of the technical terms intent, malice, premeditation, and deliberation. Blinder steered clear of that error and fell instead into preaching junk science. He thought he could explain the behavior of a single man under a unique set of circumstances. He conducted no tests, he had no precise diagnostic information about White's blood sugar level over time, he had no control group to test his prediction of when and how individuals are driven to kill. It seems to carry no weight at all that there were thousands of people who ate the same diet, hated their bosses, and lived under constant pressure but did not resort to killing. The prosecutor could have ripped this junk science to shreds on cross-examination, but he chose instead to focus on the same issues of Dan White's calculated planning that he stressed in the cross-examination of all the other experts for the defense.

As one might expect, the press picked up Blinder's testimony and savored every bit of the newly dubbed "Twinkie defense." Blinder's view of criminal behavior was no more skewed than that of his colleagues, who promoted other deterministic accounts of violent crime. Yet his fashionable attack on sugar and preservatives captured the faddist style of California thinking. He had isolated the food of the devil, the cause of crime. Yet it is not clear how much this argument influenced the jury, for there were many factors working for Dan White at the time of the trial.

As a general matter, the defense is in a favorable position in putting on a case of diminished responsibility. The client pays the full hourly rate (at the time: $50 to $60 an hour) for the time of the defense experts, both to sit and talk with him in jail and to testify at trial. Paying the piper does not mean that the defense lawyers call the tune, but they can orchestrate the trial by letting only those witnesses testify who play the argument their way. The power to choose the psychiatrists who will testify is the power, in advance, to write the score of the trial. Second, the defense can block the prosecution's psychiatrist from visiting the accused on the ground of possible self-incrimination. For example, Dr. Levy spoke to Dan White only once, and though the defense lawyers did not restrain Dr. Levy from returning, they believed they could have done so.[35] Third, the defense did not need to convince the jury that White suffered from the kind of depression that deprived his killing of malice. Rather, the prosecution had to convince the jury beyond a reasonable doubt that the defendant "harbored" the mental state of malice in the killing. Thus the defense would win if it could raise a reasonable doubt about the conditions that negate or deny malice. All the psychiatrists needed to do, therefore, was to generate a reasonable doubt in the minds of the jurors.

Good Moves and Bad

The defense parlayed these advantages by constructing a coherent defense and by capitalizing on the prosecution's mistakes. The refrain that Douglas Schmidt sounded many times was that honest and decent people do not commit murder. Dan White was an honest and decent person. Therefore there had to be an explanation for what happened on November 27 that went beyond White's character. It would not do to argue that White gave in to his evil impulses, that he was overtaken by frustration and a passion for revenge. Enter the psychiatrists and their alternative accounts of why he pulled the trigger nine times.

The prosecution had no account of the killing to match the defense's simple line of attack. Thomas Norman devoted his time to proving the obvious, that Dan White did what everyone agreed he did. This pedantic interest in completeness led him to play the tape recording of the confession Dan White made to his long-time friend Homicide Inspector Frank Falzon. After the confession was heard,

Falzon testified on cross-examination that "Dan White was an exemplary individual, a man that I was proud to know and to be associated with."[36] His only character flaw was his tendency to "run away" from problems.

The confession itself is a heartfelt, emotional recounting of the events leading up to the killings. White recounts the financial and political pressures on him and his family. The prize-winning documentary, *The Times of Harvey Milk*, claims that several members of the jury had tears in their eyes as the tape played in the courtroom.[37] Because White decided not to testify at the trial, his voice on the tape was the only exposure the jury would have to his manner of presenting himself and his understanding of what he had done. The prosecution sought to introduce a transcript of the confession, but the defense insisted on playing the full tape. The tactic was well taken. The impact of this concentrated exposure to the defendant's humanity seems to have generated some sympathy for White among the jurors.

And who were these 12 representatives of the people? Defense counsel Schmidt recalls that he was looking for a "reverse" jury—that is, a group of 12 men and women who would see in the defendant not a threat but the type of person who characteristically upheld law and order. As part of this strategy, Schmidt was resolved to keep homosexuals off the jury. Since the candidates for the jury had to declare their marital status, it was not too difficult to ferret out probable gays who would identify strongly with Harvey Milk. Schmidt could use his peremptory challenges (without any need to give reasons) to ensure that the jury reflected the same middle-class values that had gained Dan White his seat on the Board of Supervisors.

The combination of these tactics and mistakes netted Dan White his compromise verdict. More importantly, they defined the playing board for all subsequent political trials that seek to promote the interests of minorities and women. Expert testimony and the weight it deserves becomes a recurrent problem. The tension between common sense moral condemnation and the pro-defendant analysis of the experts confounds the ensuing trials of the four police officers who beat up Rodney King, the prosecution of the young blacks who assaulted Reginald Denny, and the spate of proceedings invoking the battered women's syndrome. Jury selection turns out to be a pivotal problem in all these instances of the new political trial. Gays, blacks, Jews, and women are not inclined to recognize the legitimacy of verdicts when they are not represented on the jury. Yet there are serious constitutional impediments to recognizing the right of the victim's "community" to be represented on a jury of supposedly neutral and impartial judges of the facts.

Californians responded to the Dan White verdict in sympathy with the gay community. The majority of the population concurred that there was something wrong in letting psychiatrists substitute their expertise for common sense condemnations of obvious evil. In June 1982, the voters endorsed Proposition 8, known as the "Victims' Bill of Rights," which explicitly abolished diminished capacity as a defense and sought to ban psychiatrists from testifying on the issue of malice. Though the legislature introduced parallel reforms to the criminal code, ingenious defense lawyers sought to maintain the relevance of psychiatric testimony in jury deliberations about whether a killing should be classified as murder or manslaughter. Finally, in 1991, the state supreme court decided that the voters and the legislature meant business: the defense that garnered Dan White his compromise verdict was indeed abolished.[38] Whether the courts would get the deeper point about the importance of common sense moral judgment and the danger posed by expert witnesses would remain to be seen.

These problems do not lend themselves to an easy cure. Like a virus that retreats into the nervous system, the problems of fairness to victims and their communities remain quiescent for long periods of time. The discriminatory practices of criminal justice burst on the scene when least expected. For no one knows when a man who has just bought a video camera will turn it on.

* * *

Postscript: Dan White was released from jail on January 6, 1984, after having served a little more than four and a half years. On October 22, 1985, unable to reintegrate himself into California society, he killed himself by inhaling exhaust from a car in his garage.

CHAPTER TWO

Blacks

"Can we all get along?"
—*Rodney King, May 1, 1992.*

SOOT FROM FIRES PAST HAS SETTLED ON THE VERDICT OF A federal jury in Los Angeles. On April 17, 1993, Sergeant Stacey Koon and Officer Laurence Powell suffered the legal comeuppance that most Americans had been yearning for. According to a *USA Today* poll, taken right after the Simi Valley acquittals, 79% of whites and 95% of blacks surveyed believed that the federal government should bring civil-rights charges against the four officers who had beaten Rodney King.[1] But only Koon and Powell were eventually convicted. They became felons under the law, each required to serve 30 months in prison. They lost the extraordinary power they once had to decide when and how to use force, when to swing their batons, and when to pull their guns. From being the law's enforcers, they fell subject to the law's lockup. Their offense was depriving a black man of his civil rights. The name of the crime was obscure, but the crime, the facts of the incident, seemed transparent. They lay in 81 seconds of videotape. Everyone who had access to a television set was a witness. The country knew a crime when it saw one.

In the wake of the second verdict, the National Guard packed up and went home. There would be no replay of the 1992 burning of the

South Central district. After weeks of fretting about the consequences of another acquittal, the media were almost disappointed.
This time there would be no dramatic helicopter footage of fires, of
stone throwing, and of assaults on drivers in their cars. There would
be no fear spreading northward and westward toward affluent resi-
dential neighborhoods.

Rodney King and his community emerged victorious from the
flames of May 1992. But two days after his victory in federal court he
was nearly forgotten. His case disappeared from the television screen
as the cameras shifted to the burning of a religious compound in
Waco, Texas. There the followers of a religious king hardly stood a
chance. The FBI moved in and triggered the brutal end of 81 people,
including 17 young children.[2] New violence, new investigations, new
accusations. The news rolls on, and we are left with the task of
understanding how and why California's system of criminal justice
failed so badly in Rodney King's first trial. We are left to ponder how
we could come back from the ashes and redeem, if only in part, the
possibility of justice in American courts.

Simi Valley Sorrows

Of the 23 police officers who witnessed or participated in the
videotaped beating in the early morning hours of March 3, 1991,
the state of California indicted three who actually inflicted blows,
Laurence M. Powell, Timothy Wind, and Theodore J. Briseno,
along with Sergeant Stacey C. Koon, who was the officer in charge
at the scene.[3] Under state law all the charges of assault with a
deadly weapon and using excessive force turned on the claim that
Powell's and Wind's 56 baton blows as well as Briseno's stomp
on King's back were unjustified and brutal attacks against King's
body. The defense faced the same kind of challenge that Dan
White's lawyers had encountered 13 years earlier: How could they
undermine the solid appearance of crime, this time recorded
in 81 seconds of seemingly indisputable proof? They could not rely
on the psychological condition of the aggressive cops, for there

were too many of them to claim that they were all insane, even temporarily.

There was little dispute about King's wrongdoing. He had committed several violations of the vehicle code as a result of driving much too fast and trying to get away. California Highway Patrol officers Melanie Singer and Tim Singer clocked him driving in excess of 100 mph. They were justified in signaling him to stop and in giving chase when he refused. When they finally caught up with him at Hansen Dam Recreation Park, the legal turf shifted from the highway patrol to the city police. The radio reports of the eight-minute pursuit had already prompted police vehicles, including LAPD Sergeant Stacey Koon, to converge on the scene; they were joined by a helicopter equipped with a search beam. As Tim Singer ordered the three black men out of the cornered white Hyundai, at least eight guns and an airborne searchlight were trained on them.

Significantly, the two passengers, Freddie Holmes and Bryant Allen, promptly got out of the car and assumed the passive "felony prone position" that Tim Singer demanded. Handcuffing them, the police treated the two as cooperative citizens. They were released unharmed, without being charged. From the beginning, however, Rodney King irritated the police. He would not obey orders. He waved at the helicopter. He refused to fall flat on the ground. Melanie Singer ordered him down. King responded by grabbing his buttock and shaking it. Then with gun drawn, Officer Singer approached within five feet of King. At this point, LAPD Sergeant Koon intervened. Viewing himself as the ranking officer at the scene, he ordered her to holster her gun and let the LAPD handle the arrest.

The police were justified in trying to take King into custody. That means that they could be proactive and could make the first moves against him. He had committed a crime in their presence. The traffic violations were admittedly not the gravest, but there was a possibility of booking him for drunk driving or for "felony evasion" if in the course of trying to elude a police officer he drove in "willful or wanton disregard for the safety of persons or property."[4] That King was then on parole for having committed a convenience-store holdup in 1989 was irrelevant; the arresting officers did not know about it and therefore could not claim the prior conviction as part of their justification for the arrest and the use of force.

Stacey Koon confronted an uncooperative suspect, possibly a felony suspect, one who would not lie down flat on the ground and allow himself to be handcuffed. Apart from himself and the Highway Patrol, there were at the moment only four LAPD officers on the scene. Koon could have waited; there was no sign that King was going to take the initiative and harm somebody. Yet the process of stopping a suspect has its own logic. The officers had no patience to wait, as the FBI would hold their fire 51 days in front of David Koresh's compound. They felt they had to move in and bring him under control. That is the imperative of police work. Identify a suspect and take charge. Defense lawyer Michael Stone later characterized the option of waiting to see what King would do:

> Either he's going to get in his car and leave and you are going to go back to the police station for coffee or you are going to have to shoot him. So that is why these officers determined to keep . . . Mr. King down on the ground.[5]

The only manly and responsible thing to do, apparently, was to approach and seize the suspect. If the police had had suitable equipment at their disposal, such as a net, a Velcro blanket, or a leg-grabbing device, they might have been able to neutralize King without touching him. The police commission had barred the use of upper-body-control holds, also known as "choke" holds, except as a last resort. The only option, as Koon saw it, was to move in with the four officers in a "swarm" maneuver.[6] Sergeant Koon ordered the four officers (the three who were later indicted, plus Rolando Solano) to move in; each allegedly grabbed a limb and pulled out, forcing King to fall face first to the asphalt. The situation seemed stabilized, but then, according to the police account, King rose up and shook off Laurence Powell, who was then on King's back. Events followed quickly just as George Holliday was turning on his newly purchased video camera. Koon shot an electric charge-carrying dart, called a taser, at the suspect. King was stunned but not disabled. Then a second set of taser darts shot into his clothes and body, followed by another taser blast of 50,000 volts. Stung, afraid, and perhaps angry, he got up and started either to run or to charge the officers. Powell started swinging his steel baton in power strokes.

The succession of events is debated, as is the nature of the initial blows: Were they to the head or to the body? One thing is clear: King was not following orders, and the police had just managed to convert their proactive use of force into a situation of self-defense. And they could bolster their posture of self-defense with tales of King's super-human strength, his staring straight ahead, his sweating, and other alleged signs of the power-enhancing drug PCP. Whether the claim of self-defense would fall on receptive ears would depend, in large part, on who would serve on the jury.

Against the Odds

The preliminary challenge for the defense lawyers—Michael P. Stone for Powell, Ira M. Salzman for Koon, John Barnet for Briseno, and Paul R. DePasquale for Wind—was to secure the kind of sympathetic jury that Douglas Schmidt had garnered by system-atically excluding gays from the Dan White jury. But there was too high a percentage of African-Americans in Los Angeles County to think that the defense could keep them off the jury by using its limited number of peremptory challenges. The first move, then, was to get the case relocated to a place where passions about police beatings did not run so high—ideally, to a suburb where people would be sympathetic to the tough blue line of defense against inner-city threats.

Judge Bernard Kamins in Los Angeles County, who was as-signed the case, seemed inclined to keep it at home, but he made the mistake of communicating on the side with the prosecution that they should trust him, for "he [Kamins] knows what he is doing." The Assistant District Attorney on the case, Terry White, felt ethically compelled to disclose this communication, which led to a defense motion to disqualify the judge. Judge Kamins resisted, but the appellate court decided against him.[7] The new judge on the case, Stanley Weisberg, also ruled in favor of keeping the case in Los Angeles County. But the defense appealed and won a windfall judgment from a higher court sitting in Ventura County.[8] The appellate justices reasoned that the media had so thoroughly saturated the public's thinking "that potential jurors cannot try the case solely upon the evidence presented in the courtroom."[9] The defense's constitutional right to a fair trial was in danger.[10] It did not occur to the court that the local people—in particular, the local African-American community—had a right to participate in the adjudication of one of its most fundamental grievances, namely, the recurrent and systematic suffering of police abuse.

The assumption behind this ruling was that the judge now in charge of the trial would travel with the case, wherever it was tried. The witnesses too would have to commute. Oakland resembled Los Angeles in its racial composition, but it was an airplane trip away. Riverside was close in its demographic structure, but too far for daily freeway driving. In the end, Judge Weisberg chose the nearest alternative courthouse, Simi Valley in Ventura County. Though this was a community with many retired police officers and less than 2% African-American residents, there was no legal impediment to the transfer. Once the case had been dislodged from the community in which it was rooted, it no longer had a natural home. There was, furthermore, no reason to think that white suburban residents would be less than impartial and fair in hearing the evidence and passing judgment. The jury system thrives on the faith that we can all judge one another without bias. If the videotape was really the powerful proof that it seemed, there was nothing to fear.

In the end, then, the defense had a good chance to secure a jury without the participation of the community that would have a special investment in the fate of Rodney Glen King. The practical advantages for the defense of proceeding without African-Americans on the jury are manifest. Not only would there be no one who would feel an intense identification with a brother who had suffered the kind of contact between police and inner-city blacks that had become all too common. There would also be no one in the jury room whose presence might check the innuendos and the covert dread of crime that afford the police leeway in coping with the dangerous underclass. With no one there to object, the jurors might say of the victim, "You know, we rely on the police to make sure that 'his kind' of people do not endanger our neighborhood."

The defense got the jury they wanted. Of the six men and six women finally selected, three were former security guards or had served in the military. There were three members of the National Rifle Association. One was the brother of a retired LAPD sergeant. The prosecution could have used its challenges against prospective jurors with these ties of sympathy to the police but did not. As early as 1978 the state supreme court had proclaimed that in cases of crimes "against a black victim, the black community as a whole has a legitimate interest in participating in the trial proceedings."[11] This principle should have governed jury selection in Simi Valley too, but it did not. Several African-Americans presented themselves in the jury pool. All were dismissed, some by the judge for possible bias; the last prospect, by the defense.

As the jury in remote Simi Valley was sworn in, not a black face was to be seen. The presence of one Hispanic and one Filipino juror added a touch of off-white but hardly enough for the residents of far-off Los Angeles 90057 to feel that they were included. The jury's composition would help the defense, but only if the defense presented arguments that moved these 12 lay people. Because they would presumably do their best to follow the judge's instructions on the law, unreasoned sympathy for the police would hardly carry the day. Like everyone else, they would begin with 81 seconds of video-tape revulsion. The presumption of innocence would not be enough to ward off a conviction. The lawyers had to conceptualize a defense. They had to be prepared to strike back, however weak the prosecution's evidence beyond the tape might be.

A successful criminal defense often turns on slogans that the jurors keep in mind—almost hum to themselves—as they deliberate.

The two soundbite slogans that the defense coined on behalf of the four police defendants carried what seemed to be simple truths of the conflict. The first was that the jury should judge the officers by putting themselves in their shoes. They should look at King's alleged efforts to get back on his feet the way fearful officers looked at them. They should recall Officer Powell's testimony: "I was scared to death that if he got up again he was going to take my gun away from me or there was going to be a shooting."[12] The jury should also consider the possible signs of PCP as Powell, Koon, Wind, and Briseno read the situation. The proper test for the reasonable use of force is not what the particular officers thought, but what a reasonable police officer would have thought under the circumstances. And Michael Stone, counsel for Laurence Powell, simplified the standard to what "a reasonable officer would say when facing the same or similar circumstances."[13] If the jury believed that these four were reasonable officers and that they read the facts in a particular way, then the police were home free.

The second slogan asserted that King was in charge of the situation. If he had gone prone and limp, if he had submitted to the power of the batons, the police would have ceased their onslaught. He held the keys to his own safety. What a marvelous twist! A similar argument came forward in the Goetz defense.[14] The shooting was arguably not Goetz's doing at all; the action was prompted by Troy Canty's asking for five dollars. If King was in control, then so too was Troy Canty. But the argument of control did not work for Goetz, and for a very simple reason. The police enjoy a rhetorical advantage that no one would accord Bernhard Goetz, a civilian carrying a concealed weapon. The police making an arrest become a fixed point of reference. They are not initiating action; they are merely doing their duty. The potential variation in their conduct, therefore, is not their choosing but rather a reflection of the suspect's obstinacy. If he resists, the police respond; if he is compliant and lies down motionless, the police stay their attack. This is what it means for the police to do their duty.

An expert prosecutorial team might have triumphed over these two slogans—"in the shoes of the police" and "King was in charge." Instead of countering the soundbites of the defense, the Los Angeles District Attorney responded in confident confusion. For one, the prosecutors failed to maintain a consistent image of the police. Sometimes they portrayed the police as racist and therefore indifferent to their wrongdoing. Sometimes they painted the police as feeling guilty about what they had done and therefore inclined to cover up the incident by drafting false reports. The defendants themselves tried to convey a third picture of themselves—as men who played by the rules, however tough and brutal the consequences might be.

It was not easy for the prosecution to establish the charge that the police had acted out of racial bias. The problem of racist sensibilities eludes the simplified cast of mind that most people bring to the subject. None of us is color-blind. There is no doubt that when the officers closed in on King they saw "black" as one of the factors that defined the situation. Young blacks, particularly when traveling in groups, are commonly perceived as a source of danger. Yet it is impossible to know how heavily skin color—along with King's being large and muscular, his speeding, his disrespectful and noncompliant behavior after the stop, the supposed signs of PCP—weighed in the officers' perceptions of danger. The Simi Valley jury could undoubtedly appreciate the complexity of these perceptions.

In a book published after his Simi Valley acquittal, Stacey Koon goes to great pains to argue that he had acted on behalf of blacks many times in his life.[15] This may well be true, but it does not follow that his perception of danger in King's actions turned more on King's actions than on his appearance. Koon admits that King fitted his profile of an ex-con who had had time to work out and "buff out" his build. Seeing him as an ex-con enhanced the sense of danger in the situation, and race could have been a weighty factor in this perception.

It is hard to know what to make of Laurence Powell's describing an earlier intervention that evening with African-Americans as akin to "something out of 'Gorillas in the Mist.' " We are inclined to think that one "unsocialized" remark of this sort means that Powell's perceptions of danger would be different from those of his white (or black) colleagues. I'm skeptical of such superficial inferences—as though there were two kinds of people in the world, racists and non-racists. One off-color remark does not define Powell's essence as racist and evil. He might even be more honest about his racial sensibilities than better-trained contemporaries who are savvy enough to avoid politically incorrect comments.

Yet the context of the remarks is revealing. The response over the Mobile Digital Terminal, an electronic network that police use to communicate, suggests a culture of commonplace racist slurs. The party receiving Powell's derisive remark responded, "Hahaha . . . Let me guess who be the parties." This mocking of African-American dialect reveals a culture in which the sensibilities of blacks, Chicanos, and other minorities are obviously not respected. Though it is difficult to trace the connection between talk and action, the pattern of derision raises serious concerns about the way police officers treat each other as well as lay citizens of color.[16]

The prosecutors' charge that the officers had covered up the incident brought to the fore a host of after-the-fact reactions by the police that required careful interpretation and parsing. Wind had completed the use-of-force report, and Koon had made an entry in the sergeant's log. Neither mentioned King's having been on the ground during the beating. A missing word in a written report; Powell's nervous laugh in his recorded call-in. The evidence of a cover-up is less than airtight. None of this poring over the tapes and written records added much to the power of the prosecution's case— at least in the minds of the Simi Valley jury.

More significantly, the prosecution failed to appreciate the impact of expert testimony on the jury's assessment of reasonable force. The defense's lead expert, Sergeant Charles Duke, formulated a slogan of his own that shed a favorable light on the beating. In his view, any unsearched felon is a "very serious threat."[17] King was technically a felon, at least if you assume that during the chase he was driving very recklessly.[18] A threat triggers a right of self-defense.

Thus Powell, Wind, and Koon could craft a defense for the 56 blows to King's body. Each blow, they argued on the basis of a frame-by-frame analysis of the videotape, was a response to a movement by King, a movement they interpreted as a threat, as the beginning of an aggressive action, as an invitation to a defensive response.

Sergeant Duke was more than happy to confirm the most expansive definition possible of a threat to the officers. The tape revealed King writhing and turning on the ground, in apparent agony. But in Duke's view, a rolling motion was not necessarily a response to pain. It could be seen as the beginning of a "Folsom" roll, a maneuver developed by prisoners at Folsom State Penitentiary: they would roll over to an armed guard, grasp his legs, and then reach up and grab his gun. One man's twitch, it seems, is another man's threat. Whether a movement of an arm or leg spells danger is filtered by the lens of the beholder. These officers were accustomed to seeing suspects respond to their orders. A man who does not respond, who does not comply with orders, is by definition a danger. If he does not accept the authority of the police, he might well attack them.

The state prosecutors failed to neutralize Charles Duke; their sole expert, Commander Michael Bostic, was discredited as a desk man without adequate experience on the street. He supposedly did not understand the split-second judgment required of officers on the front lines. In the same way that the prosecution lost the battle of the experts in the killing of Harvey Milk and George Moscone, the prosecutors allowed Duke to shape the jury's perception of the reasonable use of force. We have come to realize that insanity as well as malice and premeditation are legal and moral questions; as argued in the last chapter, psychiatrists should not be able to shape the jury's judgment with imperial claims of expertise. One can only wonder why we have not applied the same principle to the police. The question of reasonable force is just as moral and value-laden as were the questions of malice and accountability in the Dan White trial. In the wake of White's manslaughter conviction, Californians came to the conclusion that expert witnesses were the enemy of common-sense justice for the victims of violent crime. Now, a little more than a decade later, they seem to have forgotten that a different kind of expert can be the enemy of common-sense justice for the victims of police brutality.

The official reason for permitting Sergeant Duke to testify on departmental policies toward reasonable force turns on a peculiar logic that was never properly articulated at either the state or federal trial. The argument offered by the United States Attorney's office goes something like this. Establishing guilt for a federal civil rights violation requires proof of a "specific intent" to violate the defendant's constitutional rights. Some lawyers think that this specific intent means that the police must know that they are doing the wrong thing. If that were true, the violation of departmental policy would show at least that, by police standards, they were doing something wrong and they probably knew it. On the basis of this reasoning, the testimony of Sergeant Duke becomes relevant. The explanation of departmental policy tends to show that the police have the required specific intent to be liable under the civil rights statute.[19]

This theory about federal law does not explain why the same testimony was admissible at the state trial. The state crime requires only that the police have intended to make contact with their batons against King's body. Whether the police violated departmental policy has no apparent bearing on that question. And yet the testimony of Sergeant Duke was assumed, without discussion, to be relevant in the Simi Valley trial.

The fact is that expert testimony about departmental policy has no real relevance to the intent required either for the federal or the state offense. The assumption is that a relatively strict form of intent is required for violation of the civil rights act—perhaps that the police knew they were violating King's constitutional rights or at least that the beating was unreasonable. Yet the law has been clear for decades that, as the federal jury would learn, the defendants were guilty even if they "had no real familiarity with the Constitution or with the particular constitutional right involved." It was enough that they intended "that which the Constitution forbids." They do not in fact have to know that they were doing something wrong. Therefore, their violation of internal departmental rules has no bearing on whether they violated state and federal law. In the end, the intent required for the federal offense collapses into the simple question whether they intended to beat up King. The question of police conformity with departmental policy has no more relevance in the federal trial than it has under the state law.

Once this confusion about intent is stripped away, it is clear that another agenda drives the use of expert testimony in police brutality cases. The more emphasis directed to the expert testimony about police policy, the more the courts seem to defer to the police as a self-governing body. Their wayward officers are tried, de facto, under police regulations.

There are other signs that we treat the police as self-governing. The department itself is politically autonomous. The Chief is not subject to political control. The cop on the beat has the power to turn his back on a petty offense, to ignore a domestic dispute, or to reward a trusted informer by letting him go. Some of this discretionary power is inevitable, but the full extent of police autonomy generates an image of the men and women in blue acting on their own code of proper conduct, including their own rules on the use of force. For many cops on the streets, the binding code is not the law of the state, but the police manual as interpreted in the police academy and in the upper echelons of the department. The experts justify their role as witnesses to this process of internal law-making. They inform the court and the jury of the rules the police think they are supposed to live by.

Every trial of police brutality tests the unarticulated premise that the police should be able to govern themselves. In a drama barely visible to the participants, the prosecution and the court try to impose the law of the state on the police. With the aid of their expert interpreters of internal policy, the defendants seek judgment under their own rules of conduct. The battle for the applicable law has even greater symbolic significance than the jury verdict on the defendants' guilt. If the discourse of the trial reaffirms the centrality of their own rules, the police as a whole win. They salvage the important principle of their autonomy from the misfortune of some of their own getting convicted.

As the police affirmed their autonomy, Rodney King struggled against further loss of his. Suffering insult as well as injury, he watched the trial on television from his living room. When he heard Melanie Singer describe him as a "monster," he called state prosecutor Terry White in high dudgeon. Something had to be done. The beating was replaying itself as verbal assaults. Terry White decided—then and there, it would seem—not to call the volatile King to the stand. He thought King would add little to the prosecution's case and that, on the down side, calling him would risk exposing his criminal record on cross-examination. As a result, the prosecution's case turned almost exclusively on the videotape.

White may have had sensible tactical reasons for not calling King as a witness. The defense strategy, in this case as in many, was to seek advantage by attacking the victim. King was not a model citizen. His drinking and driving, his prior conviction, his casually violating the conditions of parole, his reckless flight from the police—none of these put him in good stead. The Simi Valley jury heard plenty of police testimony about King's unruly behavior on March 2 and 3, 1991. But why would letting the jury see and hear him talk tarnish his image even further? The only thing the jury had not heard said was that King had pled guilty to a robbery indictment and that he had violated parole by drinking and driving. They could only speculate about why he did not stop and accept a ticket for speeding. And sometimes speculation can generate a more negative image than the facts would warrant.

In light of all these factors working for the defense, the outcome of the jury deliberations need not surprise us. Nor should we be particularly surprised that arguments of police autonomy would generate rage in the black community. It seemed to observers almost everywhere that the Los Angeles police had succeeded in placing themselves above the law.

The legal system failed us for a second time, with structural similarities to the verdict for Dan White 13 years earlier in San Francisco. Two victims, King and Milk, were Americans in the shadows, members of disfavored groups who must struggle to be treated fairly. In both cases, experts distracted attention from the obvious facts of unjust violence. The response of those let down by the legal system was similar. In Los Angeles, African-American rage found a multiplier effect in the willingness of disaffected Latinos and whites to join in the rioting. If understood properly, both cases have much to teach us about why, in America, there is justice only for some.

The Federal Response

Though the Civil War ended in 1865, the struggle to eliminate the badges of slavery had just begun. The laying down of arms relegated the battle to Congress and the courts. The Thirteenth Amendment, abolishing involuntary servitude, cemented the message of the war; the Fourteenth Amendment imposed additional requirements on the way state governments must treat their citizens. For the first time, the Constitution demanded the "equal protection of the laws" for all those, black and white, born in the United States. Yet it would take more than a reform of the Constitution to end the subjugation of African-Americans. The federal government acquired a new mission. It had to remake the United States into a single nation with one standard of justice for all. If there is a single theme that explains the growth of federal judicial power relative to that of the states, it is the ever-present suspicion of Southern justice toward blacks. And the distrust of the states in the former Confederacy eventually played itself out in the federal intervention to bring about a just resolution of the conflict between Los Angeles blacks and the police. Though miles and years away, the Royball Federal Courthouse in downtown Los Angeles lies but a short conceptual journey from the Appomattox Courthouse in which General Robert E. Lee conceded the end of the states as separate and sovereign entities.

The pluralistic character of the "United States" changed with the military victory against Southern secession. Lincoln's speech at Gettysburg invokes a single "nation conceived in liberty and dedicated to the proposition that all men are created equal." The United States *were* no longer a collection of autonomous states. The country *was* unified under one constitution. Yet the constitutional amendments adopted in the wake of the Civil War do not, in themselves, give the federal courts jurisdiction to intervene in state criminal trials. All we find in the pivotal Fourteenth Amendment is a guarantee of equality and a recognition that every individual born in the United States counts as a citizen, with full protection against denial "of life, liberty, or property, without due process of law."

The "due process" clause became the conduit from the Bill of Rights to state criminal justice. The "new deal" in federal criminal justice began in the 1930s. When the Alabama Supreme Court affirmed the conviction of the nine black "Scottsboro" defendants on seemingly trumped-up rape charges, the U.S. Supreme Court intervened. Because the state court did not assign state-funded counsel to the defendants in a capital case, it had denied them a fair trial and due process of law.[20] When the Mississippi courts affirmed a conviction for murder against three African-American defendants on the basis of confessions that a local sheriff beat out of them, the Supreme Court stepped in once again.[21] In the post-Second World War period, the Supreme Court began speaking of the wholesale incorporation of specific provisions of the Bill of Rights into the Fourteenth Amendment. Not all the cases of federal intervention posed problems of abuse against black Americans, and very few of the trend-setting appeals came from the states of the former Confederacy.[22] But there is little doubt that without the special attention of the courts to the aftershocks of slavery, the federal courts would hardly have intervened so deeply and irreversibly into the procedures of the state criminal courts.

Special concern for blacks as victims of crime crystallized in Congressional efforts, beginning in 1866, to impose criminal sanctions on those who sought to keep the newly emancipated blacks in a condition of servitude. The federal government threatened criminal sanctions against private groups of people who conspired to intimidate citizens from exercising rights secured by the Constitution. And more significantly, for purposes of federal intervention against the four LAPD defendants, an 1866 statute created a category of civil-rights crimes committed by the representatives of state governments. The message was clear: No governmental unit, certainly not one formerly of the Confederacy, could seek to retain blacks in a condition of legal or de facto subservience. The statute was generalized to apply to any individual acting in the name of the government ("under color of law") who "willfully subjects any inhabitant . . . to the deprivation of any rights, privileges, or immunities secured or protected by the Constitution." The way the 1866 statute is formulated, the crime is committed not by private individuals but only by officials acting as agents of the state.

This postbellum language of the federal code did not come into active use against police brutality until the Second World War was coming to end. The federal courts initially had great anxiety about intervening in areas that should be the responsibility of the states. They were worried about the vagueness of the statute, about defining the constitutional rights protected, about the intent required for violation,[23] and about an issue that will concern us later: the violation of double jeopardy in prosecuting state officials after they have been acquitted in a state court. Perhaps the "feds" should have had doubts about applying to a southern California injustice a statute that was originally designed to combat the vestiges of slavery in the former Confederacy. But Washington never hesitated. Just three months after Los Angeles experienced the worst riot in its history, the federal grand jury returned indictments against the four once-acquitted police officers. The trial was set to begin in early October 1992 in the downtown Los Angeles courtroom of Judge John G. Davies.

Trying Harder the Second Time

In the course of the summer, the prosecution received a major psychological boost from Washington. In a case that had nothing to do with L.A.'s tribulations (but perhaps inspired indirectly by the riots), the Supreme Court finally decided that the defense may not discriminate on racial grounds in jury selection.[24] The upshot was that the second time around there would be a different emphasis in jury selection. Everyone assumed that the case would stay in the "community," namely in downtown Los Angeles, where there was a relatively large black representation in the jury pool. Further, the authority of the United States Supreme Court now stood behind stricter controls on the defense's discriminatory use of peremptory challenges.

Nothing in the Supreme Court's new rule required black representation on a jury in which a black man appeared as the alleged victim. The Constitution forbids only intentional racial discrimination. The prosecution and defense can proceed neutrally, eliminating only obviously biased jurors, and yet produce an ethnically homogeneous jury. As I sat in Judge Davies' courtroom in early October, however, I sensed that the government could not possibly go to trial without at least one or two blacks on the jury. The unwritten rule binding Judge Davies was not only non-discrimination but fair representation.

The way the jury was selected bore out my sense that the operative rule was not just avoiding discrimination but making sure that the appearance of discrimination not be repeated. The judge would bend over backwards to let black candidates on the jury. The defense tried to challenge a retired black man who had not disclosed in the judge's questionnaire about the candidates' backgrounds and attitudes that he lived in South Central Los Angeles, close to ground zero of the 1992 rage. His concealing this information suggested a desire to get on the jury in order to rectify the mistake of Simi Valley. Judge Davies ruled that in the absence of stronger evidence of bias, the defense could not keep this man off the jury. Had the candidate for the jury been Caucasian, the defense could have interposed a peremptory challenge and dismissed him without having to explain why. But under the new rule prohibiting discrimination by the defense, the race of the potential juror made a difference.

The prosecution too appeared to be indulgent on the race issue. They refused to challenge a black postal worker who said that justice was probably done the first time around. Had she been white, she would hardly have appeared to be a good bet for conviction in the federal trial. Yet whatever the law required, no one—not the defense, not the prosecution, not the judge—dared to go to trial without fair "community" representation on the jury.

This mode of jury selection raises a paradox. Representation is desirable, but assigning ethnic quotas in jury selection violates the principles of neutrality and impartiality. No one could make it onto a jury if he or she expressed loyalty to a racial or national grouping. Try to imagine how trials might be possible if jurors could be selected despite honest confessions of bias toward their own ethnic group, gender, or sexual culture. There would be biased opinions representing both the straight man accused of gay-bashing and his gay victim, both for the white police and the black victim. If juries voted according to group loyalties, we would have either gridlock in every case or compromise verdicts convicting the innocent of half the charges against them. The only mode of representation that would work in Judge Davies' courtroom was one that did not speak its name. The jurors, whatever their color, would have to swear that they would remain neutral and impartial in evaluating the evidence and applying the judge's instructions on the law.

Picking a jury was only the first stage of the battle. There was little hope that the prosecution could win unless it could cabin Charles Duke and confine his impact. To do that, they needed a credible expert on their side and also had to educate the court and the jury on the proper role of expertise in assessing the reasonable use of force. In the federal prosecution, the central question was whether the beating deprived King of his rights under the Fourth Amendment, a constitutional provision that relies explicitly on the principle of reasonableness: "The right of the people to be secure in their persons . . . against unreasonable seizures . . . shall not be violated." The Supreme Court had already decided that the use of deadly force to apprehend a youthful, apparently unarmed burglary suspect constituted an unreasonable seizure in violation of the Amendment.[25] The conclusion lay near that beating a suspect into submission was also unreasonable.

One might have hoped that in the course of the trial either the lawyers or the judge would have clarified the elementary distinction between necessary force and reasonable force. The point is simply that necessary force may sometimes be excessive. It might be necessary to shoot at a fleeing burglar, but it is excessive and unreasonable to do so. Unreasonable means "not worth the cost." Stopping a fleeing suspect is not worth the price of killing a human being. By like measure, it might be necessary to break bones to beat an unsearched and unruly suspect into submission, but this drastic measure might be excessively costly for the net gain to the police. Reasonableness requires a judgment that beating the suspect— relative to the next-best measure for effecting the arrest—justifies the added suffering by the suspect. If less intrusive measures might work, they and no more might be what the standard of reasonableness requires.

Nothing resembling this simplicity or clarity emerged in the federal prosecution of the four police officers. The top-of-the-line prosecutors Steven Clymer and Barry Kowalski never seemed to link up the issue of reasonableness in their case with the Supreme Court precedent restricting the right to use force to prevent the escape of a burglary suspect. They tried to elicit some understanding on the concept of reasonableness from the expert witnesses, particularly from the ever-present defense witness Sergeant Charles Duke, but the careful analysis of concepts was not their field. The Judge fared no better than the lawyers. He should have explained to the jury that necessary force is not always reasonable. But there is not a word to that effect in his instructions to the jury. Those instructions consist sometimes in pap bordering on tautology: "Reasonable force is that which would appear reasonable to an ordinary, reasonable officer under the same circumstances." Or sometimes in jargon with an air of seeming precision, as in this instruction:

Determining whether the arrest of a person is unreasonable under the Fourth Amendment requires careful attention to the facts and circumstances of the particular case, including the severity of the crime at issue, whether the person posed an immediate threat to the safety of the officers or others, and whether the person was actively resisting arrest or attempting to evade arrest by flight.

Careful parsing reveals the confusion created by lumping all these factors together. That the "person posed an immediate threat" is a condition for using even minimal force, as are the alternatives mentioned in the last clause: resisting or evading arrest. Even for the trained legal mind, therefore, these instructions are confusing. They miss the central point: Sometimes the police must forgo the use of necessary force when the cost of using it is too high.

The federal instructions do represent an improvement over the way Judge Stanley Weisberg instructed the jury in Simi Valley. There the jury learned:

A peace officer who is making an arrest may use reasonable force to make such arrest or to prevent escape or to overcome resistance. The officer need not retreat or desist from his efforts by reason of the resistance or threatened resistance of the person being arrested.[26]

That last sentence effectively undermines the legal and constitutional requirement of reasonable force. If the officers need not desist in the face of resistance, then they may do whatever is necessary—regardless of the cost—to overcome resistance. The federal prosecutors zeroed in on this issue when they had Sergeant Duke on the stand.

Duke had testified in both state and federal hearings that every blow inflicted by Officers Powell and Wind met the criteria of justifiable force. He opined at one point that the police use all necessary means "to beat people into submission."[27] He thought it was ludicrous "for these officers to go for cover, unholster [their] weapons, and see what the suspect is going to do."[28] Why was this less intrusive action ludicrous? Because, he thought, the baton could do the job. His bottom line: "If it takes one baton blow, then that is what is necessary to overcome resistance. If it takes a thousand baton blows to overcome resistance, then that is what it takes."[29] Duke's invoking "a thousand blows" reveals as much as one frame of a suspect in agony. Duke cultivated an imperial image of the police mission. When it comes to subduing suspects, the police cannot wait, they cannot risk losing, they cannot take seriously the costs of their actions.

In the "expert" vision of Charles Duke, the police live by their own law, and he says what that law is. Prosecutor Clymer pressed him repeatedly to provide some authority—anything in writing—to support his view that the police may use all force necessary to suppress resistance to their commands. If anything, the written guidelines for the department go the other way. Clymer confronted Duke with a note in bold letters in the manual: **"The baton shall not be used to gain compliance to verbal commands absent combative or aggressive actions by a suspect."** One would think that police policy was clear on the point. The purpose of securing compliance with commands was not sufficient in itself; the officers could not use the baton except as a defensive measure to ward off "combative or aggressive" actions.

But the manual did not impress Sergeant Duke. He relied on an oral tradition. He could have relied on the argument that King's every gesture made him "combative or aggressive." But instead he argued that one of his supervisors had told him: "We will beat people into submission and break bones, if necessary. Do you understand that, Sergeant Duke?"[30] And when he taught classes on police tactics, he repeated the same principle: "If it requires that to be done in order to overcome that resistance, then that's what has to be done."[31] In an interview with Anna Deavere Smith, Duke revealed that his "supervisor" had delivered his interpretation of official policy—"beat people into submission and break bones"—as they were standing by the drinking fountain "right by where the water is."[32] For this Duke in his kingdom, his own views, as informed by drinking-fountain banter, were the law. The police and their oral traditions constituted an autonomous legal culture, and Duke's job was to explain to the jury what that law was.

According to Duke's unwritten code of police conduct, the world of suspects is divided into felons and nonfelons. This architectonic distinction organizes his thoughts. In his testimony, his thoughts return repeatedly to the distinction between felony and nonfelony suspects. He defends the use of the baton, despite the clear language of the manual, on the ground that the officers had grounds to suspect King of the felony of evading arrest: "But when you are dealing with a felony situation . . . they can use a baton to gain compliance after some verbalization."[33] Because felons are generally more dangerous to society than people who commit misdemeanors, there is greater urgency in effecting their arrest. Duke implicitly appeals to this point by conditioning his argument on King's having allegedly committed the felony of avoiding arrest.

Yet the question whether King really committed a felony never received much discussion in either the state or the federal trial. The niceties of the legal classification really did not matter to Duke, for in the end he claimed, "We teach pursuits to be deemed a very high risk on the same level as a felony situation."[34] For Duke, King's having tried to avoid stopping was sufficient reason to treat him as though he were an "aggressive or combative" escaping felon. The argument was not that there was a greater social interest in achieving the arrest of a felon, but rather that King's felony-like driving coupled with his actions after stopping provided a sufficient basis for a reasonable police officer to infer, without more, that he was "combative or aggressive."

The felony classification also shaped Sergeant Duke's views on the proper use of the "team take-down" or "swarm" technique. Sergeant Mark Conta, the head of LAPD training, had argued in prior testimony for the prosecution that after about 12 seconds of beating Rodney King a less harmful means of controlling him was available. In his view, a group of at least four officers should have rushed King and attempted a second take-down, namely to force his arms into handcuff position. It will be recalled that the officers had tried the swarm technique at the outset and King had thrown them off. In response to Conta, Duke maintained that the swarm was not an ordinary part of LAPD training. Even if it was used in the field, he said, "It was never intended for unsearched felony suspects."[35] Duke had nothing but contempt for the tactical move of the four officers who tried to handcuff King at the outset. He repeatedly dismissed their scramble as the actions of a "gaggle of officers."[36] Apparently he would have gone for the baton even earlier.

Steven Clymer's cross-examination of Sergeant Duke deftly elicited Duke's conception of himself as the sovereign interpreter of police policy. Clymer approached Duke as if Duke were a judge opining on the law of his own jurisdiction. The questions resemble an anthropological inquiry into a curious, exotic legal system. Clymer's first two hypothetical cases elicited two benchmarks for further inquiry. Duke conceded first that there is a difference between a perceived threat and a reasonably perceived threat; not everything a police officer subjectively fears constitutes an objective threat justifying the use of force. He acknowledged secondly that the officer must be aware of the threat for it to be relevant. Both admissions rest on Duke's sense of what a reasonable legal system would require. But neither position is spelled out in so many words in the police manual, and neither is accepted everywhere without dissent.[37]

Appealing to Sergeant Duke's sense of reasonableness might not have been the best prosecutorial tactic. Once emboldened by his sense of what good law requires, Duke began to expound on the unwritten police code of action, the implicit rules governing the use of the baton and the swarm. He confronted Clymer over and over again about whether the police manual really means what it says. It is hard to fathom the exact impact on the jury of either Duke's testimony or his subsequent cross-examination. There is no doubt that both Duke and Conta carried more weight than ordinary witnesses. And the prosecution's countering Duke more effectively than did the People's representative in the state trial undoubtedly contributed to the jury's convicting Officer Powell and Sergeant Koon. But the question remains whether either expert should have been allowed to act as the interpreter of reasonable police behavior in the streets.

In the federal trial, more than in the state trial, the participants were careful to insulate the expert testimony from the ultimate legal question of reasonable behavior. Sergeant Conta limited his opinions to the judgment of what was "in policy" and "out of policy" in the mini-jurisdiction called the LAPD. Duke and the defense lawyers tried to break out of this restraint and venture opinions on the formal question that the jury would have to resolve. From time to time, Duke actually said the behavior was "justified," by which he meant of course justified according to law, not just according to the internal standards of the LAPD. While the internal standards of the LAPD may be of sociological interest, the trial never made clear why they were relevant to the legal question of using unreasonable force under the Fourth Amendment. This is a problem to which we must return in a later chapter.

More Than Guilt or Innocence

For many observers, the only relevant question was the legal bottom line. Were the police guilty and what would their sentence be? The quest for the verdict is, of course, the core of any criminal trial. Many of the disputes in the evidence can be understood only as they bear on the central question of guilt. For example, the lawyers, police witnesses, and medical experts disputed whether Officer Powell had struck Rodney King in the head. King suffered multiple fractures of both cheek bones. Hospital personnel established that he required 20 stitches. The defense claimed that these injuries occurred as a result of King's falling face-first to the pavement. Melanie Singer and Tim Singer both testified that they observed Powell strike King directly across the side of the face. The videotape did not resolve the dispute. The question was important, because it bore on the ultimate issue whether the officers intentionally used too much force.

Then there was the dispute about what the officers said immediately before and after the beating. Judge Davies had ruled prior to trial that the jury would not hear Officer Powell's reference to African-Americans as akin to "Gorillas in the Mist." This remark, with its overtones of racism, would have hurt the defense. When Rodney King finally testified, the jury did hear his testimony that the officers taunted him during the beating with the chant: "We're going to kill you nigger, run."[38] On cross-examination, King admitted he was not sure whether the officers had said "nigger" or "killer," but they had pronounced "killer" with a Southern drawl, making it sound like "killah" and thus close to "niggah." If the jury believed that race was a motivating factor in the beating, they would be less likely to credit the officers' claims of danger as reasonable.

All these factual disputes swirled about the decisions the jury would eventually reach on the four indicted officers. The two most involved defendants, Powell and Koon, ended up guilty, and the two least involved, Wind and Briseno, slipped by as not guilty in a sensible jury compromise. Some people took the compromise as evidence of political sensitivity. As Harland Braun, lawyer for Briseno, commented after the trial:

> Is it the truth of Koon and Powell being guilty?
> Or is it the truth of the society
> that has to find them
> guilty in order to protect itself?[39]

Other dramas played themselves out in the margins of the testimony and cross-examination. These subplots may have more lasting social and political effects than the time served by the two police officers in a minimum-security federal penitentiary. The trial cut a deep division between officer and officer. The code of police conduct—like the code of every profession—demands internal loyalty and solidarity. Chief Daryl Gates was allegedly the first to break with the code by publicly distancing himself from his men. He suspended, without pay, the three indicted officers who were regulars and fired Timothy Wind, who was on probation. In May 1991, Koon wrote an op-ed piece in the *Los Angeles Times* that called for Gates' resignation for having broken ranks.[40] Significantly, none of the other LAPD officers at the scene testified against their "brethren."

But Highway Patrol Officers Melanie and Tim Singer did break with the "family code." Melanie Singer delivered the most damaging evidence at the Simi Valley trial when she said that Officer Powell had struck King at the top of the cheek bone, "splitting his face from his cheekbone from the top of his ear to the bottom of his jawline."[41] On cross-examination, Michael Stone challenged her to point to signs of the facial "split" on photographs of King taken shortly after the incident. Though the photographs suggested the contrary, she stuck to her recollection. In her view there was "no reason" for a blow to the head.[42] In his book, Stacey Koon exudes contempt for her breaking the thick blue bond among those who "serve and protect." He describes her losing control as a result of King's shaking his rear end at her:

> Control and common sense were cast aside. Melanie's Jane Wayne and Dirty Harriet hormones kicked in. She drew her pistol and advanced to within five feet of the suspect.[43]

Singer had her revenge. The defense called her as a witness in the federal trial, primarily, it seems, because she would testify about King's driving in excess of 100 mph on the freeway. When she reached the point of describing the initial use of force, she broke into tears. Lawyer Michael Stone offered her a glass of water. The damage was done. Melanie Singer had become the prosecution's star witness. After the trial, her former colleagues would regard her as disloyal to the force. She and her husband accepted transfers to a desert district of the Highway Patrol, far from the sirens of the Los Angeles Police Department.

The four Los Angeles police defendants themselves suffered repeated breaches of loyalty. From the very beginning, Theodore Briseno took his own path of defense. He broke ranks in Simi Valley and testified that Powell "was out of control" and that he had hit King in the head. Briseno was charged with only one blow to King's body: a stomp to the back. Briseno is seen on tape blocking Powell's swing, and he tried to explain his stomp to the back also as a gesture designed to protect rather than harm the bloody and beaten man on the ground. The prosecution's decision to include him in the indicted four put strains on the defense. Briseno was the least likely to be convicted, but his presence among the defendants kept the defense lawyers off balance. Briseno did not testify at the federal trial— perhaps as a belated act of loyalty to his colleagues under attack. But his silence did little good. In a surprise legal maneuver, the prosecution gained permission to play the videotape of his damning Simi Valley testimony. Through it all, the defense maintained a surprisingly decorous and nominally united front.

They reserved their anger for Sergeant Mark Conta—the man from the home office who had the temerity to testify against the officers on the front line. He had no sympathy even for Briseno's stomp to King's back, which he labeled "out of policy." Yet in his brilliant cross-examination, Harland Braun established that a kick might be "out of policy" but nonetheless reasonable and lawful.

The four indicted officers had the sense that the front office had decided that they were dispensable. Chief Daryl Gates and his successor Willie Williams saw the value in triage. Thus they supposedly sent in Conta, the head of training, to testify about "police policy" as it was viewed in the Parker Building downtown. The men on the street had a different view of police policy. The division thus engendered struck the abandoned defendants as particularly disloyal behavior. In a press conference outside the courtroom, Ira Salzman, attorney for Stacey Koon, referred to Conta's testimony as "Monday morning quarterbacking." Koon himself was less temperate: Conta was a whore "looking for a promotion."[44]

The profession of policing has become like the healing professions, where, for a fee, doctors readily testify about the malpractice of their colleagues. In many countries, this is still a rare phenomenon. In France, for example, professional loyalties remain solid and tight in the face of lawyers seeking advantage for their clients. But not in the United States. As physicians can no longer count on solidarity from their peers, police officers now readily testify about the "mal-policing" of their colleagues in uniform. Faced with federal prosecution, the common mission no longer counts. Blue uniforms array themselves on both sides. A cohesive department disintegrates.

The Rodney King case also illuminates the importance of the victim as a participant in trial proceedings. There was something askew in King's absence from the Simi Valley trial. In many ways, it was his case; he should have had his day in court. Of course, he was not officially a party to the proceeding. The officers were on trial, and the state was prosecuting. Yet it was a trial that would determine whether King had suffered a justified or unjustified violation of his dignity as well as his person. He and his sense of himself lay at the vortex of the dispute. Whether or not he testified, one wants to say, should have been his decision. But that is not the way the system is structured. In the American adversary system, the prosecutor makes the case *for* the victim and the society. The prosecutor must be free to make tactical decisions in the interests of winning. Or so it is assumed. I later argue that this conception of the trial is distorted and that, in fact, victims are entitled to a greater role in "their" trials.

For now, we note the changes wrought by the events themselves. Whatever the logic, whatever the system requires, the federal prosecutors had to distance themselves from the abuses of the state case, and one way to do that was to let the victim tell his story. It was only when Rodney Glen King spoke—neatly dressed and groomed— that the press and the public realized how important his testimony was to the case. His mere presence overcame the image of a PCP-crazed, "buffed-out" black giant that the police and their lawyers had pawned off on the media and the jury. He came alive as a suffering human being. His testimony also provided a perspective on the events that we could not hear elsewhere. He explained his motives for driving fast (avoiding a return to prison), for exiting the freeway where he did (to find a liquor store), and for heading toward Hansen Dam Park (his father used to take him fishing there).

Most importantly, he gave an alternative version of why he seemed to be charging Officer Powell at the beginning of the tape. He testified that he had already been struck in the face. He lay there coughing.

> [T]hat's when he [one of the officers] said, "Oh we're going to kill you nigger. Run." And when I got up to run, I just laid down on the ground for a second maybe, just to look for a clearance in between the Hyundai—the Hyundai and the police car. And I went—I ran—I ran closer to the Hyundai than the police, and that's when I was struck.[45]

Of course, there is no way of knowing whether this version is more accurate than the claim that he deliberately charged Officer Powell. It does not matter. This is essential information bearing upon the truth of what happened that night at the Hansen Dam parking lot. The jury had a right to hear King's story, and King had a right to tell it.

King suffered the usual attacks in a cross-examination rife with innuendos. He was allegedly out for money in a civil suit. He had lied to his parole officer about whether he was drunk that night, so perhaps he was lying now. He had failed to mention the racial epithet to the grand jury. These attacks are hardly surprising. King held up well and won the sympathy of the press and presumably of the jury. The prosecutors were satisfied. After the defense finished their cross-examination, Clymer and Kowalski waived their option to bolster their case with further questions.

The press praised as a bold tactic their decision to call King to the stand. They were avoiding the pitfalls of the state case. My own view is that their decision to let King speak was as inescapable as the defense's decision to let two blacks be selected for the federal jury. This victim could no more be left invisible in the federal trial than African-Americans could be left off the jury that decided the case. This is not the law, but certain decisions inhere in the fuzzy logic of the situation. This was a trial played out against the backdrop of black rage, against the recurrent image in American justice of white police officers beating up black men. This man could be beaten but not silenced. King's victory at trial was not only seeing two of his tormentors convicted but gaining the opportunity to be heard. He emerged from the trial as a man who could be trusted, as a citizen capable of telling the truth.

Postscript: Rodney King was back in court in April 1994. On the basis of the criminal judgment, he sued the Los Angeles Police Department and the City of Los Angeles for civil damages to compensate him for the medical bills, lost wages, and pain and suffering he endured in the March 3, 1991 beating. A jury awarded him $3.8 million in compensatory damages but refused, in a separate verdict, to impose punitive damages against the individual officers.

In the spring of 1994, the two convicted defendants appealed to the Court of Appeals for the Ninth Circuit to overturn the conviction; the prosecution simultaneously appealed the sentence on the ground that it was too lenient.

The defendants argued that Judge Davies bent over too far to accept two African-Americans on the jury. As to the retired black male whom the defense sought to strike with a peremptory challenge, the argument on appeal was that the candidate changed his views about the fairness of the Simi Valley trial from the time he filled out the written questionnaire to the time of voir dire in open court. This change of heart, the Court of Appeals responded, was insufficient to justify the peremptory challenge because one non-minority juror also changed his answer and the defense accepted him.

As to the black postal worker who said that justice was probably done the first time around, it turns out that the defense sought to have her stricken when another potential juror disclosed that the postal worker also made derogatory comments about the defense's having all the blacks "kicked off" the jury in the state trial. In a hearing in the judge's chambers, she denied making the statement and Judge Davies let her remain on the jury. The Court of Appeals ruled that there was insufficient evidence of her bias to warrant a reversal of the conviction.

In light of the critique in this chapter of the intention required for civil-rights violations, the most interesting argument on appeal was that Judge Davies failed to explain to the jury how the intent required for the federal offense was indeed "a specific intent" to violate the constitutional rights of the victim. The court's opinion refers to the argument I make above on page 48 as the "paradox" of claiming that the defendants must intend to violate a constitutional right but they need not be thinking in constitutional terms. The court believes that it resolves the paradox by insisting that the specific intent encompasses "reckless disregard of a constitutional requirement that has been made specific and definite." This language reveals how confused the courts still are about the intent required for a federal civil-rights violation. First, it is odd to define a required intention by invoking the concept of recklessness; it is the legal version of explaining what an automobile is by describing a bicycle. Further, the language quoted was not included in the instructions to the jury and therefore it is not clear how the additional talk of recklessness justifies the instructions and the verdict against the two convicted defendants. Nonetheless, the court of appeals dismissed this argument along with others. On August 19, 1994, the court affirmed the convictions of Sergeant Koon and Officer Powell.

The major surprise in the appeal was that the court ruled that the sentence was far too lenient—perhaps half of what the convicted defendants deserved. Judge Davies relied on several arguments to justify his departure from the Federal Sentence Guidelines. Notable among them were the likelihood that the police officers would be abused in prison, the unfairness of the second prosecution, and King's own contribution to the incident. The appellate court rejected all of these factors and remanded the case for the setting of a higher sentence.

CHAPTER THREE

Jews

"[A]gain I heard the tinkling of the glass."
—*Survivor of* Kristallnacht *commenting on the acquittal of Lemrick Nelson.*[1]

IN 1993, ON THE SAME TUESDAY IN NOVEMBER, NEW YORK AND Jerusalem, the two most important Jewish cities in the world, voted new mayors into office. Rudy Giuliani outpolled one-term incumbent David Dinkins, and Ehud Olmert ousted Teddy Kollek, long-time mayor of Jerusalem. As the results became known, the *Jerusalem Post* ran a cartoon capturing the political reality expressed in the electoral results. Dinkins meets Kollek on a desert island, touches his elbow reassuringly, and says, "I guess we both owe our retirement to the [ultra-orthodox] communities."[2] The cartoon captures the current political divide in the Jewish world.

In Jerusalem, the right-wing orthodox vote for Olmert reflected the political struggle in Israel between the religious and secular forces for control of public monies and the definition of Israel as a Jewish state. In New York, though mainstream Jews supported Dinkins significantly more than did other white voters, the Hasidic fringe turned out in fervent opposition to the mayor, who, they said, had negligently managed the 1991 riots in Crown Heights, a Brooklyn neighborhood consisting almost entirely of black Americans and ultra-orthodox Jews. At his inauguration on January 2, 1994, Mayor Giuliani showed his gratitude by inviting Rabbi Moshe Sherer of the right-wing organization Agudath Israel to deliver the invocation.[3]

The defeat of Dinkins and Kollek illustrates the political and cultural division of Jews, who are divided today far more deeply, it seems, than either gays or blacks. All African-Americans and out-of-the-closet gays suffer with Rodney King and Harvey Milk. But when a black-hatted Jew falls victim to a bias crime, the suffering is localized. The traditional anti-Semitism of the dominant culture is reflected in a tendency of mainstream and progressive Jews to distance themselves from the crime. Among the assimilated Jews in universities and the media, very few identify with the victims of anti-Semitic hate crime; after all, they pass in black and white society and never encounter the hatred directed against their orthodox kinsmen.

When Rabbi Meir Kahane was assassinated in a New York hotel meeting room in November 1990, his sympathizers came almost entirely from the ranks of his own organization, the Jewish Defense League. When the Hasidic Jew Yankel Rosenbaum was stabbed to death on the first night of the August 1991 Crown Heights riots, his own community rose up in protest. Though dismayed by the killings, most New York Jews did not see themselves as directly threatened. After all, Kahane was a right-wing political activist and Rosenbaum was a devotee of a separatist culture that upwardly mobile secular Jews have left behind.

Hasidic Jews (the *Haredi* or "strict ones" as they are called in Israel) set themselves apart from Gentiles as well as from other Jews. They are to Jews as the Amish are to Christians. The difference is that the dominant American culture treats the Amish with bemused respect. The Amish are allowed to keep their children out of public high school, even though they have no alternative educational opportunity to offer. The desire of the Amish to insulate their children in a rural agricultural culture is treated as a First Amendment right, the "free exercise of religion."[4]

No similar respect is accorded to the "strict Jews"—neither by

Jews nor by the dominant culture. Philip Roth describes the contempt of secular Jews for their devout but distant cousins in his short story "Eli the Fanatic." A Hasidic Jew causes consternation and fear when he moves into a suburban neighborhood of reform and assimilated Jews. Richard Goldstein made the point well in the *Village Voice*.[5] The Lubavitch Hasidim, the group victimized in the Crown Heights riots, practice outreach toward assimilated Jews. They approach people in public places and ask them whether they are Jewish. If the response is "Yes," they try to induce the wayward modern Jew to engage in an immediate act of religious worship. In a moving article on the August 1991 racial confrontation, Goldstein confessed that until the riots, when approached in this manner and asked whether he was Jewish, he would respond to the Hasid, "Not if you are." Would a Christian respond with this amalgam of shame and contempt to an evangelical Amish brother or a Catholic nun who addressed him? I doubt it.

Jewish self-contempt internalizes anti-Semitism. As the Jewish cop Robert Gold says in David Mamet's film *Homicide*, "There has been so much anti-Semitism in the last 4000 years, the Jews must have been doing something wrong." Anti-Semitism attacks not only the inner peace of Jews; it may have distorting effects on the judicial process. And, significantly, the impact may be strongest when Jews emerge as victims, as in the killings of Meir Kahane and Yankel Rosenbaum.

There are, to be sure, dangers of convicting innocent Jewish defendants on the basis of anti-Semitic stereotypes. A subtle presumption of guilt works against some Jewish defendants as it does against some black defendants, though the bias attaches to different stereotypes and different crimes. When the charge implicates Jews in behavior disloyal to their country of citizenship or shady financial dealings, less evidence may be sufficient for conviction; and even if the conviction is deserved, the penalty may well be greater than that accorded a non-Jewish defendant who committed the same offense.

There is more than a hint of this pattern in the experiences of

Julius and Ethel Rosenberg, Jonathan Pollard, and Michael Milken. The Rosenbergs were convicted of espionage in 1953 on the testimony of a single witness. A Jewish judge, Irving Kaufman, sentenced them to death because, in his curious view of history, they were also responsible for the deaths of American soldiers in the Korean War of 1950–53. Jonathan Pollard was convicted in 1987 of committing espionage for Israel and was sentenced to life imprisonment. Though there is no doubt of his guilt, many have argued that the penalty was excessive and unfair in view of his agreement to a plea bargain with the prosecution. Michael Milken innovated junk bonds on Wall Street and made a return emblematic of the financially overheated 1980s. For the crime of using inside information in trading, a federal jury convicted him and Judge Kimba Wood sentenced him to ten years in jail, presumably to set an example for others. The Jewish factor was close at hand in all these cases, for these were crimes of disloyalty and greed—the traits typically ascribed to anti-Semitic stereotypes.

Jewish victims receive their share of prejudiced verdicts. These perversions of the law parallel the effects of homophobia and racism in the Harvey Milk and Rodney King trials. The impact of subtle anti-Semitism on a Gentile jury might be to render the crime less serious and thus make the jury inclined either to acquit or, as in the Harvey Milk trial, to convict on a less serious charge. After all, if the victim is not "one of us," there is less reason to treat an intentional killing as a murder. This may have been the case in the surprising not-guilty verdicts of the two men charged with the killings of Meir Kahane and Yankel Rosenbaum. Before indicting the legal system on these grounds, however, we need to define and track the elusive phenomenon called anti-Semitism.

There are at least five ways of articulating anti-Semitic stereotypes. In a recent survey of attitudes toward Jews conducted by the Anti-Defamation League, four of these ways were evident. The ADL submitted 11 generalizations about Jews to a fair sampling of the American public. Seven of them probed the popular image of Jews as working together as a group to exercise power over Gentiles:

1. Jews stick together more than other Americans.

2. Jews always like to be at the head of things.

3. Jews have too much power in the U.S. today.

4. Jews have too much control and influence on Wall Street.

5. Jews have too much power in the business world.

6. Jewish businessmen are so shrewd that others don't have a fair chance in competition.

7. Jews don't care what happens to anyone but their own kind.

The fear of Jewish conspiratorial power is apparently one of the driving forces of anti-Semitism, in the United States as well as in Europe and Japan. One of the 11 questions asked was whether Jews are more loyal to Israel than to the United States. One assayed social anti-Semitism. (Do Jews have a lot of irritating faults?) And two tested the once widespread view that Jews are money-hungry, dishonest businessmen. (Are Jews more willing than others to use shady practices to get what they want? Are Jews just as honest as other businessmen?) Missing from the survey was a query about the historically pervasive Christian foundations of anti-Semitism: a question whether Jews deserve to suffer "because they killed Christ." The ADL seemed primarily interested in whether the public perceives Jews as possessing certain characteristics that may trigger fear, anger, or contempt. The survey omitted characteristics that speak favorably of Jews, such as generalizations about Jewish talent, intelligence, family values, and aversion to heavy drink. Respondents who affirmed six of the negative generalizations about Jews were classified as "anti-Semitic."

The disturbing conclusion of the ADL study is that 20% of all Americans entertain a negative stereotype of Jews. More significant for our purposes is the greater tendency of African-Americans to affirm the stereotype of the power-mad, conspiratorial Jew. The replies of black Americans, on the whole, ran 37% in favor of that stereotype, and among those with no university education the

figure was a frightening 46%. To this disturbing figure we should add
the impact of Christian anti-Semitism, which was left out of the
survey. In view of the relatively high rate of Christian observance
among African-Americans, hostility toward "Christ-killers" might
run higher than in the population as a whole.[6] In view of the fact
that jury service draws the less-well-educated (and presumably more religious) segment of the public, the likelihood that black
jurors will harbor anti-Semitic attitudes approaches one in two. The
American Jewish Committee has come to slightly different conclusions on the basis of its own surveys, but the differences are matters
of degree on such questions as whether black anti-Semitism increases or decreases with college education.[7] Whatever the details,
we should be concerned about the risk that anti-Semitic attitudes
may influence jury deliberations. Of course, screening potential jurors with careful questions might eliminate some of the more obviously bigoted, but the danger of distortion in jury deliberations
remains too serious to be ignored.

The assumption that Jews engage in shady dealings makes it
easier to convict a Jew charged with fraud, insider-trading, or other
crimes of financial manipulation. More intriguing, for our purposes,
is the way in which anti-Semitic attitudes distort the process of
judgment when Jews are victims. When a gay was a victim in the
prosecution of Dan White, critics of the verdict argued that anti-gay
sentiments made it easier for the jury to downgrade the gravity of the
killing. When a black was the victim in the trial of the four police
officers in Simi Valley, the fear of black crime arguably drove the
jurors into supporting the police as the "thin blue line" protecting
suburban peace. Our concern here is whether in the homicide trials
arising from the killings of Meir Kahane and Yankel Rosenbaum
anti-Semitic attitudes played a part in generating acquittals in defi-
ance of the evidence.

This is a subject difficult to assay in a responsible manner.
Discussions of racism in criminal justice fluctuate between the all-
knowing pretensions of the victim groups and the blind eye of those

charged with bias. Either the matter is too obvious for proof or there is no need to probe it at all. My own view is that there is a serious risk of biased distortion in all the cases we have discussed, but the charge is one that eludes proof. Without in-depth psychological investigations of the jurors who served on these particular juries, there is no way of knowing how much they were influenced by prejudiced assumptions about gays, blacks, and Jews.

The most I can claim for the discussion in this chapter is that it explores the mechanism by which anti-Semitism might have influenced the jury deliberations in the Kahane and Rosenbaum trials. In neither case did a Jew serve on the jury; in both cases there were six African-Americans, few of whom appeared to have a university education. The danger of statistical studies about thinking in stereotypes is that they generate their own stereotypes, namely the profile of the less-well-educated black anti-Semite. Nothing could be more unfair to the 12 black jurors who served on these two juries than to assume that they, or any one of them, fell into the ADL's category of "anti-Semitic." Yet the danger is there, and the disturbing consensus reached by these two juries requires that we explore how they could have reached their surprising verdicts.

The Trial of El Sayyid Nosair

The alleged assassin of Meir Kahane was Arab immigrant El Sayyid Nosair, 36 years old, a U.S. citizen since 1989. He worked as a boiler tender in the courthouse in which, coincidentally, he would be put on trial. It is not clear how or why he came to hear Kahane speak on a Monday evening, November 5, 1990, at the Marriott Hotel in midtown Manhattan. He could not have expected Kahane to say anything he would enjoy hearing. Kahane had begun his career as an American religious leader with a spiritual mission. His ambitions turned nationalist. In the 1960s he organized the Jewish Defense League to protect Jewish interests on the streets of New York. He then emigrated to Israel, where he organized the right-wing political party Kach. When tensions began to develop in the late 1970s in the occupied territories, his political line turned hardhearted and brutal: He advocated various means of expelling the Arab population from the territories or at least of inducing them to leave. Nosair could only have expected to be angered by what he heard. His mere presence at the speech, therefore, reeks of political purpose.

At the end of Kahane's speech, shots ripped through the audience. Kahane lay wounded. Several witnesses saw Nosair holding or apparently secreting a gun immediately after the shooting. As Nosair tried to run out, a 72-year-old man, Irving Franklin, tried to stop him. Nosair shot him in the leg. Down the block from the hotel, he commandeered a taxi driven by Franklin Garcia by holding a pistol to his head. When the taxi stopped for a red light, Nosair fled and ran into the path of a uniformed postal service officer, 56-year-old Carlos Acosta. In an exchange of gunfire, both men were wounded. According to ballistic experts, the .357 Magnum found lying next to Nosair was the same as that used in the shooting of Kahane.

The only weak link in this tight chain of incriminating evidence is Nosair's connection to the gun. Maybe it was not his gun at all. Maybe the police or one of Kahane's people had put it next to him. In any criminal case, there is room for fanciful hypotheses to explain away overpowering evidence. But typically one needs evidence to support alternative explanations of how the suspect gets implicated in a web of evidence. When there is no counter-evidence, as in this case, the only option for the defense is to argue that a conspiracy— typically implicating the police—has sought to "frame" the defendant and use him as a "fall guy" to take the penalty in place of the real culprit. When the victim is a Jew, and the representative of a Jewish organization, this strategy is particularly easy to ply. All one needs to do is invoke the popular myth of the conspiratorial Jew. A jury with anti-Semitic leanings is likely to believe this canard on the basis of chimerical evidence. If only some of the jury members are anti-Semitic, they at least will be sympathetic to the view that Jews conspired to frame the defendant.

This is the best reconstruction of the strategy that William Kunstler and his associate Ronald Kuby used to nourish a reasonable doubt in the jurors' minds. I ascribe no motives to Kunstler except the understandable aim of winning for a client who insisted on pleading not guilty.[8] From jury selection to final argument, the defense played on the possibility that the jury might believe that Jews would conspire to bring about a false conviction. This strategy would not surprise Alan Dershowitz, who said, with a mixture of scorn and respect, "Kunstler knows better than anybody in America how to manipulate the ethnic prejudices and biases of a jury."[9]

Kunstler did everything he could to get a jury of, as he put it, Third World, nonwhite voices. He wanted people "who had been pushed down by white society."[10] Why should he have wanted that kind of jury? There is nothing about the conflict between Jews and Arabs that resolves itself into an issue of white vs. nonwhite. There are many black Jews and many Caucasian Arabs. The only way this strategy would make sense is to assume that some black jurors would regard Jews, particularly organized and religious Jews, as the vanguard of an oppressive white society. Accordingly, the defense used its first nine peremptory challenges against prospective white jurors.

The defense was behaving according to the pattern we noted in the Harvey Milk and the first Rodney King trials: Keep men and women off the jury who might identify with the victim. But this time the discriminatory sickle cut deeper. Suspect were not only Jews but all whites. When the pattern became clear, Justice Alvin Schlesinger intervened and applied the newly declared New York rule that prohibited both the defense and the prosecution from discriminating in jury selection.[11] After that point, the defense had to justify its peremptory challenges in racially neutral terms.

After the judge clamped down on the defense's practice of discrimination, the prosecution nearly succeeded in placing a Jewish woman on the jury. Leona Kaplan presented herself for jury duty. Defense counsel Kunstler questioned her about her ties to the Jewish community. Some 32 years before she had taught at the Memphis Jewish Academy, a day school for Jewish students. She and her husband had also contributed to Israeli charities during the Six-Day War. Referring to the charities as supporting the "Israeli war machine" and thus demonstrating bias against Arabs, Kunstler challenged Mrs. Kaplan for cause—that is, on the ground that she was unlikely to be impartial. The Judge denied the motion. Then Kunstler sought to use a peremptory challenge—for which formerly no cause need be shown—to remove her from consideration for the jury. Now under the principle of non-discrimination, the question became whether the defense had a convincing nonracial reason for challenging Kap-lan. Kunstler repeated his arguments based on the assumption that practicing Jews could not be fair toward Arabs. This is undoubtedly an article of faith for Kunstler. He and co-counsel Michael Warren tried repeatedly to remove Jewish Justice Alvin Schlesinger on grounds of being biased against Arabs. And they subsequently tried, with no greater success, to challenge Orthodox Jewish Justice Michael Mukasey in the World Trade Center bombing trial. They must really believe that Jews (Kunstler excluded) cannot be fair-minded when judging crimes allegedly committed by Arabs. If they do not believe it, they are willing gratuitously to insult their judges, perhaps to put them on the defensive.

Over Kunstler's repeated protests, Justice Schlesinger rejected the use of the peremptory challenge against Mrs. Kaplan. He decided that Kunstler's arguments were purely racial in character. It appeared that Mrs. Kaplan would be sworn in as the 11th juror in the panel. Her presence on the jury would have been as important in securing an impartial trial as the presence of black jurors on the Rodney King jury. There was reason to rejoice. She was sworn in, but she never served. What happened?

Twixt the cup and the lip, there's many a slip. There are fewer between being sworn in and actually serving on a jury, but one of them tripped up Leona Kaplan. As the clerk was about to administer the oath to her, he asked both sides, as was his wont, whether they were satisfied with the juror. The prosecution said Yes, but the defense bellowed No. Nonetheless Leona Kaplan took her place among the jurors. Then a prosecutorial aide sitting in the audience noticed that Mrs. Kaplan looked familiar: perhaps she had once associated with the aide's parents. The aide called home and verified the association. The general principle is that jurors should have no personal ties either to the prosecution or to the defense. This was a remote instance of personal association. Nevertheless, the prosecutor William Greenbaum felt bound to call the matter to the attention of the Judge. At the same time Kunstler sought to challenge Mrs. Kaplan once again, this time on the grounds that she had heard Kunstler disapprove of her serving on the jury (the earlier debate about Jewish connections was beyond the earshot of the jurors). It was not Kunstler's fault that the clerk had asked whether Kunstler approved. He had given a truthful reply. The clerk should not have asked the question after the judge had rejected a peremptory challenge. But the harm had already been done.

The two grounds together—the personal association, however remote, and the possibility of bias produced by Kunstler's verbal rejection—proved too much for the prosecution. Though Mrs. Kaplan maintained that she could judge independently and impartially and prosecutor Greenbaum argued to keep her on the jury, the judge felt constrained to dismiss her. Chance had its way. The clerk's mistake, the honesty of the prosecutorial aide—in these peripheral human dramas, trials are won and lost. There would be no second chance to secure a juror of the same ethnicity as the victim Kahane. The most the prosecution could get was a non-Jewish woman who had worked for some years in an Israeli bank. The defense thought that she too was tainted, but she made it onto the jury anyway. The clerk had learned not to ask the question that gave the defense an additional ground for dismissing jurors it did not trust. As the trial began, there sat in the jury box six blacks, one Latino, and the rest non-Hispanic, non-Jewish Caucasians; nine were women and three were men. One of the jurors described the educational level as a mixture of high-school and college graduates.

The prosecutor, William Greenbaum, had reason to remain confident. His case seemed airtight. There was not much to do except present the array of witnesses and physical evidence linking

Nosair to the shootings of Kahane and the three resulting victims, the wounded Franklin, the coerced cab driver Garcia, and the wounded postal worker Acosta. Greenbaum hammered home the obvious, with 51 witnesses. One witness saw Nosair holding the gun near Kahane moments after the shooting. The ballistic experts linked the .357 Magnum found next to Nosair with bullet fragments found near Kahane. With so much evidence on the surface events, Greenbaum made the tactical decision not to elicit the political context of the assassination. The Middle East conflict would remain in the background.

Greenbaum was afraid to remind the jurors that the victim was a radical nationalist. He thought the term "Zionist" would carry the connotations of racism once expressed in a nefarious United Nations resolution, recently repealed. He made this connection explicit in a standard question used to prepare potential jurors for the trial and to filter out those obviously biased: "Would you reject the rest of what that person is saying solely because of your intensive strong feelings about them being racist or Zionist or nationalist?" This is an extraordinary coupling of suspect views. If the association between racism and Zionism seemed plausible to Greenbaum, he understandably sought to suppress the Middle East conflict and Kahane's image as a Zionist leader.

For Greenbaum, the facts spoke for themselves. He would create the equivalent of a videotape showing the surface events: Nosair approaching Kahane at the end of the speech, firing the .357 Magnum, and fleeing the room. There was no need for the jury to understand why Nosair went to the meeting, why he might have hated Kahane, why he had a strong motive to assassinate him. The case, it seemed to the District Attorney's office, would be won on the array of witnesses documenting Nosair's many crimes on that November night.

The prosecution's evidentiary overkill wrought its own problems. Fifty-one witnesses generate too many stories, with too many minor inconsistencies. Everyone sees and recalls the events differently. Discrepancies are normal. Yet when the defense has no real case, it can generate an obsessive interest in discrepancies. Some heard two shots, but only one bullet was recovered. That anomaly gave the defense an opening. The police found bullets in Nosair's pockets, but they disagreed on which pocket. Again, a wedge to work with. In the end, the jurors wanted to compare the precise details presented by the prosecution's witnesses. During deliberations they asked the court reporter to read back, in part, testimony from 40 of the prosecution's witnesses. They were content with what they had heard from the defense's six witnesses the first time around.

The prosecution's failure to articulate a motive left a clear field for the defense to speculate about how and why the killing really occurred. The defense devised the story that someone in Kahane's organization, the Jewish Defense League, killed him in a dispute over funds. The genius of this story is that it permitted Kunstler and his associates to refer repeatedly to a "Jewish Defense League Conspiracy."[11] After the conspiratorial Jews supposedly decided to eliminate Kahane, they hit upon Nosair as the best available fall guy. In their infinite cunning, they planted the .357 Magnum next to him as he lay on the sidewalk, wounded from his shootout with Carlos Acosta. Greenbaum branded the defense's theory ludicrous, as it undoubtedly was. But Greenbaum himself had left the grounds of Nosair's action uncovered. The defense moved in where the prosecution, mistakenly, feared to tread.

The defense pursued this theme by questioning all the prosecution's witnesses about their involvement with Kahane's Jewish Defense League and the Israeli party Kach. Midway during the trial, the prosecution moved to restrict this insinuating form of questioning, and Judge Schlesinger sensibly ruled that the defense could not pursue its "wild speculations" (Greenbaum's term) without substantiation. But there were other ways to play the ethnic card. Kunstler repeatedly stressed that Kahane's family refused to submit the deceased's body to the customary autopsy. Orthodox Jews regard it as their duty to respect the bodily integrity of the dead, partly because they believe that the Messiah's coming will lead to bodily resurrection. The corpse, therefore, must be buried intact. Accordingly, the family also insisted on burying Kahane's bloodstained clothes with him. Kunstler claimed that these moves frustrated the collection of reliable evidence about the cause of death. Yet the medical experts had no doubt that it was the shooting that had done the mortal damage.

Lawyers often argue that some bizarre event intervened between a homicidal act and the victim's death. If the intervening act was the true cause of death, then the defendant is not guilty of homicide. Kunstler tried this tactic by devising the tale that Dr. Steven Stowe, an orthodox Jew, had boarded the ambulance with Kahane and had killed him en route to the hospital. Stowe had alienated the medical staff at the scene by insisting on using his own method, namely manipulating the neck, to maximize Kahane's chances of survival. Of course, eccentric medicine hardly indicates a homicidal intent. But the speculative charge of intervening homicide, together with the emphasized absence of an autopsy, generated questions about the precise mechanism of Kahane's death.

Kunstler had many opportunities to remind the jury of the antagonism between passionate Arabs and nationalist Jews. The hostility expressed itself in the courtroom. So many supporters of Kahane and Nosair showed up for the trial that the guards decided to limit friction between the two camps by separating them on the opposite sides of the courtroom. Thereafter the guards admitted precisely 24 Arabs and 24 Jews at each session. It was as though the abortive 1947 United Nations resolution to partition Palestine had been realized in the courtroom. Some jurors seemed to be as attentive to the interaction between these opposing camps as they were to events in the trial itself. This point became clear when one of the jurors made the unusual request to speak to the judge in chambers. He had noticed that the witness on the stand, a young JDL member, and another Jew in the audience, also wearing a yarmulke, had made signs to each other during the witness's testimony. It turned out that the person in the audience was the witness's brother; his signs were designed to get the witness to raise his voice. What is significant about this little vignette is that the juror noticed the transaction at all.

His eyes were obviously turned to the young, exotically dressed religious men in the audience.

Kunstler lost no time in cross-examining the witness at great length about his associations with all the other Jews in the audience who wore yarmulkes. The more he stressed Jewishness and the more he pointed to signs of Jewish separateness, the more he could bolster his innuendos of Jewish conspiracy. The jury became so sensitized to the question of who was Jewish and who was not that many of them sought to classify witnesses by religious ethnicity. One witness, Ben Styger, a hotel concierge, spoke with a thick Dutch accent. One of the jurors (not the one who had noticed the gestures from the audience) petitioned the Judge to find out Styger's religion. Jewish or not? Incredible. Sensibly, the Judge would not answer the question. But it must have been apparent that the single defining feature of this trial had become the Star of David.

To those who move only in polite, well-socialized circles, talk of the conspiratorial Jew seeking to oppress blacks and other minority groups seems, as Greenbaum said, "ludicrous" and repellent. This is the language of the anti-Semitic tract "Protocols of the Elders of Zion," forged and disseminated in tsarist Russia. We had all assumed that modern enlightened society had buried these lies forever. Yet they are emerging again, with particular virulence, on Eastern college campuses. The speeches of Louis Farrakhan, his associate Khalid Abdul Muhammad, and CUNY Black Studies Chairman Leonard Jeffries draw enormous crowds. They do not deny the Holocaust; they make light of it. Muhammad asks: What did the Jews do to trigger Hitler's wrath? They speak highly of a current, historically deceitful pamphlet called "The Secret Relationship Between Blacks and Jews." Among other historical absurdities, this anti-Semitic tract claims that Jews owned 75% of the slaves in the antebellum South. To the dismay of other students and media observers, many black students seem to take these malicious innuendos and outright lies seriously. And when Jews criticize irresponsible allegations being passed off as "black history," their criticism is taken to be further proof of their conspiracy to suppress black people.[13]

No one knows, of course, whether this anti-Semitic propaganda had seeped through to the minds of either the blacks or the whites who voted to find Nosair not guilty of homicide. There is evidence that at least one black juror fought hard for conviction.[14] The jurors as a group tended to cite evidentiary gaps in the prosecution's case in explanation of their verdict. They were disturbed by inconsistencies in the testimony, by the failure to locate the bullet that killed Kahane, by the absence of an eyewitness to the shooting, and by the sloppy police work at the crime scene. Admittedly, the police should not have passed the gun found at Nosair's side back and forth between them. New York police officers often handle evidence in this casual way. (As we shall see, all these factors re-emerge in the trial of Lemrick Nelson, and the jury's mode of justifying its verdict repeats the same concerns about discrepancies in the multiple sources of proof.)

After four days of stormy deliberations, on December 21, 1991, the jury reached a compromise verdict. They acquitted Nosair of murder and all lesser charges connected with Kahane's death, but convicted him of assault against both Franklin and Acosta and of criminal coercion against the taxicab driver Garcia for commandeering his cab. Also, because Nosair did not have a license, he was guilty of possession of the gun with unlawful intent. Many commentators faulted the jury for not convicting Nosair of attempted murder against Acosta. It appeared inconsistent that his shooting could constitute assault but not assault with intent to kill—or attempted murder. It would have been easy for the jury to reason, however, that the killing had occurred in a spontaneous gunfight and therefore contained a blend of self-defense and aggression.

On the only charge that carried political implications, the jury's decision not to convict Kahane's apparent assassin appeared to be much worse than the reduction of the charge in the slaying of Harvey Milk and the Simi Valley acquittal in the beating of Rodney King. After all, the jury did convict Dan White of manslaughter. Though the jury's action in the King case might have been wrong, the defense had managed to articulate a compelling excuse based on the officers' perception of danger. The acquittal of Nosair had no logic to it. The jurors insisted that they had acquitted him because there was no eyewitness to the shooting. As one acerbic observer remarked, "People don't commit rape in a Macy's window."[15] The jurors asked for too much.[16] The judge too was outraged by the verdict. In another unusual move, he said publicly that the verdict was "against the overwhelming evidence and was devoid of common sense and logic."[17] As Kahane's Jewish supporters screamed "Death to Nosair" outside the courtroom, he sentenced the defendant to a maximum term of 7⅓ to 22 years for the array of minor charges on which he had been convicted.

Nationalistic Jews took to the streets in Israel as well as in New York. A hundred people marched across the Brooklyn Bridge and burned Nosair in effigy in front of the courthouse. In Israel, in eerie anticipation of the February 1994 Hebron massacre of Arabs kneeling in prayer, protesting Jews warned of retaliation. As satirical author Howard Jacobson reports from his firsthand observation of the Israeli response:

> A Baruch Somebody-or-Other, speaking on behalf of Kahane's followers, has promised that "if justice is not done, then a Jew will rise up who will do justice in this matter."[18]

Whether the speaker was Baruch Goldstein, who later committed the Hebron massacre, obviously did not seem important at the time.

An adequate explanation for the jury's wayward decision might be that some of the jurors got carried away with their role as amateur detectives. In the middle of the prosecution's examination of a witness, a juror waved his hand and asked permission to put questions directly to the witness. The judge agreed, provided the question was submitted to him first in writing.[19] This deviation (most lawyers have never heard of this legal option) may have encouraged the jurors to measure the state's evidence against that which they, as investigators, might have looked for. Shortcomings in the state's evidence thus loomed larger than usual.

Either as an alternative or a supplementary account, the

defense's manipulation of potentially anti-Semitic attitudes can not be disregarded. The repeated invocation of the "Jewish Defense League conspiracy" played into widely held biases and anti-Jewish stereotypes. Attacking the state's evidence for want of an autopsy suggested that somehow the victim's "peculiar" religion had contributed to the supposed holes in the state's case. Standing alone, the acquittal of Nosair on homicide charges might seem like a simple aberration in the administration of justice. A less charitable view emerges, however, as we compare the structure of this acquittal to the equally surprising outcome in the aftermath of the Crown Heights riots and the killing of Yankel Rosenbaum.

The Trial of Lemrick Nelson

Yankel Rosenbaum died on the first night of the worst race-motivated riots in New York City's post-Second World War history. Both Jews and African-Americans saw ghosts of their past in the events that began on August 19, 1991. The three days of looting and assaulting rekindled terrifying memories of European pogroms. More than the members of any other American subculture, the 15,000 black-coated observant Jews in the Crown Heights section of Brooklyn live in daily proximity to their past. Biblical legends have the immediacy of current events. The Holocaust has left fears of imminent persecution burned in their skin. Crowds yelling "Get the Jew" and the racist stabbing of Yankel Rosenbaum became a symbol of their worst fears: It can happen here too.

The triggering event for the black attack on the Jews was an automobile accident in the heart of the neighborhood where African-Americans, blacks from the Caribbean, and Hasidic Jews have lived for several decades in uneasy co-existence. A Mercury station wagon driven by a Hasidic Jew collided at an intersection with an oncoming car and careened onto the sidewalk, pinning two black Caribbean children against a brick wall. It remains disputed whether or not the station wagon entered the intersection after the traffic light had turned red; there is room to argue that the driver,

Yosef Lifsh, had been criminally negligent in causing the accident. This event too triggered specters from the past. As Arthur Herzberg described the accident "[B]lacks saw the ghosts of slave masters riding into their quarters and not caring whom their horses might trample."[20]

The careening car was the third in a police-guided motorcade that regularly accompanied the late revered leader of the Lubavitch sect, Rabbi Menachem Schneerson (the "Rebbe"), on his biweekly visits to the graves of his deceased wife and father-in-law, the previous Rebbe, at a cemetery in Queens. These visits were major events in the life of the late Rebbe and visible signs of his power and prestige in the community. On every trip, as on August 19, 1991, he received a police escort. It is unusual, at the least, for a religious leader to have a police escort every time he ventures forth into other neighborhoods. It is also unusual for the police to close off certain streets in Crown Heights on the Sabbath and on major holidays. The streets are closed in Brooklyn, as in Jerusalem and other religious centers in Israel, to protect the sensibilities of orthodox Jews for whom driving is a desecration of the holy day. The rerouting of buses and other traffic might be justified, on secular grounds, as a means of protecting the thousands of Hasidic pedestrians who spill from sidewalks onto the streets. The price paid by non-Jewish neighbors is not trivial. Dr. Vernon Cave complained, for example, that during his Saturday office hours patients had to walk several blocks from their parking places to reach his office.

These practices understandably generated a sentiment among the black residents of Crown Heights (80% of the local population) that the Jews received "preferential treatment" from the authorities.[21] Those familiar with religious politics in Israel will recognize a familiar pattern. As African-Americans resent special privileges for the religious Jews among them, so secular Jews in Israel object to restrictions imposed on them to ensure the sanctity of the Sabbath. This pattern of resentment accounts for the residents' particular sensitivity to the accident. Here was the Rebbe's motorcade, displaying the power and prestige of a seemingly privileged segment of the population, wreaking harm on the local residents.

The first reaction of the crowd that gathered at 8:20 P.M. at the scene of the accident was that even in tragedy Jews received better treatment. A private ambulance run by the Hasidic community, the Hatzoloh service, attended immediately to the Jewish driver and passenger and, in the perception of the crowd, ignored Gavin and Angela Cato, the children pinned under the car. As the first officer arrived at the scene, the African-American crowd was already pummeling the Jewish passengers in the Mercury station wagon. A police officer advised the Hatzoloh crew to remove the endangered Jews from the scene.[22] The crew's driving off without aiding the pinned children contributed to the impression of privileged treatment for Jews and indifference to the needs of the black victims of the accident.

As the members of the crowd grew angrier, they turned on their Hasidic neighbors. Blacks started throwing bottles at Jewish homes. By 10:30 P.M. "rocks and bottles were raining down at the scene of the accident."[23] The two or three reported assaults in the neighborhood were marked by anti-Semitic epithets: "Jew get out of here." An hour later, five long blocks from the scene of the accident, 29-year-old Yankel Rosenbaum, a Hasidic scholar from Australia, encountered a group of some 10 or 15 black youths. A few minutes later he had been stabbed four times in the chest and lay bleeding on the hood of a car. With the area becoming saturated by police, patrol cars converged quickly on the scene.

The first two officers, Richard Sanossian and Leonard Milazzo, happened fortuitously upon the fray. They saw a group of black youths crouched over a black-frocked Hasid. When they sounded their siren, the group dispersed. Sanossian said he noticed that one of the group was a young black male wearing a red shirt and a baseball cap. He broadcast a call for help over his portable radio and says that he mentioned "the red shirt" in his description.

Within minutes, officers arrived from several different precincts and police units. The major players were Officer Mark Hoppe and

Robert Lewis, a transit cop. Hoppe saw a black male wearing a red shirt running down the street. He knew that another officer was in pursuit of someone, but he did not who it was or why. Hoppe gave chase. The youth in the red shirt jumped over a fence into a private yard, with Hoppe in pursuit.

What happened in the aftermath suffers from the problems of reconstructing history from witnesses caught in the heat of the moment. As Rosenbaum lay bleeding on the hood of the car waiting for medical aid, the police raced off in different directions to find suspects of the stabbing. So far as we know, they brought four young blacks to Rosenbaum for identification. Of a 15-year-old youth named Cleon Taylor, Rosenbaum said, "He was one of them," though apparently not someone who had stabbed him.[24] He rejected both a "chubby kid" and a young man named John Anderson as his assailants.[25] Then Hoppe came up the street with 16-year-old Lemrick Nelson.

According to Officer Hoppe, he had found Nelson on the other side of the fence crouching behind a bush. He ordered him into the prone position, frisked him, and took a knife from his right front pocket. He opened it, noticed blood on the blade, closed it, and put it in his right rear pocket. As we shall see, another officer at the scene would give a slightly different account of these events.

Accompanied by several other officers, Hoppe and Nelson walked toward the crowd around Rosenbaum. As they approached, Hoppe took off Nelson's hat, presumably to expose his face more clearly. When Rosenbaum saw Nelson, he lifted himself up and spat at him. Rosenbaum then said, according to various accounts, "Why did you stab me?"[26] "The red shirt. The red shirt, that's him."[27] "Why did you do this to me?"[28] "He is one of them, the red shirt, I remember the red shirt."[29] "You were tough then but you're not tough without your friends."[30]

Rosenbaum's identification prompted Nelson's arrest. Various officers handled and traded Nelson back and forth, until about 3:00 A.M. the next morning he found himself in an interrogation room alone with Detective Ed Brown of the South Brooklyn homicide division. Yankel Rosenbaum had died a half-hour before. He was the second victim of the events of August 19. Gavin Cato had died on the way to the hospital.

Alone with Ed Brown in the interrogation room, Nelson apparently confessed to having stabbed Rosenbaum once in the left side. But the circumstances attending the confession were unusual. Detective Brown had facilities neither for tape recording nor video recording. He said later that he had read Nelson his Miranda rights, but Nelson had signed nothing at the time. Later, Detective Nemesio Abraham replaced Brown in the interrogation room and, according to him, Nelson confessed again in substantially the same form. No mode of interrogation could inspire less confidence.

Events were heating up outside. Though it was the middle of the night, Gavin's death brought one set of demonstrators to the 71st Precinct; Yankel's death brought another. With demonstrators facing each other across the barricades, the scene resembled the audience jeering at each other and at the authorities in the Kahane case. Under orders to take the prisoner to a Coney Island precinct, the detectives passed in front of the crowd with Nelson. It was a fateful moment. Nelson asked, "How much trouble am I in?" Having become aware of his situation, he changed from cooperative prisoner into fighting suspect. When the detectives asked him later to sign his confession, he refused.

Officer Hoppe had searched Nelson again at the station house and found three bloodstained dollar bills. These bills, together with the bloodstained knife, found their way eventually to Detective Abraham, who registered or "vouchered" them as evidence some 36 hours after the stabbing. Thus began the long process of preparing for trial. The bloodstained knife, the dollar bills, Nelson's pants, all were sent to the lab for testing. A week later, a grand jury indicted Lemrick Nelson on two counts of murder in the second degree and one count of criminal possession of a weapon.

The officers began conferring with Assistant District Attorney Sari Kolatch about their diverse perceptions of events on the night of August 19. The case for the prosecution was beginning to come together. They had Rosenbaum's identification of Nelson and Nelson's own confession, however irregular it might have been. They had the murder weapon in the pocket of the accused. Then the results came in from the lab. The blood on the knife and pants was definitely not Nelson's and was identical with Rosenbaum's (though consistent as well with that of another 11% of the U.S. population). Confidence reigned in the offices of the Brooklyn District Attorney Charles Hynes and his assistants. They were so sure of their position that they did not bother to locate the two African-American transit officers who were at the scene and had participated in the arrest.

Apparently, Nelson's lawyer Arthur Lewis knew nothing about those two transit cops until early in September 1992, a month before the trial. In response to Lewis's motions to suppress the key items of evidence—the knife because Nelson was unlawfully searched, the identification because it was tainted by police suggestions, and the confession because it had not been voluntary—Justice Edward M. Rappaport convened a suppression hearing. Lewis's motions were all ultimately denied, but the defense gained an unexpected prize from the hearing.[31] In the course of recounting the events of August 19, 1991, Officer John Marinos mentioned two African-American transit cops who had been present and assisting at the scene of Nelson's apprehension. At that point the prosecution did not know that their names were Robert Lewis and Gerald Wheeler. Defense counsel then demanded that the prosecution produce these two witnesses. The judge, a former criminal defense lawyer, gave the prosecution tips on how they could track down the two transit officers, which they soon did. Their failure to do so before and their apparent indifference toward interviewing the only two African-Americans in the entire cast of police carried the unfortunate suggestion that they wished to write a trial transcript with white officers only.

As the trial opened and jury selection began, the prosecution faced an even greater hurdle in getting victim representation on the jury than William Greenbaum encountered in the Kahane case.

Though Jews constitute 16% of the Brooklyn population and about 20% of the population eligible for jury service, fewer than 5% of the names on the list of potential jurors in the Nelson case were Jewish.[32] There would be no Leona Kaplan in Brooklyn who would even come close to making it onto the jury. As in the Manhattan trial, African-Americans constituted half of the jury; of the remaining six, three were Latinos and three were white.[33]

The selection of Nelson's jury took place in September 1992, when the embers of the Los Angeles riots were still glowing just below the surface of everyday speech. Defense counsel Lewis reminded the jurors of the ongoing conflict between blacks and the police. The backdrop of distrust for the police made it plausible for him to repeat the kind of conspiratorial charges that had run through the Kahane trial. Lewis tried to characterize the three days of violence as hostility directed not against Jews but against the police. "But for the behavior of the police that day," Lewis claimed, "the circumstances would not have escalated to what we have described as a police riot."[34] He claimed that a police officer had shoved Gavin Cato's father at the scene of the accident. The evidence of the epithets shouted at the scene, however, pointed to anger toward the Jews as the impulse for four nights of rioting.

Of course, it was not hard to make out a case of police incompetence, in this instance as in many others. The police failed to get the names of witnesses at the site of the stabbing. They failed to voucher the knife for 36 hours. They interrogated Nelson without any means of preserving his confession for use at trial. Yet the customary incompetence of the New York police hardly points to evidence of a "police riot."

Directing the jury's attention toward the police provided a convenient screen for the anti-Semitic hints that might have scored with the Nelson jury as they had with the Nosair jury. Again, the charge of Jewish conspiracy carried the weight of covert anti-Semitism. As Lewis claimed over and over again, the police, acting in collaboration with a Jewish civilian patrol, decided to frame Nelson. When cross-examining the prosecution's witnesses, he asked them repeatedly whether they had heard of the "Rabbi's roll call." The reference was to the supposed collaboration between the police and Rabbi Joseph Spielman, chair of the Crown Heights Community Council and liaison with the District Attorney's office. The charge of conspiracy never became as elaborate as in the tale spun by the defense in the Kahane case, but here it was, a screen for tempting the jurors to see the prosecution as an exercise of Jewish power. And Jewish power was not hard for them to find. It was all around them. Both the trial judge and the head prosecutor were observant Jews, and they conferred from time to time, in front of the jury, about their observance of the Jewish high holidays that fell during the trial.

Arthur Lewis propounded a clever tale to implicate the victim in a Jewish conspiracy. Rosenbaum "had a purpose for being out on the street that day."[35] According to Lewis, he was there to protect his "houses of worship" from vandalism.[36] He was a member of the civilian patrol. He knew karate. He was a fighter. This man who had come from Australia for a brief stay had supposedly enlisted immediately in the Jewish patrol and was no longer an innocent civilian. He was a combatant in the exercise of Jewish power in the neighborhood. This accounts for the curious line that Lewis used repeatedly at the trial and in press conferences afterwards: "Yankel Rosenbaum sacrificed his life on the evening of August 19th."[37] The notion that Rosenbaum made a "sacrifice" makes him partly accountable for his own ill fortune. He entered the fray. As Rodney King was supposedly "in control" of his own beating,[38] Yankel Rosenbaum walked into danger by leaving his home and patrolling the streets at 11:00 P.M. on the night of growing disturbances. There was no serious evidence for any of this, but for the defense it was a tale worth concocting.

Our understanding of anti-Semitism is so primitive that we do not know how a skilled African-American lawyer (and Lewis is black) might trigger these biased sentiments in the minds of the jurors. My hypothesis as I began to watch the trial on videotape was that Lewis's strategy would be to put himself in the role of a victim fighting back, and thus elicit the jury's sympathy and induce at least the six black jurors to identify with his resistance against the Jewish power arrayed against him in the courtroom. The more overbearing the Judge came across, the more sympathy and identification might flow forth from the jurors. The hypothesis is only partially validated by what one sees on the videocassettes recorded by Court TV. Lewis's behavior alternates between polite cooperation and rudeness seemingly intended to provoke the Judge into overbearing, chastising responses in front of the jury.

Generally, the judge did display an overbearing manner, but it was directed at both the prosecution and the defense. He would interrupt frequently and start questioning the witnesses himself. Lewis, for his part, made more mistakes under the rules of evidence than is common for well-trained lawyers. It almost seemed that he did not understand the limits on what he could ask witnesses. This meant that the judge often had to intervene against him, sometimes to the point of instructing him on how to ask questions. When Lewis asked an inappropriate question of the first witness, Esther Edelman, the judge corrected him, and Lewis responded, "You're not going to let me question the witness?" The judge told him to sit down. This kind of interplay recurred dozens of times in the course of the trial.

Many of the fights were beyond the ken of the jury. At one point, Lewis requested that the judge procure postmortem photographs of the victim. Justice Rappaport balked. When Lewis got angry, the judge interjected, "What do you think, we're out in the street? This is a courtroom."[39] To which Lewis responded, "Let's conduct it that way."[40] At times, however, the jury got a fair taste of this unprofessional behavior. At one point the question arose whether the police officers were eligible for rewards, as advertised at the precincts, for furnishing leads in the Rosenbaum case. Lewis wanted to probe the witnesses on this question, but the judge intervened and took over the questioning, as was his general practice. In an angry tone, Lewis complained that the judge was breaking into all his questions and trumpeted, "You can ask it if I don't get to it."[41] The judge heightened the tension by proclaiming, "We won't have this in front of the jury"[42] and called for a conversation beyond the jury's hearing. It did not take many exchanges of this sort for the jury to get the point that Lewis was fighting back against an overbearing judge.

To be fair, Justice Rappaport made an effort, informally and in his own words, to keep the jury informed of legal complexities as they arose. Yet, on the whole, he lacked a professional sense of decorum and restraint. He often sucked candies during the trial. He took telephone calls while he was on the bench. He attacked Steven Brill, president of Court TV, from the bench for having made a negative comment about him in public. But Justice Rappaport's worst fault was his failure to exercise restraint and to let the lawyers run the trial. He acted as though justice depended exclusively on him. In his arrogance, he committed the most unjust intervention in the trials discussed in this book.

The fateful intervention came during Transit Officer Robert Lewis's testimony. Officer Lewis validated the key points offered in the testimony of the other officers. Most importantly, he confirmed that Rosenbaum had identified Nelson as one of his assailants without first receiving cues from the police that they regarded Nelson as their prime suspect. Lewis added the sentence to Rosenbaum's supposed response, "You were tough then but you're not tough without your friends." There was only one slight inconsistency. Hoppe had not remembered seeing Officer Lewis at the scene of Nelson's apprehension and pat-down in the private yard. Lewis said he was there and indeed that he and his partner Gerald Wheeler were among the first to handle the knife. Hearing this, the judge lost his temper. He fumed in anger, "I will tell you this. The court wants Hoppe and Marinos back here on Monday. Do you follow me? I want them back."[43]

Sensing that something favorable was happening, attorney Lewis provoked the judge, "And what about Litwin?"[44] Detective Litwin had also testified about the sequence of events without mentioning the role of the transit police. The judge then shot himself in the other foot: "We will deal with Litwin. We will have Litwin back too. This is bad."[45] It may have been, but what Justice Rappaport did was "bad" beyond repair.

When a judge blurts out disbelief in the prosecution's case, he obviously assists the defense. And worse: A mistake that benefits the defense is not subject to correction. Why not? Because only mistakes that affect the outcome of the trial are subject to appeal, and a mistake in the defense's favor can, at worst, generate an acquittal. (If the defendant is convicted anyway, the mistake has no harmful impact.) The rub is that the prosecution cannot appeal an acquittal. Thus a mistake in favor of the defense, one that contributes to an acquittal, never reaches the higher courts for review and criticism. And so Justice Rappaport inadvertently put his thumb on the scale and tilted it in Nelson's favor. There was nothing the prosecution could do about it.

Prosecutors Sari Kolatch and James Leeper considered asking for a mistrial, but they were afraid that New York precedents would be interpreted so as to prevent their retrying the case.[46] The best they could do, therefore, was to avoid advertising the judge's *faux pas*. But the progress of the trial only compounded the judge's error. The defense recalled Officers Hoppe, Marinos, Milazzo, and Detective Litwin. It was unlikely that the court or the jury would learn much about the petty inconsistency between Officers Lewis and Hoppe: Did Lewis go over the fence or did he not? No one changed his testimony, and no one supported Lewis's version of the facts. My own sense is that Officer Lewis may simply have recalled the escapade with an exaggerated sense of his own importance.

With a second crack at the police witnesses, the defense gained an edge. First, the very return of the officers to the trial implied that the prosecution's case was running aground. Attorney Lewis had an opportunity to remind the jurors that the inconsistencies ran along the racial fault line. He could ask the white officers over and over again whether they saw black officers at the scene. Further, having the officers on the stand once again enabled Lewis to provoke embarrassing tremors about past charges of police brutality. He questioned them about complaints lodged against them with the police review board. He probed Hoppe, Marinos, and Milazzo about several incidents of reported assaults, thus setting the background for impermissible and unanswered insinuations that they had mistreated not only Lemrick Nelson but other African-Americans whose lives were touched by the events of August 19. At the close of his interrogation of Officer Hoppe, Lewis said he had one more question; the judge invited him to go ahead. In fact Lewis did not have a question, but a groundless accusation: "You sit here and say that you did not punch out Carmel Cato [the father of Gavin Cato], did you?"[47]

Insinuations of this sort are always ruled out of order, but they take their toll nonetheless. The jury hears them. The judge reminds the jurors that they should not consider blind charges unsupported by evidence. Yet when the charges are repeated over and over again, they acquire a kind of plausibility that comes from familiarity. They are as close as defense lawyers can come to propagating propaganda for their clients. In cutting corners, violating the judge's orders, and manipulating the jury with patently improper questions to the witnesses, Lewis approached the nadir of ethical behavior. Controlling him became Justice Rappaport's preoccupation.

The biggest blowup between attorney Lewis and the judge occurred as the defense started to put on its own case. Arthur Lewis wanted to develop his tale that Yankel Rosenbaum, the karate expert, "sacrificed" his life as a combatant in the civilian patrol. When he started calling witnesses, he wanted to question them about the patrol and how it collaborated with the police. This would support a general image of Jewish power, as expressed in influence with the police. According to the testimony of John Anderson, a black youth who himself had been briefly suspected of the stabbing, Rosenbaum came to the scene in a patrol car, jumped out, approached a group of black youths, and provoked the fight with a karate kick. If this story could be made plausible, the defense would have an argument. The entire strategy hinged on Rosenbaum's having been a member of the patrol.

Justice Rappaport ruled that he would not allow questions about the patrol unless Lewis could present "an offer of proof" about Rosenbaum's participation in the patrol. In other words, how did Lewis intend to prove it? If Rosenbaum had not been a member, then the inquiry about the patrol and its influence with the police would be irrelevant. There would be no anchor for the claim that Rosenbaum "sacrificed his life." Yet Lewis did not appear to understand the request for "an offer of proof." He thought he had a right to probe the witnesses about the Jewish patrol and its power without making the questions specifically relevant to the guilt or innocence of Lemrick Nelson.

As a result, Lewis and Rappaport started arguing in the style of a barroom brawl. No doubt to Lewis's regret, the jury was in the next room. He would have relished the role of the browbeaten black lawyer. In the end, however, the judge made his most sensible ruling of the trial: Lewis could not inquire of his witnesses about the Jewish patrol and the "Rabbi's roll call" unless he could link the patrol to the activities of Yankel Rosenbaum, and that Lewis could not do. There was no evidence for the grand conspiracy that Lewis hoped to infer from the myth of Jewish power. The ruling ran parallel to Justice Alvin Schlesinger's decision that defense counsel could not cross-examine witnesses about their role in Kach or the Jewish Defense League.

In the end, the prosecution had a much stronger case than William Greenbaum presented in the Kahane trial. As prosecutor Sari Kolatch stressed in her summation, the case for guilt traded on the testimony of the two most knowledgeable participants in the crime, the victim and the defendant. The victim made an unambiguous identification and the defendant made an unequivocal, if not properly recorded, confession. Add to this the blood on the knife, linked indubitably with the blood of the victim rather than with the blood of the defendant, and the evidence appeared overpowering. But that evidence, even the results of the blood testing, came into the trial by way of testimony. If the jurors experienced resistance to the witnesses, they would never appreciate how compelling the evidence was.

The Jury on Its Own

Judges typically think that jurors follow and comprehend the intricate legal instructions read to them at the end of a trial. And so Justice Rappaport must have thought as he droned on for several hours explaining the technical differences between the various kinds of murder and manslaughter. I know from experience that law students can barely comprehend these arcane legal points. There could be no greater fantasy than the assumption that jurors could hold all these "elements" and distinctions in their minds. Lawyers would like to think that when jurors retire to deliberate among themselves, they weigh the two sides presented to them and choose the more compelling version. In fact, jury deliberations often bear only tangential and accidental connections to the arguments presented at trial.

This was particularly the case with the jury that deliberated the fate of Lemrick Nelson. Because Governor Mario Cuomo initiated an investigation of the jury's acquittal of Nelson, we know more about the curious and tortured process of deliberation in this case than in the others under study.[48] Sitting alone in the jury room, the men and women, blacks, whites, and Latinos, began to look for common ground. Whom could they believe? What test could they use to determine whom to trust, whom not to trust? It turns out that this jury's starting points—the premises they could all agree on—had little to do with the lawyers' arguments.

The jurors seized on a minor fact barely mentioned at trial. Some of the officers, including Hoppe, Marinos, Milazzo, and Sanossian, had applied for a special commendation—an internal departmental reward—for apprehending Nelson on August 19. Hoppe wrote a report of the arrest describing his activities but omitting reference to the role of Robert Lewis in the pursuit over the fence into the yard. Neither Lewis nor Sergeant Brian Wilson, a minor player in the events, had applied for a commendation. To an apparently influential group among the 12 jurors, that difference provided a benchmark of credibility. Hoppe, they thought, was not credible because he had to stick to the story in his commendation report. If he deviated, many thought erroneously, he could be held liable for filing a false document.[49]

For this reason, and because the judge drew attention to the inconsistency between his and Hoppe's testimony, Transit Officer

Lewis became the pivotal figure in the case. Many jurors thought that the prosecutors' bringing him into the case at the last minute revealed a "cover-up." These speculations should have helped the prosecution, for Lewis confirmed the crucial points in the prosecution's case. As far as he was concerned, there was nothing untoward in the behavior of the other officers that would undermine the force of Rosenbaum's identification of Nelson as one of his assailants. Attorney Lewis was so disappointed and angry at Robert Lewis's testimony that he began his cross-examination by saying, "I am going to put in for a name change right after this trial."[50] At the end of his questioning, attorney Lewis added snidely, "You were used again."[51] Robert Lewis had done his job, but attorney Lewis treated him as a disloyal black brother.

The jury seems to have responded more to the form than to the content of Lewis's testimony. Here was an African-American brought into the case at the last minute. He had not applied for a commendation. His testimony was sufficient to force the judge to recall four other police witnesses. Without regard to what Lewis actually said, his presence was enough to sow doubts in the jury's mind. Yet more significant in the jurors' view were some details in the testimony of Sergeant Brian Wilson, another officer who had not applied for a commendation. The most important thing Wilson had done was to conduct the show-up—the presentation of Nelson to Rosenbaum for identification. His two critical admissions on the stand were first that Hoppe had shown him the knife at about the time he was conducting the show-up, and second that after he identified Nelson, Rosenbaum spat a gob of blood at him. These two admissions, buried among a thousand other details, provided the threads for the jurors to spin their instincts into doubts about Nelson's guilt.

Although Sergeant Wilson, along with every other witness, including Robert Lewis, denied that anyone had shown Rosenbaum the knife prior to the identification, the jury did not believe it. They thought that Rosenbaum must have seen the knife and therefore they were inclined to throw out his identification of Nelson as tainted. The gob of blood was even more significant. Wilson was the only witness to mention that there was blood in the spittle. If Rosenbaum's blood-laden spit had landed on Nelson's jeans, that would explain why the blood found on the pants matched Rosenbaum's blood but not Nelson's.

It sounds, then, that beginning with a totally irrational premise—namely that the officers who did not apply for commendation were believable and the others were not—the jurors could begin to couch their sympathies for Nelson in arguments that sounded almost logical. The jurors prided themselves on other sleuthing moves. They noted that the taped police record of communications on August 19 included the calls put in by Officers Sanossian and Milazzo. But contrary to those officers' testimony, the tape did not contain a reference to a "red shirt." The tape might have been wrong, or the reporting officer might have been reading later knowledge back into the initial moments. Either way, the detail was tangential. Yet the jurors came to speculate about why this discrepancy occurred and what it implied.

Another slip-up that stimulated the jurors' imagination was the late disclosure that Nelson is left-handed. This did not come into evidence until his teacher, Nancy Casella, testified. What, then, about finding the knife in his right pocket? That needed explaining. Even more significantly, when the jurors examined Nelson's pants in the jury room, they discovered blood stains on the left pocket. Yet there had been no lab test on those stains. They were beginning to get the feeling that the prosecution could not be trusted to put on the case properly.

The biggest single mistake that the prosecution made, however, was one that the jury did not even notice. The prosecutors had a secondary theory on which they could have convicted Nelson. Suppose he had not stabbed Yankel Rosenbaum. If he was present in the mob and if he encouraged the others to hit and kick the victim, he was complicitous in the assault and liable at least for manslaughter. The most famous example of this form of complicity is a notorious

New Bedford, Massachusetts gang rape, popularized in the Jodie Foster film *The Accused*, of a pack of beer-swilling bar hounds cheering on their comrades as they rape a woman who started dancing in the bar. The guys in the background, who never touched the victim, are held liable for rape. Encouraging, supporting, participating—all are sufficient to make one complicitous in the crimes of another. Most of the jurors believed that Nelson was with the mob as it attacked Yankel. But they had doubts about whether he actually put knife to flesh. Under these circumstances, it should have been easy to convict Nelson at least on a theory of complicity.

No one in the courtroom seemed to understand the relevance of complicity. The prosecution never mentioned it. As a result, Arthur Lewis had no reason to worry about the theory and respond to it. For him, mob rule was not a basis of complicity but a reason to excuse someone who was caught in the mood of the group. As Paul Robinson commented about the effort to excuse Damian Williams for brutally beating Reginald Denny in the April 1992 Los Angeles riots: "Riot used to be an offense; now it's a defense."[52] The same could be said of complicity: It used to be a ground for conviction; now it is a ground for sympathy.

The judge did instruct the jury on "acting in concert"—an arcane expression ordinarily used in tort law and which has no place in criminal law. And when he did invoke the phrase, he typically misused it as a qualification on the defendant's liability rather than as an independent basis for conviction. The issue of liability, as Justice Rappaport formulated it for the jury, was always whether Lemrick Nelson, "while acting in concert with others," kicked or stabbed Rosenbaum. The implication of this grammatical formulation is that if Nelson was not acting in concert, he was not guilty of anything. It is true that buried in his instructions of several hours, one finds a few sentences on aiding, abetting, and complicity. The jurors said that they did not understand the doctrine.[53] Neither they nor the prosecution seemed to appreciate that they all had an easier route to conviction.

Rosenbaum and King

In the politics of protest, the Rosenbaum case quickly came to be linked with the Simi Valley acquittal of the four Los Angeles police officers. In the aftermath of the Los Angeles riots, the New York City Council unanimously passed a resolution "lambasting the jury" in Simi Valley. It may seem like overreaching for a city council to condemn any jury, not to speak of one that deliberated on the other side of the continent. But the injustice seemed apparent to everyone. After the seemingly equivalent betrayal of Yankel Rosenbaum, Jews on the city council, particularly Noah Dear from Brooklyn, expected similar support for a resolution to condemn the wayward jury. Jews were disturbed not only by the verdict but by the apparent mood of celebration afterwards. The jury in Simi Valley had the decency to retire from the public eye. Eleven members of the jury that acquitted Lemrick Nelson joined Arthur Lewis the next night at a festive dinner with Nelson and a few reporters. Yet as the Jewish demand for solidarity grew louder, the city council balked. Mr. Dear complained in distress, "Is Jewish blood different from black blood?"[54]

When a seemingly unjust acquittal occurs, particularly in a case that offends the dignity of a minority group, the immediate demand becomes: federal action now. As nearly 5,000 Hasidic Jews gathered in protest on the night after the verdict, their thoughts were on Washington. American Jews have learned from African-Americans. They too march to the beat of "No justice, no peace." And they too clamor for intervention under the mantle of the federal civil-rights laws. This was the demand made after the assassination of Meir Kahane, to little avail. But in December 1992, with a trial pending in Los Angeles to erase the stains of Simi Valley, Jews felt justified in insisting on a federal civil-rights trial of their own.

The stumbling block was not double jeopardy but the terms of the statute. When agents of the state—and there are no more visible agents than police officers—commit a wrong, the federal authorities

have good grounds to intervene. Thus there was solid grounding for
the Los Angeles prosection. But when private persons commit a
wrong, the feds have trouble finding a legal hook on which to hang
their prosecution. There are two provisions in the current civil-rights
laws that could come into play to support a federal prosecution
against the killers of Yankel Rosenbaum. The first imposes liability if
"two or more persons conspire to injure, oppress, threaten, or intimidate" anyone in the exercise of a constitutional right.[55] The other
applies to individuals who injure any person because of his religion
provided he is enjoying a "benefit, service, privilege, program, facil-
ity, or activity" under auspices of the state.[56]

Under the first provision, the government could readily establish
a conspiracy to attack Rosenbaum; the problem is whether the point
of the attack was to interfere specifically with a constitutional right.
The latter provision is drafted more broadly to cover not only constitutional rights but any benefit provided by the state. The argument
for the prosecution is that public streets are a benefit conferred by the
state. There are no precedents that precisely support this point, and
therefore Attorney General Janet Reno understandably dragged her
feet in responding to the demand for federal intervention.

Jewish organizations began a campaign to secure prosecution under this provision of the civil-rights laws. In September 1993, the Senate passed a resolution urging a federal investigation. Then, in
January 1994, Brooklyn D.A. Charles Hynes also petitioned the Justice Department to convene a grand jury to investigate the murder of
Yankel Rosenbaum. He had concluded that the state could go no further in investigating the case. There were rumors of another possible
suspect, Ernesto Edwards, but Hynes did not think he could convict
him in state court. Finally, Janet Reno announced that she would
convene a grand jury to investigate the killing.[57] In August 1994, the
investigation ended in an indictment and the promise of another trial.

The new form of political trial puts extraordinary pressure on the
federal government to provide the court of last resort in all cases of
apparent jury breakdown. The state systems of justice, coupled with
appeal to the Supreme Court on constitutional issues, provides am-

ple protection for criminal defendants. What the states have not developed, however, is an adequate system for protecting the interests of victims. This failure has become politically urgent in cases where the victim captures the frustrations of a minority group. The sad tales of Harvey Milk, George Moscone, Rodney King in Simi Valley, Meir Kahane, and Yankel Rosenbaum teach us that some form of appeal is imperative when juries fail to convict. The only solution we have found so far is the use of federal civil-rights laws as a fail-safe remedy against wayward juries.

Yet other remedies are imaginable. We begin our study of those alternatives by turning to a story in which the victims have fought back and won. This is not the story of a minority, but of the majority gender that for too long has received short shrift in American criminal justice.

Postscript: Plus ça change, c'est plus la même chose. The more things change, the more they remain the same. By the fall of 1994, the same defendants and the same lawyers, with some shifts, were back in court defending against charges based on the same crimes. In August 1993, the federal government had indicted El Sayyid Nosair along with 14 others under a federal racketeering statute for conspiring to engage in acts of terrorism, including the murder of Meir Kahane. William Kunstler and Ronald Kuby were preparing to defend one of the defendants, Ibrahim A. Elgabrowny. But in September 1994, Judge Michael Mukasey, already challenged by the two as Jewishly biased, disqualified them on grounds of conflicts of interest with other clients.

In early August 1994, a federal grand jury indicted Lemrick Nelson, by then 19 years old, for having violated Yankel Rosenbaum's civil rights on August 19, 1991. In the curious packaging of the law, the violation consisted not in killing him but in depriving him, because he was Jewish, of the use of the public streets. The indictment was kept secret because the judge assigned to the case, Judge David G. Trager, still had not decided whether to try Nelson as a juvenile or as an adult. Because he was under 18 at the time of the alleged crime, Nelson was still regarded as presumptively a minor under federal law.

Michael W. Warren, one of the lawyers for Nosair in the state trial, replaced Arthur Lewis as counsel for Nelson. He immediately displayed the same style he and Kunstler used in defending Nosair. He challenged Jewish Judge David Trager as biased, the reason being that the head of the selection committee that recommended Trager for the bench was also the head of a Jewish organization that called for a federal investigation of the Crown Heights killing. If this were the standard for recusal, no Supreme Court justice appointed by the president could rule on one of the president's policies. Instead of rejecting the motion out of hand, Judge Trager postponed his ruling, thus lending credence to the possibility of his bias.

CHAPTER FOUR

Women

"It ain't men bashin', it's female assertin' "
—*Interview with Monique Mathews in Anna Deavere Smith,*
Fires in the Mirror *(1993).*

GAYS, BLACKS, JEWS, AND OTHER MINORITIES FEEL, FROM TIME TO time, burned by the system. When compassion flares for the accused, victims often get trapped in the backdraft. In one way or another, defense counsel puts *them* on trial. The blame shifts from one side of the courtroom to the other. The defendant is convicted on a lower charge or gets off altogether because, according to the jury's sentiments, the defendant does not deserve more severe condemnation for the crime. So it was in the Harvey Milk case when the defense managed to highlight the peculiarity of the "gay lifestyle." The attack on the victim was more serious in the Rodney King prosecutions, as the defense tried to insinuate to the jury that King was a dangerous monster on PCP. The notion that he was in charge of his own beating made him appear at fault for the action shown on the videotape. Allegedly, he could have stopped the beating at any time, and therefore he brought about his own suffering.

Black victims are routinely put on trial, as were the four youths who surrounded Bernhard Goetz in a Manhattan subway. Defense lawyer Barry Slotnick went so far as to claim that his client was not

Goetz but "the people of New York" and they had an interest in vindicating frontier justice underground. Jews have received the same treatment. In no case was the turnabout more obvious, however, than in the groundless and incessant references to the Jewish conspiracy to frame El Sayyid Nosair and Lemrick Nelson. The charge was so insidious and so unrelated to the evidence that the prosecution never adequately responded.

Blaming the victim has become an effective defensive tool when the victim represents an unpopular minority. Where did all this begin? Where did lawyers learn that the way to win a case is to convict the victim? The place to look is in the long tradition of defending men accused of rape.

Defending Rape by Blaming the Victim

As we are now becoming aware, women aggrieved of sexual mistreatment have had, for centuries, to run the gauntlet from suspicious police to hesitant prosecutors to hostile courtrooms. The woman's sexual virtue has always been on trial; her testimony has always been treated as suspicious. As expressed by a late-17th-century commentator, the general sentiment has been: "Rape is . . . an accusation easily to be made and hard to be proved, and harder to be defended by the party accused, tho never so innocent."[1] No group of victims has ever been treated with so much suspicion.

Susan Brownmiller, in her call to men and women to wake up to the injustices of the past, dubbed this suspicious attitude a "cherished male assumption that female persons tend to lie."[2] The suspicion comes into Western culture, she claims in her 1975 bestseller *Against Our Will: Men, Women and Rape*, as the moral teaching of the story of Joseph and Potiphar's wife in Genesis 39:14. When Joseph, then enjoying Potiphar's trust, refused her sexual entreaties, she grabbed his cloak and used it to accuse him of coming to her with the intent to seduce her, thus making light of both his master and his master's wife. Potiphar's wife, the rejected, lascivious woman, has become a cultural artifact in the West. She is memorialized in the words of the poet William Congreve:

Heaven has no rage like love to hatred turned,
Nor hell a fury like a woman scorned.[3]

The suspicion that rape complainants are enraged, scorned women took on more sinister overtones when Freudian social commentators, in particular psychologist Helene Deutsch, began to argue that women entertained masochistic rape fantasies.[4] Whatever a responsible statement of the psychiatrist's position might be, lawyers are prone to vulgar versions of the prevailing wisdom. Thus the great evidence scholar John Wigmore fell prey to mid-20th century intellectual currents of skepticism toward rape victims. In an oft-cited and oft-criticized passage, Wigmore wrote that "errant young girls and women" suffered from "multifarious" "psychic complexes" that resulted in their "contriving false charges of sexual offenses by men."[5] One wonders whether wholesale propositions about "errant young girls and women" have any more reliability than the charges of Jewish conspiracy that fueled the defense in the Kahane and Rosenbaum cases.

Wigmore's language illustrates the general strategy for attacking women who filed rape charges in the recent past. The effort was to prove that they were "errant" because they had had prior sexual experience and therefore, as the argument went, they were likely to have consented and to be lying if they said the contrary. Until well into the 1970s the courts permitted defense counsel to question the complainant about her sexual experiences with other men and to get witnesses to comment on her reputation for "chastity." Once the "unchastity" of the "prosecutrix" was established, the jury was told that they could infer consent to sex with the defendant from her apparent disposition to sleep around.

In 1970 California had a standard jury instruction, available in a bound volume in every judge's chambers, that permitted an inference of consent from a state of "unchastity" established by prior sexual experience. It was difficult if not impossible to convince judges not to use this standard instruction; they were afraid that if it did something to worsen the position of the defense and a conviction followed, the conviction would be reversed on appeal. As an assistant district attorney in Los Angeles County, I tried to convince a judge not to use the standard instruction by arguing that the concept of chastity was no longer applicable in California law. Unchastity refers to unlawful intercourse—that is, fornication outside marriage. But, as I maintained, fornication was not a crime in California and therefore it made no sense to describe a witness who admitted prior sexual experience as having engaged in "unlawful intercourse." The judge listened politely to my argument and then gave the jury the standard instruction on "unchaste" sexual behavior and what it implied.

And what did "unchaste character" imply? We need to indulge in a bit of moral archaeology to excavate what the judges might have been thinking. They seem to have assumed that unconstrained female sexual desire was something like a propensity for violence. If released repeatedly in the past, it was likely to be exercised randomly in the future. In the way an aggressive male might attack anyone who looks at him the wrong way, a lustful female is likely to consent to sex with anyone who looks at her the right way. The message was simple: Bad girls are likely to consent; good girls say no.

A more insidious implication of "unchaste character" was that there was no great harm in forcing intercourse on a woman who was already fallen. Once damaged, the goods cannot be further defiled. This view of the "experienced woman" impressed itself on the California Supreme Court in an otherwise sound precedent of the mid-1960s. A young man named Francisco Hernandez technically committed statutory rape and was convicted for sleeping with a young woman who was three months short of 18 years, the official age at which a woman's consent then made intercourse lawful. On appeal, Hernandez explained that she looked older than her years and that in fact he had no reason to suspect that she was "jailbait."[6]

To generate sympathy for the convicted defendant who had slipped innocently into the statutory vise prohibiting sex with minors, the court approvingly cited language from a 1923 Missouri opinion that reeks with prejudice toward young women who dare to enjoy sexual freedom.[7] The young female, who should have enjoyed the statute's protection, was branded a prostitute. As the California Supreme Court quoted the Missouri opinion:

> This wretched girl was young in years but old in sin and shame. A number of callow youths, of otherwise blameless lives . . . fell under her seductive influence. . . . They did not defile the girl. She was a mere "cistern for foul toads to knot and gender in." Why should the boys, misled by her, be sacrificed?[8]

No language could better illustrate the Madonna-prostitute complex of the courts: There are virtuous women who are not "errant," who do not have complexes, who are not seductive. And there are prostitutes whom one cannot "defile," for they are already contaminated by their loose behavior. The California Supreme Court gave young Hernandez a break and reversed his conviction. But it did the right thing for the wrong reason—or at least in part wrong. The courts can do justice to a defendant without endorsing gratuitous attacks on the complaining witness's character. The question is whether they want to.

When judges dared to resist this traditional way of blaming "loose" women for their own fate, they ran into trouble on appeal. As late as the early 1970s, we find appellate decisions reversing convictions because the judges did not give instructions favorable to the defense. In one federal case against multiple defendants that originated in the Virgin Islands, the trial judge instructed the jury that just because the alleged victim of rape "may have been promiscuous with some of these people [i.e. the defendants], or all of them at different times, does not give them a vested interest in their demanding that she perform it at their pleasure."[9] That sounds like a reasonable view of the law, but the defendants appealed and won on the ground that the judge should have given an instruction that the complainant's bad reputation of unchastity was "of substantial probative value in judging the likelihood of her consent."[10] The issue was nominally consent, but in fact the victim was chastised and blamed for being a loose woman.

By the mid-1970s, as a harbinger of greater activism, the National Organization of Women began intervening in appellate cases to argue against the use of jury instructions incorporating outmoded views of sexual morality. In a Virginia appellate case, NOW won a partial victory when it claimed that a trial judge correctly prohibited male witnesses from testifying about their sexual relations with the woman complaining of rape. The judges did reverse the resulting conviction, however, on the ground that the male witnesses should have been able to testify about the alleged victim's reputation for unchastity.[11]

These anachronistic biases ached for reform. Rape reform became as important in the feminist agenda as the repeal of punishment for abortion. But as *Roe v. Wade*[12] wound its way toward a successful resolution in the Supreme Court, feminists wisely gave up on the courts as the vehicle for rape reform. There was only so much one could do to counteract the judges' fear of ruling against the defense and risking reversal on appeal. The fight shifted to state legislatures. And, surprisingly, these naturally conservative, male-dominated bodies got the message. One state after another legislated to protect rape victims against intrusions of Victorian moral hypocrisy. As early as 1974, California countermanded by statute the inference from prior sexual activity to consent in a particular case.[13] A specific provision outlawed the use of the term "unchaste character" in rape prosecutions.[14] In an effort to expunge memories of injustice, the legislature branded the words themselves as taboo.

Yet this was hardly enough. The legislature had to root out the innuendos that sprang from prior sexual history, and they could do this only by restricting inquiry altogether into a woman's past sexual encounters. Thus in the late 1970s and early 1980s, one state after another enacted a "rape shield" statute designed to protect complaining witnesses against embarrassing and prejudicial questions about their sexual histories.

The Indiana legislature adopted a typical provision in 1981. The basic idea is: no testimony at all about prior sexual experience.[15] But that is a promise that goes too far. What if there is no dispute about whether the complaining witness had intercourse on the date alleged but the defendant insists that he was not the guy? He claims that it was, let us say, John. In order to prove this claim, it would be useful to elicit testimony from the alleged victim that she often had sex with John. For this and other special cases, the statute plausibly permits questioning the complaining witness about her sexual history.

One dubious exception permits examining the alleged victim about prior sexual acts with the defendant. One wonders why. A sexual partner can change his or her mind at any moment. That she has consented in the past does not mean that she consented on the night in question. Including this exception implies, at least in Indiana, that a man might properly infer, say from customary foreplay, that his sexual partner has consented once again. But if that is the case, then perhaps a man might infer consent from any number of acts that occurred prior to the moment of intercourse—enthusiastic necking, voluntary stripping, and perhaps even entering the man's room in the middle of the night and sitting down on the bed.

Thinking about these bases for inferring consent lands us in the thicket of the most difficult and controversial question in the contemporary law of rape. When does a woman consent? Susan Estrich popularized the slogan "no means no."[16] Granting this tautology, we still encounter the problem of proving that the woman said no. Here we have no videotape. There are no signed consent forms, as there are in hospitals, and there are no witnesses. There would be no trial unless the man claimed that the woman had said yes. So how do we know? And what happens if we can never know for sure?

The Credibility Trials of 1991–92

That was the question that dominated the news of 1991 and early 1992 as two celebrities—one a scion of the Kennedy family, and the other a famous heavyweight boxer—found themselves charged with ignoring the protestations of women who said they had said no. At the end of March 1991, 30-year-old William Kennedy Smith, a medical student, started dancing with like-aged Patricia Bowman in a Palm Beach bar. She went home with him to the Kennedy estate and, according to him, took off her pantyhose along the way, left her undergarments in the car, and went with him for a walk along the beach. Further, he testified, she participated actively in intercourse, twice, on the estate lawn. She charged him with rape, because, as she claimed, what really happened was that he tackled her and forced sex on her.

Mike Tyson met Desiree Washington a few months later, on July 18, at the Miss Black America beauty contest in Indianapolis. Tyson flirted with several of the contestants but left with Washington's hotel-room phone number and her expressed interest in seeing him on a date. At 1:30 A.M. the following morning, Tyson called Washington from his limousine. Though she was ready to turn in, she agreed to meet him, spent 15 minutes preparing herself, and then joined him in the back seat of his limousine. They then drove to Tyson's hotel and walked to his suite together. When they entered the suite, she accompanied him into the bedroom and chose to sit on the edge of the bed. There is some dispute about whether they kissed in the limousine but generally, to this point in the story, Washington and Tyson agree on what happened.

After the point of her sitting on the bed, the stories diverge, hers pointing to forced intercourse, his to consensual sex. Yet the two did concur on at least four aspects of the sexual encounter. Tyson performed oral sex before he penetrated her. At a certain point, he asked her whether she wanted to be on top. Saying that she did, she mounted him. He did not use a condom, which made her fearful of pregnancy; he withdrew and ejaculated externally. After the sexual encounter, he asked her to spend the night, but she declined and descended alone to the waiting limousine.

Of course, each of these stages of the sexual interaction takes a different spin in the respective stories. For example, she claimed that she chose to be on top because it would then be easier to get away. Despite the general agreement framing the events, there is disagreement about if and when Washington said "No. Stop!" If you believe her, she was raped; if you believe Tyson, she agreed to sex and made up the charges of rape some 24 hours later.

In neither of these cases was there much evidence corroborating either the man's story or the woman's story. Admittedly, Patricia Bowman had to deal with some anomalous facts, such as her leaving her pantyhose in the car and the absence of signs of rough handling on her clothes. Also, she claimed that she had screamed. But guests at the estate, sleeping nearby with their windows open, heard nothing. Washington offered tighter testimony, but with some anomalies. She seemingly gave different stories to different people—either that the incident occurred on the floor or that she screamed or that Tyson prevented her from screaming. In her support, a medical expert testified that she displayed two slight vaginal bruises suggesting forcible intercourse.

In the end, both cases turned on her word against his. In the old days, when Wigmore's views on the psychological propensities of women were taken seriously, the state would probably have refused to prosecute either case. But this was 1991. Feminists had been fighting back for nearly two decades. These were charges of date rape. Though this type of rape is hardest to prove, the suspected rate of unreported abuse between acquaintances had been of increasing importance on the reform agenda. With these two celebrity defendants, the prosecution could not turn its back on feminist critics of the law. Now was the time to prove to the supporters of Patricia Bowman and Desiree Washington that women receive equal justice.

The result was not so equal. A middle-aged, conservative Florida jury of six acquitted William Kennedy Smith, the young aspiring medical student, after 77 minutes of deliberation. A racially diverse

Indiana jury also reached a consensus quickly. In ten hours they concluded that Tyson was guilty as charged, on all counts. Both deliberations were much shorter than is normal in difficult cases. Why the disparity? Why was it so obvious in one case that the woman was lying about Smith; in the other, that the woman was credible enough to send Tyson to jail for six years (three years with good behavior)?

Another test of female credibility, the Senate Judiciary Committee hearings on Clarence Thomas's nomination to the Supreme Court, began between the Palm Beach and Indianapolis trials. The public was challenged to believe the cool, lawyerly testimony of Anita Hill that Thomas, in private conversation, had said nasty things about pubic hairs and sexual prowess. Hill charged harassment by talk. There was no improper touching. But still it mattered greatly whether the public believed her (at the time, the majority did not). 1991, it seems, was the year in which the American public had to reevaluate traditional attitudes about whether women had an inclination to lie, like Potiphar's wife, about the sexual aggression of men with whom they had had a falling out.

Some people think the different outcomes were grounded in race: A black man, even a heavyweight champion, supposedly cannot get a fair trial; a Kennedy is going to get all the breaks. Clarence Thomas tried to play the race card to his advantage when he complained of a "high-tech lynching." Would that the matter were so simple. Both Smith and Tyson had first-rate lawyers. Roy Black for Smith and Vincent Fuller for Tyson were as good as you can find. Thomas—or was it Hill?—was "tried" before an all-male committee, a fact that in itself generated a rage among women comparable to the later reaction of African-Americans to the all-white jury in Simi Valley. Race may have mattered, but its bearing on one white-on-white and two black-on-black cases requires a subtle analysis of divergent cultural mores. There may indeed be localized variations in the way men speak to women and the assumptions they make when women condone and accept treatment that others might regard as unacceptable.

Apart from these mores of gender, class, and race, we should attend to certain structural differences between the two trials. The state could bring William Smith to trial without the need for a preliminary grand jury and indictment. This was important, because it meant that Smith was not tempted to make statements on the record that could later be used in a search for inconsistencies in his testimony. Tyson went to trial only after appearing before a grand jury, and his grand jury testimony provided a record that the prosecutor could use to probe the consistency of his trial testimony about what had happened in the course of those fateful minutes with Desiree Washington. As a result, the prosecutor was able to elicit several anomalies for the jury to ponder.

According to Tyson's testimony at trial, he had bluntly propositioned Washington on their first meeting at the beauty pageant. He had supposedly said, "I want to fuck you," and she had supposedly responded, "Sure give me a call. That's kind of bold."[17] Earlier, before the grand jury, his recollection of the exchange had been more circumspect. Also, he described Washington's clothes in radically different ways on the two occasions. Most significantly, in September, before the grand jury, he claimed that while he and Washington were in the bedroom his bodyguard Dale Edwards was in the parlor of the suite. If this had been true, it would have provided convincing evidence that Washington could have sought help but chose not to. Other witnesses testified, however, that Dale Edwards was not in Tyson's suite at that time. In his memoir of the trial, prosecutor Gregory Garrison claims he had forced Tyson to defend himself with the feeble response: "That's where he was supposed to be."[18] So far as the jury noticed inconsistencies in Tyson's testimony, the prosecution profited from the availability of pre-trial statements.

William Smith had no such problems to contend with. Instead, his lawyer, Roy Black, insisted that Smith make no pre-trial statements. Thus Black could shift the focus to inconsistencies in Patricia Bowman's testimony. He did not have to do much to put her on the defensive. A bare 17 days after the incident, *The New York Times* published an in-depth portrait of the 29-year-old single mother who

filed charges against Smith; the newspaper created a flap by naming
her in print. By refusing to name a woman who had known Bowman
in high school and who said Bowman "had a little wild streak," the
Times was more respectful of its sources than it was of Bowman
herself.[19] Every pebble in Bowman's past was turned, including her
having received 17 traffic tickets in 18 years. The spin was clearly on.
There was little sympathy in the press for a woman who would dare
endanger the reputation and medical career of a young Kennedy.

In case the media missed anything, the defense could and did
force Bowman, as complaining witness, to submit to a deposition, an
interrogation before trial that would be used later as a check on the
consistency of her story. Bowman found herself increasingly alone.
After Smith's acquittal in rapid-fire deliberations, law professor Bar-
bara Babcock wrote a suggestive article complaining that even the
prosecutor, Moira Lasch, had abandoned Bowman. She "never
seemed to form a bond with either the jury or the alleged victim."[20]
The only person at trial who can represent the victim is the prosecutor. And in many of the trials we have canvassed as well as in the
Smith trial, the prosecutor remained aloof and distant, preoccupied
with his or her task of representing the People instead of the victim.

In fact, if we look back on the seven trials we have examined in
depth across four distinct groups of victims, a rather striking correlation comes into focus. In four of the cases, the prosecutor was a
member of the same class or group as the victim. Terry White and
Rodney King are both African-American; William Greenbaum,
Meir Kahane, Sari Kolatch, and Yankel Rosenbaum are all Jewish;
Moira Lasch and Patricia Bowman are both women. In all four cases
the prosecutor did a professional job but maintained emotional
distance from the victim. In all four cases the prosecution went down
to defeat. In two cases, the prosecutors bore no apparent ethnic or
other similarity to the victim. Federal prosecutors Steven Clymer
and Barry Kowalski could not have differed more sharply from
Rodney King, and middle-aged white male Greg Garrison came
across as the polar opposite of Desiree Washington. Yet in both
instances the prosecutors developed a passionate, committed, and

crusading alliance with their client, the victim. In both cases the victim testified brilliantly. And in both cases the prosecution won a conviction.

There are obviously many variables in these defeats and victories. But the pattern is worth noting. A victory in these high-profile cases requires a strong identification between prosecutor and victim, both as person and as member of a group. If the prosecutor comes from the same group as the victim, his or her sense of professionalism may well inhibit the emotional bond necessary for a convincing presentation to the jury. At the very least, a prosecutor who is not visibly identified with the victim can convey a stronger commitment to the case without appearing biased and parochial.

Despite the lackluster performance of Moira Lasch, the state of Florida might still have secured a conviction of William Kennedy Smith had it not been for a watershed ruling by trial judge Mary Lupo. The state sought to secure the testimony of three women who had come forward and were willing to say that Smith had made strong, aggressive sexual advances toward them as well. In one of the three cases, the woman had had intercourse with Smith, allegedly when she was too drunk to resist; the other two did resist, successfully. If witnesses like these had surfaced in the Hill–Thomas hearings, they would undoubtedly have torpedoed Thomas's appointment to the Supreme Court. Yet criminal trials are not the same as free-ranging Senate hearings. Susan Estrich believes that the judge in the Smith case should have let the witnesses testify, if only to bolster the credibility of the complaining witness.[21] Yet the defendant cannot fairly be expected to fight four charges from four different directions all at the same time. Even if Smith had been previously convicted of rape, the prosecution could not have used the prior convictions to prove that he was likely to have raped Patricia Bowman (though they could have been used to undermine Smith's credibility as a witness). Prior convictions are simply too prejudicial. They can prompt the jury to convict on the theory: "There he goes again." And if that is true about prior convictions, it should surely be true about allegations of prior

misconduct that never even led to an arrest. Trial judge Mary Lupo
sensibly turned down the motion to admit these three witnesses
and thus protected Smith against being labeled a man who forces
himself on women. When the jury began to deliberate, his reputation was intact.

The Metaphysics of Consent

Three witnesses were the key to the Tyson trial too. But they were on
the other side. After the trial had begun and Desiree Washington had
already testified, three women told the defense team that they had
seen Mike and Desiree embracing and kissing in Mike's limousine
when it was parked in front of Desiree's hotel. They then saw the two
exit the car and walk, hand-in-hand, into the lobby. Now this would
seem like rather substantial evidence in Tyson's favor. Heavy petting
in the car ("They were all over each other," in the words of one of the
three) would have given the couple a likely motive for going up to
Tyson's room. If they were amorous at the outset, isn't it probable
that they were so inclined a half-hour later?

There were only two catches, at least in Indiana. First, the
defense had learned of the three witnesses late in the game—too late,
Judge Patricia Gifford was inclined to think. It would not be "fair"
to let the prosecution suffer a surprise move after its key witnesses
had already committed themselves to testimony without knowing of
the events in the limousine. This is an argument we will take up in
the next chapter. The second reason for excluding the evidence, is,
for now, more intriguing. Judge Gifford concluded that the testimony, even if it accurately portrayed what had happened in the
limousine, was "not vital" for the defense; it was "cumulative" and
therefore superfluous to the question whether Tyson reasonably
believed that Washington would consent to sex some time in the
future. Only after conviction and appeal to the court of appeals do we
find a full account of Judge Gifford's curious logic. According to the
two judges on the appellate court who affirmed the conviction, this is
the reason the jury had no need to know about what had happened
in the limousine:

> [A]n honest and reasonable belief that a member of the
> opposite sex will consent to sexual conduct at some point in
> the future is not a defense to rape or criminal deviate conduct.
> The only consent that is a defense is the consent that
> immediately precedes the sexual conduct; it is the defendant's
> honest and reasonable belief at that point in time, and not at
> any other point, that is relevant. Therefore, the trial court
> exercised sound discretion when it determined that the
> proffered testimony that Tyson and D.W. were "hugging and
> kissing" in the limousine and that they walked into the hotel
> hand-in-hand or arm-in-arm was not vital.[22]

Before parsing the logic of this argument, we should remind
ourselves why voluntary sexuality has always served as the foundation for the emancipation of women from patriarchal domination.
For women to feel and to be treated as equal players in modern
society, they must be able not only to say no to sex but to say yes,
without repercussions. Birth control and abortion guard the sexual
act against one form of repercussion, and that is why they are critical
to the women's movement. Being treated as prostitutes, not worthy
of belief when they are sexually mistreated, is another repercussion,
and that is why the rape-shield statutes are so important. The issue
here seems to be not ceding to others, particularly to male suitors, the
power to decide when one, as an adult, will enter into intimate
relations. This is the power to say yes. And women might reasonably
disagree about some aspects of the debate, such as responsibility for
pregnancy. In the date-rape cases of 1991, however, the primary
question was not saying yes without suffering, but being heard when
saying no.

No one can be regarded as a person unless he or she can say no,
effectively, about the things that matter most. It is unquestionably
desirable to get the point across to men that they should take no for an
answer and risk the loss of sexual pleasure, even if the female secretly
wants them to persist. They should not nourish their fantasies of
sexual power in the poetry of another time. In modern America, we

do have "world enough and time" and "coyness is no crime."[23] And a woman does not consent in law if "whispering 'I will ne'er consent,' [she] consented," in the poetry of Lord Byron.[24] It may be going too far to insist, as does the 1993 Antioch code of sexual manners, that students secure "affirmative consent" from each other for each stage of sexual exploration. But the moral point is important. No means no, at least when we must decide what to do in the future.

Three different perspectives get intertwined when we begin to think about consent in date-rape cases. There is the right to say yes, the right to say no, considered prospectively, and the fact of no having been said, considered as a problem of proof under the disputed facts of the typical criminal trial. The conflict among these three perspectives accounts for the confusion that emerges in the paragraph quoted from the Indiana Court of Appeals.

A number of themes converge in this convoluted judicial statement. First, the court seems to concede that, even if M.T. and D.W. were necking voluntarily in the car (their right to say yes), that was irrelevant to whether they were fornicating consensually a few minutes later in the hotel room. The support for this counterintuitive claim comes in the next sentence: "The only consent that is a defense is the consent that immediately precedes the intercourse." But the defense was not arguing that Washington's consent to necking *was* consent to intercourse. There was no suggestion that she was estopped from changing her mind. Of course, she had the right to say no once they got to the room. It is just that, by common experience, we know that if she was necking at 1:30 A.M., then we should recognize the increased probability that in fact she consented to sex at 2:00 A.M. The question is not whether she had the right to say no in Tyson's bedroom but how the state may prove and the defense disprove that she said no in fact.

Judges cannot decide that in Indiana common-sense odds do not hold, or that we should alter them in order to express a policy of protecting alleged rape victims. The question is whether if you were betting on consent and all other factors remained the same, which scenario would you pick? The scenario in which they are seen necking a half-hour before intercourse, or the scenario in which they are seen conversing at arms-length? If you are a rational better, you would probably bet that consensual necking is more likely than polite conversation to breed consensual sex.[25]

This elementary fact of nature is well known in Indiana. Why else would the Indiana legislature have included an exception in the rape-shield statute for a prior sexual relationship between the alleged victim and the defendant? The assumption must have been that prior sexual acts provide evidence of ongoing consent. Also there is something revealing in the proposition that the only relevant consent is consent "that immediately precedes the intercourse." Again, the assumption must be that consent immediately prior to the intercourse implies that consent continues for the entire time of physical contact. Yet the legally trained mind gravitates to the problematic word "immediately." Is one second before the intercourse soon enough? Or one minute? Or five minutes? And why shouldn't the woman be able to withdraw consent after penetration has occurred? There is no easy answer to any of these questions, and the reason lies close at hand.

Sexual relations carry the potential for deep emotional bonding. But when that potential is abused in dissonance, the victim suffers scarring in place of romantic union. The only buttress between abuse and bonding, between rape and love, is the thin prop of consent. Yet we are not entirely sure what we mean by this chimerical assertion of personality called consent. We do not know well enough what happens in the mind or the heart for us to say that a woman wants and decides in favor of sexual union with a man. One wonders whether consent to sexual intercourse is ever fully autonomous—unaffected by circumstances, atmosphere, romancing, or the promise of emotional reward. And if consent is as shaky as it appears to be, we should pay more attention to what it means for men as well as for women to consent.

Yet the focus of law reform in the 1990s is on the vindication of women's dignity by accentuating their power to say no to sex. In the days when we spoke of a woman's chastity, her "honor" was a prized possession. Now it is her dignity that, as Immanuel Kant said, is beyond pricing. That dignity is expressed in her control over her own body. The contemporary effort to raise the status of women has led to a mystification of that inner moment called consent when she commits her personality. Yet that inner moment is so difficult to fathom that we encounter the most wild swings in contemporary discussions of female sexuality. Because actual consent is so ephemeral, some radicals, such as Andrea Dworkin, claim that women never actually consent to intercourse. Whether and when women actually consent to sex may be a question too elusive for courts and juries to ponder.

One way to talk about this problem—a way that the law frequently adopts—is to shift from whether the person really has consented to whether the outward signs of consent are so strong that the other party may reasonably rely on the show or appearance of consent. What counts in the end is not the inner life of the person consenting but the reasonableness of the person who relies on the external indices of willing cooperation. This is the way the law approaches contractual agreements and consent to medical operations. In a criminal trial, there is even stronger reason to focus not on the victim's actual consent but on the defendant's reasonable or unreasonable perception of consent. After all, the focus of the trial should be on whether the defendant is sufficiently blameworthy to suffer conviction and punishment.

Given our uncertainties about the magic moment of actual consent, apparent consent may be all that we can safely rely on. If there are outward signs of consent and the defendant has relied on them, then we have a sound basis for evaluating his conduct as morally reasonable. The three witnesses who never testified in the Tyson case would have provided strong evidence of this apparent consent. If Washington appeared to be consenting a half-hour before the events in the bedroom, there is a stronger basis for understanding why Tyson thought she was also consenting in the bedroom. The trial court's ignoring Tyson's allegedly reasonable reliance on the signs of consent shifted the focus of the trial away from his behavior toward an ineffable moment in Washington's psyche. He became guilty or not guilty not on the basis of what he did and thought but on the basis of what the jury perceived that she thought.

The effort to analyze these questions often gets bogged down in irrelevant ideological disputes, such as whether a woman has a right to go to a man's room in the middle of the night and then say no to sex. Of course she has that right. But it does not follow that she *always* or even probably will say no under those circumstances. Establishing a woman's rights in the abstract has little to do with doing justice, retrospectively, in a disputed case of rape. If there is a trial in a date-rape case, we can assume that the woman claims and may even think, in good faith, that she said no. And we can also assume that the male defendant believes that he heard yes. Thus we enter the world of conflicting perceptions where both parties may have some truth on their side. How do we accommodate these conflicting perceptions in a trial that presupposes a single truth?

Conflicting Objectives

The Indiana Court of Appeals had it right when it wrote that "the defendant's honest and reasonable belief" in the woman's consent was relevant to liability. Paradoxically, however, it confirmed the trial court's decision not to give the jury any instruction on reasonable mistake about consent. The jurors had no option to acquit if they believed that Tyson had an "honest and reasonable belief" that Washington had consented to have sex with him. Many courts decide the issue of mistake in this way. And they all engage in a tragic error. Recognizing the relevance of mistake—of the defendant's "honest and reasonable belief"—provides a splendid means of reconciling conflicting objectives in a criminal trial.

One goal of the trial is to provide guidance for the future. The other is to do justice to the particular criminal defendant on the unique facts of the case. Criminal convictions can mediate between these conflicting objectives. They can inform the public that nonconsent means rape. If the woman says no and nonetheless suffers a sexual imposition, she has been raped. But it does not follow that the particular defendant, the man standing in the dock, need be held responsible for the rape. If he was insane at the time of the deed, he should not be treated as morally accountable for his criminal actions. Similarly, if he acted under an honest and reasonable mistake about consent, his actions may have been wrong but he should be excused on the ground of moral innocence.

When a court fails to make this distinction, when it links the defendant's guilt to whether the alleged victim consented or did not consent, it increases the pressure on the defense to attack the victim. That is the only recourse the defense has. The battle reduces to a zero-sum game: his victory or hers. If the court recognizes its conflicting duties both to guide future behavior and to do justice to the past, the defendant can concede the victim's nonconsent and defend on the grounds of honest and reasonable mistake. Thus to protect the victim at trial as well as to seek justice for the accused, the court should recognize a two-tiered inquiry: First, was the woman raped (did she suffer nonconsensual sex)? And second, is the defendant to blame for the rape? If he is not fairly to blame—say, because he was honestly and reasonably mistaken—he is not morally responsible for the rape and should not be convicted.

All this makes sense, but the courts are often blind to sensible solutions. In the *Hernandez* case, mentioned above, the California Supreme Court did recognize that an honest and reasonable mistake of fact about the girl's age should negate responsibility. Its reasoning was very simple: No one should be convicted without a "criminal intent." This is one of the basic maxims of the criminal law, and the court interpreted it to mean that the intent to have intercourse was not "criminal" if the defendant was morally innocent. And in the court's view he was innocent if he reasonably thought the girl was of age.

The general pattern in these cases, however, is to ignore the mistake altogether. Even the Supreme Court of California abandoned the *Hernandez* rule in a later case.[26] It does not matter whether the mistake was about the age of the girl or the consent of the woman; the courts have typically followed a strict line: Sleep with her at your peril! If you are wrong about her age or about her consent, you are in deep trouble. This either/or frame of mind forces the defendant to attack the character of the victim, as in the Missouri opinion on the "wretched girl [who] was young in years but old in sin."

One would think that in the Tyson trial, without the option of defending on grounds of the defendant's reasonable mistake, the defense would have had little choice but to attack the character of the alleged victim. Yet in contrast to the character assassination of Patricia Bowman in the William Kennedy Smith trial, the defense had few ways of getting at Desiree Washington. The trial court would not allow cross-examination of Washington's parents with regard to their daughter's possible motives for making up a rape charge. And even though prosecutor Garrison had effectively profiled her as a "good Christian" who was not the "same girl" after the bout with Tyson, the defense could not—under the rape-shield statute—undermine this image of "chastity" by eliciting her sexual history.

In a novel strategic move, the defense lawyers sought to shift responsibility to Washington by undermining the image of the defendant himself. According to prosecutor Garrison's account, they portrayed Tyson as a known womanizer, as a champion of seduction. Any woman who accepted a date with him, particularly after he had spoken bluntly to her about sex, would know what she was getting into. She was running the risk! Instead of calling witnesses who could testify to Tyson's good character, the defense called people who could help establish the image of the heavyweight "as so insensitive and crude that no right-minded person could have any sympathy for him."[27]

The defense team's effort to undermine Tyson's character carried a whiff of racial stereotyping. Would the defense attorneys have taken this approach with a white athlete? I doubt that they would have portrayed Babe Ruth, also a reputed womanizer, in the same way. The claim that "people expect it"[28] conveys a slight contempt ordinarily not associated with the hero status we accord our athletes. Perhaps the defense was covertly communicating a different point: People expect this behavior of black men who are all brawn and no brain. One black sports writer, Sonja Steptoe, branded Vincent Fuller's tactics a "damnable defense" that traded on racial bias.[29] Yet the defense lawyers were desperate. They were forced to shift the blame to Washington because they could not build a defense around Tyson's reasonable misperception of her interest in having sex. This is one of the tactical distortions produced by the trial judge's ignoring the defense's sensible efforts to introduce evidence of the couple's amorous interaction a few minutes before their apparent falling-out in the bedroom.

Ignoring a defendant's mistake about the alleged victim's consent is a harsh line to take. It seems so clearly unjust that the courts sometimes overreact and go to the opposite extreme. No cases better illustrate this than a series of kinky decisions by the English House of Lords in the mid-1970s. In these cases the defendant informs his drinking buddies that his wife, waiting patiently at home, enjoys forcible intercourse. She may resist and fight back, but in fact she wants to be taken violently. They come home together from the bar and the husband's friends accept his invitation to force intercourse on the crying, tormented wife. In the leading case, *Morgan*, the husband, and his friends were all convicted of rape. The co-defendants complained on appeal that they honestly believed that the wife, despite her tears, was consenting.[30] The House of Lords came to the amazing conclusion that, in principle, the defendants had a good defense.

More surprisingly, the Lords argued that this defense lay in the logic of rape. Their reasoning went something like this: The "prohibited act in rape is non-consensual sexual intercourse."[31] The criminal intent required for rape should encompass these essential features of the crime—nonconsent as well as the fact of intercourse with a woman. It follows, as "a matter of inexorable logic,"[32] that the defendant would not have the intent to engage in nonconsensual intercourse if he believed that Morgan's wife had consented. If this is legal logic, it is also blind and fallacious logic. There is nothing in either the statutory definition of rape or the traditional view of rape that requires the result.[33] The Morgan decision testifies to the intellectual rigidity and moral insensitivity of many judges.

Even more disturbing than the decision by the House of Lords is the apparent support it has received in many quarters of the legal profession. Shortly after the decision, two leading English professors of criminal law wrote to *The Times* of London to express support for the decision.[34] I find their opinion not only ill conceived but embarrassing. Yet the support for the result in *Morgan* continues to this day. The Canadian courts follow the rule that if a man sincerely thinks that a resisting woman has in fact consented, the jury should acquit him of rape charges.[35] In recent months I have met a surprising number of criminal-law scholars who think that this is the right rule. Something is obviously wrong in the temple of law.

The decision in *Morgan* went to the extreme of recognizing all mistakes about consent. The court in *Tyson* went to the opposite extreme of accepting no mistakes as relevant. The sensible solution is a compromise: An honest and reasonable mistake implies that we cannot fairly blame the defendant for thinking that his partner wanted sex. Yet, as an additional embarrassment to their profession, lawyers and judges do not seem capable of even discussing this compromise coherently and persuasively.

The debates in the Tyson appeal passed each other in a fog of conflicting premises. The appellate team, led by Alan Dershowitz, sought to justify the elementary point that if Tyson had acted without a "guilty mind" (which would be true if he was reasonably mistaken about Washington's consent), he should not be found guilty of rape. The argument of the appellants' brief merely tracks the formal logic of the relevant Indiana statute, which in turn follows the logic of the Morgan decision. Mistakes are relevant so far as they negate "culpability," and the "culpability required for the offense" must be "intent to have sex without her consent" or knowledge "that she did not consent."[36] *Morgan*-style formal logic did not move the court of appeals, for neither the judges nor the lawyers seemed to be

interested in the basic principle that if a man acts in moral innocence
he should not be guilty of rape.

For its part, the state made almost no effort in its brief to justify
the injustice of convicting a man who may have acted in moral
innocence. Yet the court of appeals came up with its own quirky
argument about why the jury should not have been permitted to
decide whether Tyson reasonably believed that Washington had
consented. Without any authority to back it up, the appellate court
simply assumed that a relevant mistake about consent must derive
from an interpretation of "equivocal conduct." And, the court reasoned, the evidence at trial pointed to the incompatible opposites of
actual consent and compelled intercourse. Since Washington's version of the events supposedly did not reflect "equivocal conduct,"
there was nothing about which Tyson could have made a reasonable
mistake.[37] The appellate court seemed to forget that the truth may
have lain somewhere between the two accounts and that Tyson's
version may have been a reasonable perception of that irretrievable
reality.

The court's novel theory of "equivocal conduct" cannot withstand two minutes of serious analysis. Suppose that a man in an open
field spots what clearly appears to be a scarecrow and shoots at it. It
turns out that the target is a man who, for reasons of his own,
donned the costume of a scarecrow. There is nothing equivocal
about his likeness to an object that may be shot with impunity, and
the shot kills him. According to the Indiana Court of Appeals'
reasoning, the shooter would be guilty of murder, for he could not
assert a reasonable mistake of fact as a defense—namely, that he
thought the object he shot at was a scarecrow and not a man. There
would be no "equivocal conduct" that triggered the shooter's interpretation of reality. Yet this is a textbook case of a reasonable mistake
negating the intent to kill. If the mistake was indeed reasonable, the
shooter would not be convicted in any court in the country. The
point of this exercise is to show that the alleged requirement of
"equivocal conduct" has no grounding in reason or in law. The
Indiana Court of Appeals simply created it to justify the trial court's

disregard of Tyson's claim of reasonable mistake and moral innocence.

Justice Sullivan had the good sense to dissent from this mélange
of contrived reasoning and bad law. He would have admitted the
testimony of the three witnesses and he would have required the jury
to determine whether Tyson acted reasonably and innocently. More
significantly, he pinpointed the connection between hearing the testimony of the disputed three witnesses and having the jury resolve the
question of whether Tyson's mistake was reasonable:

> The manner in which Tyson and D. W. acted toward each
> other shortly before the acts complained of has great relevance
> to whether or not Tyson, at the time, might have reasonably
> believed, from all the surrounding circumstances and events,
> that D. W. was consenting—even though as a factual matter
> she did not consent.[38]

Occasionally, common sense triumphs, but alas in too small a dosage
to keep Mike Tyson out of jail.

One senses in this distortion of justice the heavy hand of the new
political trial. The prosecution of Mike Tyson became the symbol of
a movement. This was a case in which law-enforcement officials,
aligned with the feminist movement, would send a message to men
who took sexual liberties with women. No should mean no. Fair
enough. But defending the interests of victims need not derogate
from the rights of criminal defendants. When the supporters of a
victim-based cause are willing to make an example of a morally
innocent man, we encounter the downside of politics.

The Indiana Court of Appeals developed an odd theory of consent that, in effect, privileges the testimony of the alleged victim in
rape cases. If she testifies clearly to conduct of resistance, that she
said no instead of maybe, there is no "equivocal conduct." It is
important to defend the interests of women as victims, but not to go
so far as to accord women complaining of rape a presumption of
honesty and objectivity.

Battered Women Strike Back

Women have fought back effectively in the corridors of power. They lobbied legislatures successfully in the 1970s to ban "unchaste character" from the discourse of American rape trials. They followed up in the 1980s with legislation shielding rape victims from embarrassing and prejudicial questions about their sexual history. The campaign for women in the 1990s has shifted from women as rape victims to women as victims of domestic violence. Though the roots of the battered-woman syndrome go back to the early 1980s, there has been an explosion of concern and compassion in the 1990s for abused women as criminal defendants.

The term "domestic violence" has become synonymous with men assaulting women at home.[39] The figures are indeed alarming. Donna Shalala, President Clinton's Secretary of Health and Human Services, quoted some of them in a speech portraying women and children as the exclusive victims of violence in the home.[40] About one in four women can expect that their men will assault them at least once in the course of their lifetime. But this figure obviously includes hostile contact that varies from a slight slap to life-threatening attacks. A more revealing figure comes in reports of women who make visits to emergency rooms for redress of their wounds. A large but disputed%age of these women report that their injury was received in an altercation at home.[41] Some people claim that more women are injured in domestic assaults than in car accidents, muggings, and rapes combined.[42] In 1991, about 1,300 women were killed by their domestic partners.

If the police and the courts stay aloof from this suffering, they become complicitous in it. The blood of battered women is on their hands. But there is blood on the other side as well. In the same year 1991, almost half as many women killed their husbands or boyfriends. So roughly 600 women a year are investigated and probably charged with criminal homicide. Many of these women are victims themselves who claim other victims. Many of them kill, justifiably, in self-defense.

Prior to the intensive media coverage of O.J. Simpson's alleged killing of his wife, Nicole Brown Simpson, there were no celebrity cases in this morass of domestic violence and counterviolence and no cases in which either the victim or the defendant had become a household word. Lorena Bobbitt achieved notoriety in late 1993 for having cut off her husband's penis sometime after he allegedly abused her by coercively sodomizing her. She ran out the door with the penis in her hand and threw it out her car window. The husband got his penis back but was charged in a separate trial for marital sexual abuse. The jury acquitted him, presumably because they blamed her for the terrible things she did to his front, and another jury acquitted her because they blamed him for the terrible things he did to her rear. Blaming both victims meant that neither side took the stigma alone.

More typical cases of battered women are one-sided affairs. They arise between pairs of victims whose misery and cruelty the rest of us would rather ignore. A controversial case from the 1980s illustrates the general pattern. John Norman engaged in systematic dehumanizing actions toward Judy Norman, his wife. Beginning about five years after the wedding, he started drinking and while drunk assaulted her, threw glasses and bottles at her, extinguished cigarettes on her body, and crushed food on her face. In addition, he forced her to engage in prostitution to earn income for their household and mocked her streetwalking in front of "family and friends." When he was not satisfied with her earnings, he beat her and called her "dog" and "whore." On a few occasions, he made her eat pet food out of the pet's bowl and forced her to sleep on the floor. Apparently, according to her testimony, he kept up these degrading practices for about 20 years—until the day in mid-June 1985 when she shot him in the back of the head.[43]

Of course, her testimony may have had a self-serving spin. But there is ample corroboration of her story in the words of others. For example, her daughter Phyllis testified that her father had beaten her mother "all day long" immediately prior to the shooting. Also, Judy Norman had appealed with complaints to the police and to a domestic abuse center at the local county hospital. The police would not intervene unless Judy took out a warrant for John's arrest, and that she feared to do; she had experienced beatings in retaliation for prior efforts to leave the scene of her suffering. The situation went from bad to worse. John was enraged and out of control, as a boarder testified, for having been arrested on a drunk-driving charge. At that point he forbade Judy to eat for three days prior to the shooting. The family tried to get food to her, and her mother sent groceries. But Judy Norman feared retaliation and a beating if she disobeyed her tyrannical husband. The words "abuse" and "mistreatment" are too vague to capture these anti-human conditions. This was a gulag she called home.

There is a temptation in these cases to condone the battered wife's taking the law into her own hands. If ever there was a case in which the victim had it coming to him, the killing of John Norman was it. But however tragically Judy Norman's appeals to the authorities went unheeded, she could not put herself in the position of judge and executioner. If the authorities had responded and prosecuted John Norman, they could not—for all his wickedness—have imposed the death penalty. There may be justice in his dying, but it is not a form of justice that the legal system can readily accommodate.

A defense for Judy Norman would have to rely not on what John had already done but on what he might yet do. A sound claim of self-defense would require proof of a threatened attack that put her in "reasonable fear of imminent death or great bodily harm."[44] If John was coming toward Judy with the declared purpose of severely beating her, there would be little doubt that she could respond by killing him. The problem in her case—and in the cases of many battered wives—is that the husband is sleeping when he is shot. Now one might well understand that a terrified woman might have to seize whatever opportunity presented itself, but she would have a problem justifying the killing as the fear of imminent attack. A further problem in Judy Norman's case was that she would have to explain why she did not seize a less extreme means of avoiding

John's brutality—namely, running away. Why didn't she simply leave? This question recurs routinely in cases of battered women charged with killing tyrannical husbands and lovers.

These barriers were sufficient for the jury to convict Judy Norman and for the judge to sentence her to six years in prison. The trial judge refused even to instruct the jury that the killing might be justified as a matter of self-defense. The Supreme Court of North Carolina upheld the conviction, largely because, as the majority reasoned, the feared attack was not about to happen: it was not sufficiently imminent. The jury had heard expert testimony about the battered women's syndrome. Judy was allegedly a paradigm of women addicted to abuse. In sober intervals, John was kind to her (he was a "good guy"), though there was no evidence that he engaged in the remorseful re-wooing of his wife that is supposedly characteristic of the battering syndrome. None of this moved the jury to vote an acquittal out of sympathy for Judy Norman.

Yet the professional writing in this area is motivated largely by political solidarity with women like Judy Norman. There must be a way, most observers assume, to circumvent the restrictive and cramped thinking of the North Carolina Supreme Court. In many courts around the country, the major battle of the 1980s was gaining access to the courts for psychologists who claimed expertise in this new psychological condition, diagnosed as "learned helplessness." Some legislatures intervened to win the experts a place in influencing the course of these prosecutions. In 1991 California enacted a curious statute that declared expert testimony on the "battered women's syndrome" admissible whenever relevant but failed to specify the question to which it would be relevant.[45] The California legislature also sought to resolve a scientific question: "Expert opinion testimony on battered women's syndrome shall not be considered a new scientific technique whose reliability is unproven."[46] Yet, for many reformers, securing the respectability of expert testimony about the consequence of domestic violence was not enough. In their view, the law itself should be loosened up to accommodate more possibilities for the defense.

The arguments for reform have taken off in different directions. One influential line of thought in the early literature stressed the important distinction between excusable homicide and justifiable homicide. The North Carolina Supreme Court decided the way it did largely because it could think of self-defense only as a reason for vindicating the killing, for declaring it lawful, for saying it was the right and proper thing to. Those who defend women who kill—particularly when their victims are asleep or otherwise non-threatening—could effectively invoke an older tradition in the law of homicide, one that conceded that the killing was wrong but nonetheless blameless and therefore excusable, particularly under the conditions of terror and deprivation that marked the fate of Judy Norman. Excusable homicide requires a showing only that the defendant had no plausible alternative. Judy's back was literally against the wall and there was no other way out. The advantage of this approach is that it brings into these disputes a fair recognition that the husband too is a victim, that he has been wrongly and improperly killed, but that the wife, because of her personal circumstances, cannot be fairly blamed for the killing.

The approach of excusable homicide parallels the recognition of reasonable mistake as an excuse in cases like Tyson and Kennedy Smith. As their actions might well have been rape, objectively considered, the killing of a sleeping husband is definitely criminal homicide. But as these wrongful impositions on women might be excused on grounds of reasonable mistake, striking back against violent men, nonaggressive for the moment, could well be excused on grounds of personal necessity. Affirming the convictions was wrong both in the Tyson rape case and in the Norman homicide case. The jury should have been allowed to consider grounds for excusing Mike Tyson on grounds of mistake and Judy Norman on grounds of overwhelming personal necessity.

Admittedly, I had a role in developing a version of self-defense that would claim that the battered woman's striking back was not justifiable but only excusable. When feminists first addressed the legal plight of battered women, they relied on several of my early articles on the theory of excuses published in the 1970s. As the movement matured, however, excusing women no longer seemed enough. The call crystallized for total vindication of the victim-women—for justification of the killing as justified and proper. Sometimes this demand sprang from theoretical ignorance, sometimes from the felt need to think of the woman's striking back as justice on the domestic frontier.[47]

The drive to treat killings by battered wives as justified meant, in effect, that feminist lawyers wanted to adopt the venerable technique of blaming the victim for his own demise. What was harmful to the goose would now become noxious to the gander. In order to demonstrate the wife's plight, the defense could dwell in detail on the years of abuse. The subtext became: The bastard got what was coming to him. If he had not been so abusive, if he had not driven her to it, the wife would not have had to respond with deadly force. Thus there emerged an independent argument never officially endorsed: A history of abuse could actually justify homicide.

This replay of the old strategy of blaming the victim always simmers below the surface, camouflaged by arguments on loosening the legal requirements of self-defense. Some reformers say let's get rid of the imminence requirement. The only issue should be the necessity of the response, and Judy Norman clearly acted out of necessity.[48] Some say let's simply make the perception of imminence dependent on the defendant's anxious fear of abuse. As the dissent in the Norman case reasoned: "In the context of the doctrine of self-defense, the definition of 'imminent' must be informed by the defendant's perceptions."[49] As we shall see, this maneuver came home to haunt the legal system in the 1993 trial sensation, the prosecution of the Menendez brothers in Los Angeles.

None of these maneuvers in the law of self-defense required testimony from experts about the battered women's syndrome. The point of this expert testimony about trapped wives, when it was first considered in the early 1980s, was to counteract the claim that women like Judy Norman could have left their dens of torture and sought protection with the police or in one of the centers set up to house refugees from domestic violence. An innovative and enterprising psychologist, Lenore Walker, almost single-handedly generated the new style of perceiving female manslayers as victims escaping conditions of abuse. Her 1979 book *The Battered Woman* and her indefatigable lecturing to jurors as an expert witness on her "discovered" syndrome changed the discourse of American law. The key contribution was the catchy slogan "learned helplessness," which explained why women beaten into submissive behavior did not dare to leave the scene of danger.

The language of sympathy for battered women defendants rapidly became the politically correct way of perceiving conflicts that ended in the victimization of men. Even the California legislature admonishes us not to be skeptical about the "reliability" of this current mode of expert testimony. But skeptics there have been. One of the first was David Faigman, who wrote a thoughtful student comment in the *Virginia Law Review* questioning the scientific basis of "learned helplessness."[50] Walker had based her scientific argument on an analogy between dogs and human beings. Research into the behavior of dogs demonstrated that "laboratory dogs, after being subjected to repeated shocks over which they had no control, 'learned' that they were helpless." The upshot was that when they had a chance to escape, they stayed put.

Now there are many differences between captive dogs and women rendered submissive by a cycle of violence, apology, and tenderness followed by renewed violence. But the most significant difference is the way battered women eventually respond to their condition. It is hardly a sign of helplessness to acquire a gun and to kill one's psychological captor. Concluding that laboratory experiments on learned helplessness of dogs should have no bearing on the legal quandary, Faigman sums up the contradiction: "For a battered woman to realize that she alone has to protect herself is antithetical to the notion that she is unable to assert control over her environment."[51] Lenore Walker also bases her conclusions on interviews with battered women, but the casualness of her methodology

(Faigman claims five major flaws) makes one wonder about the neutrality of her "scientific" inquiry.

Faigman's critique has taken a feminist turn. In a recent critique of Walker's theories, Anne Coughlin picks up the fallacy of drawing an analogy between dogs who are helpless and women who kill.[52] As she points out, "the animal studies that Walker cites do not appear to report any incidents in which one of the dogs suddenly attacked the experimenter who was doling out the electric shocks."[53] So much for the relevance of laboratory research to the law of self-defense.

Coughlin stresses that "women, unlike dogs, are the products of culture."[54] Women are bought up to "take responsibility for maintaining the significant relationships in their lives even when those relationships inflict suffering on them."[55] Women remain loyal to their husbands even when their self-interest dictates the contrary. They submit to battering because presumably they think that there might be some way of resolving the problem with their husbands and making the relationship work. The point of Coughlin's writing is to sharpen our perception of women's responsibility for their own choices. If married women can now be held liable for their crimes (though in the recent past they were exempt on the grounds of presumed coercion by their husbands), they can be held accountable for their failure to leave abusive husbands. Autonomous people bear responsibility for their actions.

Appreciating women's responsibility for killing implies a recognition of men as victims. What could it mean to act wrongfully unless there is a victim—or a likely victim—on the other end of the action? Yet, as other researchers have underscored, there is a tendency to think of battered women who strike back not as killing men but merely as exiting their predicament.[56] The real purpose of the woman is to get out; the man happens to be in the way. The killing comes into focus, then, not as a malicious act of manslaying but as an unfortunate accident.

These academic rumblings are hardly the beginning of a backlash against letting women off too easily for resorting to deadly violence. On the contrary, politicians are getting the message that compassion for battered women can yield dividends with a good half of the electorate. At the end of 1990, Ohio's Governor Richard Celeste granted mass clemency to 25 women convicted of killing or assaulting their allegedly abusive partners. Governors of many other states, including Maryland, Missouri, Illinois, and Massachusetts, have followed suit. A poll in California revealed that 83% of women and 62% of men favored the option of clemency for battered women convicted of killing in alleged self-defense.[57] In this political mood, no one is going to pay much attention to scholarly critiques of learned helplessness and its extension to self-defense cases. Indeed we are witnessing the beginning of a transformation of the battered women's syndrome into a general defense of abuse as a justification for retaliation.

Abuse, Abuse, Everywhere

When we look back on the 1990s, we are likely to call it the decade of abuse. The argument most likely to win sympathy in court today is that the defendant was abused, particularly as a wife, lover, or child. The perpetrators of this abuse go far beyond the husbands and lovers responsible for the battered-wife syndrome. The list has come to include homosexual lovers (male and female), teachers in nursery schools, parish priests, Boy Scout leaders, and, of course, parents responsible for all sorts of abuse. The sexual and psychological abuse that lay dormant for decades came alive in questions put by social workers to children and by explorations under hypnosis. Some of it originated in the minds of the social workers and hypnotists; some of it was unquestionably real.

In the 1990s, abuse became the standard explanation for doing evil. Lorena Bobbitt could complain, effectively, of sexual abuse as well as sexual selfishness by her husband. Tonya Harding could invoke abuse on her side as an excuse for allegedly participating in an assault against competing figure skater Nancy Kerrigan. Against charges of aggravated mayhem for pulling truck driver Reginald Denny from his cab and smashing his skull with a brick, Damian Williams could seriously claim that he would never have become a violent person if his father had not abandoned him as child. Thus in a world in which violent crime became the number-one social concern, people were bending over backwards to listen to tales of scarring in bad relationships.

There was no case in which the public was more eager to listen and the defendants more willing to spin a tale of abuse than the trial of the millionaire Menendez brothers in the Los Angeles of late 1993. The city was temporarily at rest between riots and natural disasters. The people were eager for tantalizing television distractions. At first it did not seem as though there would be much controversy about the guilt of Lyle and Erik Menendez, who in the summer of 1989, at the ages of 21 and 18, had entered their own home with shotguns just purchased in San Diego and had emptied 16 rounds into their father and mother, Jose and Kitty Menendez. Yet as the trial unfolded, the televised parade of surprising and shocking witnesses became the emblem of the "abuse" decade. In the end, this trial of two young men revealed unexpected implications of the movement to correct the position of women as victims in criminal court.

Some feminists may have thought that advancing the battered women's claims of self-defense would help women as a special class, a group that deserved special protection after centuries of discrimination. The battered-women syndrome would represent something like affirmative action in the courts; it would compensate for all the prejudice that had accumulated against women, particularly in rape cases. But if there is any principle guiding legal thought, it is the egalitarian impulse toward generalization by analogy. The courts cannot recognize a defense for the blue-eyed and refuse it to the brown-eyed. There is no way of limiting a new defense to a privileged class. If the "syndrome" relaxes the criteria of self-defense for women, it must have the same impact for battered men and battered children. This was obvious to Leslie Abramson, Erik's lawyer, who made it clear from the outset that the defense would develop a defense for battered children that would draw on the innovations developed for battered women.

The plan was this: The boys would testify that each had been subject to years of sexual abuse by both father and mother, that a few days prior to the killings Kitty had pulled Lyle's toupee off his head, and that this event had generated sympathy in Erik, the younger brother, for Lyle's embarrassment. Erik then confessed to Lyle that his father had sodomized him for the last 12 years; this revelation prompted Lyle to go to his father and insist that the abuse cease or he would make it public. Jose supposedly responded with a threat to kill the two boys. Thus a defense of self-defense began to come into relief.

The problem that Erik and Lyle faced was the same as the typical problem in the battered-wife cases. On the day they were killed, the parents did nothing to indicate a threat to their sons. They were sitting at home, watching television. They were no more overtly aggressive than the sleeping husbands in cases like Judy Norman's. How could the brothers overcome this obvious impediment? The basic rule in California was the same as in North Carolina. Erik and Lyle could claim self-defense only if they were in "reasonable fear of imminent death or great bodily harm." And surely this was not the case.

Yet California sports a doctrine called "imperfect self-defense" that permits a defendant to rely on self-defense even if his or her fear is unreasonable. This defense derives its force from the assumption that a killer who fears an attack, however unreasonably, does not act with the malice aforethought necessary for murder. The doctrine makes some sense: A person who kills in self-defense acts, more or less, in good faith, and good faith is incompatible with hatred or malice toward the victim. North Carolina recognizes this principle too, but it could not help Judy Norman on appeal. Even if the jurors had found that this fear-based good faith prompted the killing, they should have convicted her of manslaughter, and Judy had been convicted only for manslaughter.

Going into the Menendez trial, public outrage strongly backed the Los Angeles District Attorney who was committed to seeking the maximum conviction and punishment, including the gas chamber for the cold-blooded murder of the two people to whom, if morality means anything, the Menendez boys owed the most respect. Yet when Lyle and Erik began testifying about their sexual abuse at the hands of their father and the participation by their mother, the public began to sway to their side. Lyle gave such a good performance that as he stepped down from the stand several jurors were in tears.

The appetite for details only increased as Erik testified and defense lawyer Abramson tried to create the impression that some hard evidence corroborated the brothers' testimony. In fact, virtually no evidence, except a truncated photograph of the defendants as nude children, supported their tales of abuse. And there was compelling silent evidence on the other side. They both complained of forced sodomy; yet there was no sign of bruising or tissue damage to their anuses, which at the outset were the tiny openings of young boys. When they confessed their crime to their psychiatrist Jerome Oziel, they failed to mention their fear of a preemptive parental attack. No members of the family had witnessed any parental behavior that could qualify as physical or sexual abuse. In the end, the defense's case turned almost entirely on the persuasive but self-interested performance that Lyle and Erik gave on the stand.

Yet some members of the public and of the jury were eager to believe. An abusive parent is an enemy—much more of an enemy, apparently, than a child who puts a shotgun to his mother's face and blasts away. The case for the defense degenerated rather quickly into an attempt to convict the parents. This was the real strategy from the outset. As Leslie Abramson said as the defendant's testimony began to make its impact:

> "If people would just think for a minute, there are some fundamental precepts of family life. Precept No. 1 is that children love their parents. Good parents do not get shotgunned by their kids. Period."[58]

The nub of the defense, therefore, was that the parents must have done something to deserve their fate. This is the classic strategy of blaming the victim.

The claims of abuse provided good cover for reciting every detail of the parents' life, however intimate. Kitty's personal sex life, her interest in pornography, her intimate letters to her husband, would (or should) be shielded against inquiry in a rape case, but, paradoxically, not in this murder prosecution. No card was left unplayed in the defense's effort to destroy the reputation of both parents. And yet as William Kennedy Smith was protected from provocative, incriminating evidence about his history of sexual aggression, so these two defendants could keep from the jury evidence of their homicidal propensities. The jury never learned, for example, that 20 months before the shooting Erik had written a play that features a young man who shotguns his parents to death for their money.

The most disturbing aspect of the transformation of the case into a trial of the parents for abuse is that journalists took the testimony of abuse seriously and accepted the wildcat defense theory that prior abuse somehow made the killing acceptable. As the distinguished *New York Times* reporter Seth Mydans formulated the "core question" of the trial: "to what degree [can] a history of child molestation . . . justify parricide?"[59] This is a truly remarkable perversion of the trial and its legal doctrines. First, the formulation of the question presupposes that there was "a history of child molestation." At a certain point in its coverage, the mainstream press simply lost its critical judgment and assumed that where there was testimony, there must be facts. One striking exception was Dominick Dunne, who wrote a series of biting trial reports for *Vanity Fair*. Dunne remained convinced to the end that the boys were lying, and his diagnosis of their deception will, I am sure, some day be proved correct.[60]

Even if we assume that there was a "history of child molestation," the suggestion that this history could *justify* the killings would come as a great surprise to Judge Stanley Weisberg, who at least nominally decided the law of the trial. The most that could be said under his instructions to the jury was that a fear of "imminent death or great bodily harm" would negate the malice required for murder. There was no reference in the judge's rulings to the possibility of justifying the double parricide. "Justification" carries roughly the same meaning in law as it does in ordinary language. If you are justified, you have done the right thing. You are not guilty. To make it clear that this was not an issue, Judge Weisberg instructed the jury to focus on the choice between murder and manslaughter. Yet the distortion reflected in Mydans' article spread across the country.[61] Many people seemed to think that the issue was whether a history of child abuse can justify taking the lives of defenseless parents.

On the legal questions as they were actually formulated by the Judge, two juries—one for Lyle and one for Erik—could not make up their minds. After an average of three weeks of stormy deliberations (19 days for Erik, 25 for Lyle), the representatives of the people remained divided, roughly half voting for murder and the other half for manslaughter. Erik's jury split on the gender line. Six women accepted the story of abuse and voted from the outset for the less severe verdict. The six men remained skeptical to the end. Five held out for first-degree murder, one was willing to compromise on second-degree murder. It is not clear why the women were so easily persuaded. One would expect that they would have identified with Kitty, who was brutally murdered for nothing more than being there. The most likely supposition is that the cry of abuse resonates so strongly with women that two female defense lawyers, Abramson and Jill Lansing, persuaded them that this was another instance of the phenomenon that has plagued women as victims of rape and domestic battering. Yet associating the alleged abuse of Lyle and Erik with the condition of women who demonstrably suffered, as did Judy Norman, illustrates the tendency of good ideas to find their cheapest common denominator. Judy Norman could not escape without fear of being caught and beaten, as she had been beaten in the past. Nothing stopped the monied Menendez boys from getting in their Alfa Romeo (a recent present from their allegedly abusive father) and driving and driving and driving. If they motored their way to San Diego to buy a shotgun, they also could have found a non-violent way out of their silver-lined unhappiness.

My own view is that Judge Weisberg made a tragic mistake in admitting the evidence of abuse in the first place. Nothing in California law required him to open the trial to the knee-jerk reactions of the "abuse decade." The legal point that governed his decision was exactly the same as in the Norman case. To claim a relevant fear of "imminent death or great bodily harm," the threatened attack must indeed be imminent. It must be about to happen. But even if we assume that the boys' story is true and that their parents were indeed going to attack when they exited the den where they were watching television, the feared attack was not imminent. No jurisdiction recognizes self-defense for preemptive attacks, and this killing was clearly preemptive—whether there was reason to fear Kitty and Jose Menendez' long-range intentions or not. It should have been necessary for the boys to wait at least until their parents approached them in a manner that appeared to be threatening. As it was, the defendants' alleged fear was irrelevant to the charge of first-degree murder. And if their fear was irrelevant, so was the argument of abuse that supposedly rendered their fear plausible. The judge should have ruled all of it inadmissible.

Yet contrary to the indications of common sense and California law,[62] Judge Weisberg implicitly followed the dissenting opinion in *Norman*: "In the context of the doctrine of self-defense, the definition of 'imminent' must be informed by the defendant's perceptions."[63] In other words, if the defendants believed that the attack was imminent, they could escape liability for first-degree murder. It is not clear whether the jury even cared whether or not Lyle and Erik believed the attack was imminent. So long as the defendants could devise an argument for treating the evidence of abuse as relevant (it supposedly explained their fear of attack) they could testify about their "history of child molestation," put their victim-parents on trial, and thus secure a balancing of their wrong against their parents' wrong. We should never forget the 1993 Menendez trial, for it illustrates the great myth that juries and the public care about legal questions as they are formulated in instructions to the jury. No matter how precisely the judge defined the issue of imperfect self-defense, the press and their readers would view the dispute as a question whether "a history of child molestation can justify parricide."

The striking fact of putting Jose and Kitty Menendez on trial for child abuse is that they were not there to defend themselves. They received no benefit of counsel. They enjoyed neither a presumption of innocence nor evidentiary rules to protect their privacy. They were an exposed target for all the fears and biases of the time. Nothing could have been more unfair to the defenseless victims. Their posthumous plight recalls the tendency of lawyers to expose complaining witnesses in rape cases to unfair attacks against their character. Now there are other victims who are abused by zealous efforts to seek compassion for criminal defendants. But the question of fairness to both victims and defendants remains as urgent as ever.

Postscript: Lawyers for Mike Tyson continued, indefatigably, into the fall of 1994 to seek a reversal of his conviction. They sought a new trial on the ground that they had discovered fresh evidence, not available at the time of the first trial, that Desiree Washington and her parents had a financial incentive to lie. The claim was that Washington was interested primarily in securing civil damages as well as book and movie rights from a successful prosecution of Tyson. The Indiana Court of Appeals held against the defense on this point, but nonetheless granted another hearing on the question whether the prosecution had violated its constitutional duty to disclose all the information concerning Washington's financial incentives.

In the field of women as victims, no trial of the decade was more important than the prosecution of O.J. Simpson for allegedly having killed his wife Nicole Brown Simpson and Ron Goldman on June 12, 1994. In the early stages of the proceedings, lawyers for Simpson attempted to cast him in the role of victim—African-American on the verge of suicide when faced with arrest, a defendant already convicted in some quarters of the media, a man who could not get a fair trial. On the other side, feminists identified strongly with Nicole, primarily because the press gained access to the tape of a 911 emergency call that reveals O.J. to be a violent and jealous husband. He pleaded "no contest" to a charge of marital assault in May 1989 and was placed on probation.

Yet prosecutor Marcia Clark did very little to identify herself with the victims. She was not photographed with the surviving families, and she did little to show that she shared the pain felt by the families of Nicole Simpson and Ron Goldman. It is possible, as argued on pages 118–119, that the District Attorney made the mistake of picking one attractive white woman to prosecute in a case where the victim was also an attractive white woman.

Feminists had good reason to focus their energies on the O.J. Simpson trial. This was the case of a reputed and convicted wife-batterer who, out of jealousy, allegedly went too far and killed her to avoid her being with other men. They had hoped that this case would dramatize the dangers of domestic violence as the Rodney King case had brought police brutality to the center of media attention. There were some problems, however, with the hypothesis that an abusive husband is likely to kill. First, the motives for battering and killing are different. Battering expresses a desire to dominate and control. Batterers want their victims to remain alive so that they may continue the cycle of abuse and repentance. About 1,200 men kill their wives every year. By any estimate the number of batterers is greater by a multiple of 1,000 or 10,000. The odds, therefore, that any particular batterer will kill are very low.

The conflict between opposing camps in the O.J. case came to a head in early September 1994 when Gil Garcetti, the Los Angeles District Attorney, decided not to pursue the death penalty. He was left with the embarrassing contradiction of retaining the threat of the gas chamber in the pending second prosecution of the Menendez brothers but waiving it in the case of another double murder by a celebrity defendant. Garcetti described his decision as a "no-win" situation. Either he alienated African-Americans sympathetic to the defendant or women sympathetic to the victims.

CHAPTER FIVE

The Quest for a Fair Trial

"The quality of a nation's civilization can largely
be determined by the methods it uses in the
enforcement of its criminal law."
—*Justice Walter V. Schaeffer, Illinois Supreme Court, 1957.*[1]

AMERICANS AND OTHER ENGLISH-SPEAKING PEOPLE SHARE AN
obsession with fairness. We have coined the phrases "fair play" and
"fair trial" and have bequeathed them to the Western world. Many
of our neighboring cultures simply incorporate the word "fair" into
their vocabulary as an untranslatable American idea. Thus you can
hear Germans and Israelis using the word "fair" as though it were
their own. The French try in vain to translate it as *équitable* or *juste*.
But these and cognates in other Romance languages overlook the
procedural bedrock of fair dealing.

Americans learn the notion of fair play as soon as they begin
playing with other children. Enter any kindergarten and watch children playing with a single ball or Lego set. Sooner or later one of
them will complain that another is not sharing, that he or she is "not
fair." The charge of unfairness is a tool that children quickly acquire
to protect their interests. Not sharing is paradigmatic unfairness. So
is not playing by the rules.

Understanding the idea of fair play has become a challenge to the two dozen European countries that have ratified the European Convention on Human Rights, which provides that in all criminal as well as civil cases, "Everyone is entitled to a fair and public hearing."[2] The requirement of a fair trial also emerges in the newly enacted Canadian Charter of Rights and Freedoms, which provides by analogy to the European charter that everyone charged with a crime is presumed innocent until proven guilty "in a fair and public hearing."[3] Yet surprisingly, the term "fairness" does not appear in the United States Constitution. There is no explicit right in the Bill of Rights to a fair trial.

Though the Bill of Rights omits the word "fairness," the idea of a fair trial runs through our basic rights and renders them coherent. The most basic idea of justice in the Constitution, due process of law, is commonly defined as fair procedure. As the Supreme Court put it: "A fair trial in a fair tribunal is a basic requirement of due process."[4] Fair procedures take the place of substantive justice. The demands of justice—as opposed to fairness—elude the basic documents on human rights. No basic charter of any modern society requires the just punishment of all criminals. The reduced verdict for Dan White, the acquittal of the four officers in Simi Valley, the verdicts in the El Sayyid Nosair and Lemrick Nelson cases, the finding of not guilty in the William Kennedy Smith trial—even if contrary to the evidence, these verdicts would not violate national or international rules of criminal justice. The law demands not a just outcome but a fair procedure. After the East Germans achieved unification with the Federal Republic, they expected some retribution against the Communist big brothers who had oppressed them for 45 years. They soon came to recognize that the cumbersome demands of due process precluded quick and easy justice. They complained: We wanted justice and we got the rule of law.

Fair procedures triumph, then, over our passionate demands for justice now. This is the way of the law and of moral philosophy. In John Rawls' influential 1971 book *A Theory of Justice*, a fair procedure of negotiation becomes the guideline for the principles of justice that should bind society. This idea lies at the heart of Rawls' doctrine, "justice as fairness." His faith in fair procedures runs deep. If we deal fairly with one another, he argues, we will invariably end up with principles that we can accept as just.

The best explanation for this faith in fairness lies in our cultural roots. To appreciate this point, we need only pause to reflect upon our everyday speech, which abounds in sporting metaphors. A fair competition is one in which the playing field is level, the dice are not loaded, the deck is not stacked. Fairness consists in playing by even-handed rules. Neither side hits below the belt. No one hides the ball. You don't sandbag the opposition by passing on the first round and then raising your opponent's bet. In a fair competition, both sides have an equal chance of winning. And the winning side should gain the upper hand without cheating, without playing dirty, without hitting the other when he or she is down. These idioms pervade the English language. No other European language relies so heavily on sporting metaphors to carry on the business of the day. As British civilization was forged on the playing fields of Eton, Americans learn their principles of fair trial by shooting marbles in sandlots, playing poker, and participating vicariously in professional sports.

Note the way the dissent in *Tyson* formulated the issue of the case:

> Rather, the issues involve whether the prosecution and the defense were afforded a *level playing field* upon which to put forth their respective cases. This appeal is quite simply about whether Michael Tyson received *a fair trial*.[5]

The gist of fairness is equality. On a level playing field, both sides have an equal chance of advancing the ball. If everyone plays by the rules, the better side will win—fair and square. For purposes of criminal justice, the basic principle is expressed in these oft-quoted lines from an 1887 Supreme Court decision:

> Our criminal justice system requires not only freedom from bias against the accused, but also from any prejudice against his prosecution. Between him and the state the scales are to be evenly held.[6]

But do we really think of our criminal trials as providing even-handed treatment for the prosecution as well as for the defense? Consider our ingrained attitudes toward the presumption of innocence. For centuries scholars of criminal justice have claimed that it is better for ten guilty persons to go free than to convict one innocent defendant.[7] Some have urged a ratio of 20 to one.[8] Thus to achieve justice we skew the odds in favor of acquittal. The scales of justice are not balanced. They dip heavily in favor of the defendant.

This is the paradox of fairness. We are not quite sure whether fairness demands that David and Goliath are of equal size or whether fairness requires guarantees against an innocent David's losing the battle. Sometimes we insist that the playing field be level; other times, we insist that it slant in favor of the defendant.

However we solve this paradox, we know that justice for the victim may be at odds with fairness toward the defendant. The more one demands a conviction in prosecutions like those against Dan White, Laurence Powell, Lemrick Nelson, and Mike Tyson, the less one will be concerned about convicting an innocent defendant. The new political trial, typified by these cases, prompts us to reevaluate the fairness of the battle. If the defendant had a good hand before the new assertiveness of gays, blacks, Jews, and women, that hand might be trumped today. The point is simple. If the victim gains, the defendant loses. Or at least it seems that way.

Some victims' rights groups seek to cut back the procedural guarantees that defendants gained under the decisions of the Warren Court. They want to abolish the exclusionary rules that protect suspects against unconstitutionally secured evidence and involuntary confessions. They want suspects to suffer easier convictions. But these are not my goals. I stand by the liberal advances of the Supreme Court in the 1960s and 1970s. The question is whether we can continue our solicitude for the rights of the accused and at the same time heighten our sensitivity to the needs of the victim.

Impartiality

There is at least one principle of a fair trial that mediates even-handedly between the demands of victims and the demands of defendants. Judge and jury should not tender loyalties to either side. The principle is as ancient as Leviticus 19:15: "Thou shall not respect the person of the poor, nor honor the person of the mighty." If we know nothing more about a fair trial, we know that those who judge must be free of personal ties to the victim, to the prosecution, and to the accused. This explains why Leona Kaplan was unable to serve on the jury that decided the fate of the man who seems to have killed Meir Kahane. One factor was that a junior member of the prosecutorial staff had distant family ties to the Kaplans. Though Leona might not have recognized the prosecutor in court, the connection could have surfaced in the course of the trial. The other factor was that lawyer William Kunstler was given the opportunity to disapprove of Mrs. Kaplan in front of the jury. This generated the fear that she might resent the lawyers for the defense. These factors created risks of partiality, risks that outweighed the desirability of having a Jewish woman on the jury that decided whether the accused had murdered a Jewish nationalist.

But that factor too—Jews deciding Jewish interests—flouts the principle of impartiality. Even though there is something disturbing about a jury that excludes people who identify with the victim, the principle of impartiality cannot tolerate those who do identify with the victim. There is no easy solution. We are disturbed by an all-white jury deciding the fate of the police officers who assaulted Rodney King. But we would not accept a black on the jury who proclaimed a commitment to vindicate the interests of black people.

The ideal of impartiality explains a misstep in the early stage of the Rodney King proceedings. The judge who originally presided over the case sent a private message to the prosecution. Once he did that, there was no way he could redeem the presumption that he was beyond partial ties to one side in the case. The duty to maintain the appearance as well as the fact of impartiality also accounts for a curious twist in the *Tyson* appeal. While the decision was pending before the Court of Appeals in Indiana, Alan Dershowitz, who had argued the case, was sought out by Amy W. MacDonell, the wife of Indiana Supreme Court Justice Randall T. Shepard, at a law-school reunion. She offered unsolicited advice about how to handle his representation of Tyson in Indiana. Not a lawyer, Ms. MacDonell might have been excusably ignorant about the risks of meddling. Nonetheless she put both her husband and Dershowitz in an embarrassing position. It now seemed that the wife of a supreme court justice was offering advice to Tyson's lawyer on how to handle the case. Shortly thereafter, in November 1992, Justice Shepard officially decided not to participate in any further proceeding concerning Mike Tyson.

After losing the appeal in August 1993, Dershowitz filed a petition to the state supreme court to transfer the case to the higher tribunal; the justices divided, two against two, on whether they should hear the appeal. A tie vote means a negative decision. Hoping that Justice Shepard would break the tie in his favor, Dershowitz petitioned the judge to countermand his recusal. The judge declined in a written opinion.[9] For him, the critical factor was not "whether the judge's impartiality is impaired in fact" but whether there was "an appearance of impropriety" and his participation would undermine "public confidence" in the neutrality of the court. He also faulted Dershowitz for "lying in wait" until after the Indiana Supreme Court had voted not to hear the Tyson appeal. Dershowitz, in turn, faults the judge for seeking to protect his wife and concealing his reasons for his recusal until after the decision by the supreme court.

In the end, appearances mattered. The problem with Leona Kaplan is that no matter what she said, other people, reasonable people, might think she was biased against the defendant Nosair. For Justice Shepard, the problem was that because of a chance conversation between his wife and a defense lawyer, his "impartiality might reasonably be questioned."[10]

The apparent partiality of trial judge Patricia Gifford fueled

Dershowitz's effort to get the United States Supreme Court to hear the Tyson case. To take the case from the state to the federal level, he needed an issue under the United States Constitution. His best bet, he thought, was the practice in force during the Tyson trial that permitted the prosecution to select the trial judge from a list of six in the county. Prosecutor Greg Garrison chose former sex-crimes prosecutor Patricia Gifford. If this had happened in a Communist country, the immediate reaction would have been: There they go again, rigging the trial. The Indiana Court of Appeals concluded that letting the prosecutor pick the judge "lacks the appearance of impartiality that is required to maintain the confidence of the public and the accused in the system."[11] The court recommended changing the system. Yet it was unwilling to assume that Judge Gifford had actually ruled partially or unfairly. Dershowitz had brought to light a serious constitutional issue, but the Supreme Court in Washington refused to intervene in criminal justice, Indiana style.

Tyson Fights for a Fair Trial

As the one case in our series in which the prosecution won a conviction, *Tyson* exhibits a variety of skirmishes in the borderland of fairness. The metaphors of matches in rings and games on diamonds do not provide an attractive model for lawyers in court. The search for justice can easily degenerate into a contest won by the lawyer with the best timing. In competitive games on the law's court, bad timing can be a fault that looms larger than the commitment to finding the truth. And so it was with Dershowitz, who waited too long to file his request that Justice Shepard countermand his decision to stay out of the case.

Even more critically, the issue of timing dominated the debate about whether the three belatedly discovered witnesses would be allowed to testify about what they had seen in Tyson's limousine minutes before the encounter in the hotel room. In civilian criminal trials, common to Western and Eastern Europe, this evidence would undoubtedly have had a bearing on the defendant's guilt or innocence.

These originally inquisitorial legal cultures are committed to the search for truth; the combat between the lawyers means less. Yet for a common law judge—as in England and its former colonies—the main question is whether considering late evidence is fair to the other side.

Prosecutor Greg Garrison fought hard against what he informally called "trial by ambush";[12] letting the "late bloomers"[13] testify would give the defense an unfair advantage. The normal remedy to his problem would have been to request a continuance—"time out" to bring the playing field back to level. But this would not do for Garrison; he claimed that because the jurors were sequestered, they could not endure an extra few days of isolation from the world. What really irked Garrison, however, was that his well-orchestrated march would lose its beat. He had departed from ordinary rules of trial presentation by having Desiree Washington testify first rather than last. He wanted her performance to remain the main event, as originally staged, without the distraction of conflicting testimony and the prospect of recalling her to the stand.

The delay by the defense lawyers was hardly significant. They learned about the three witnesses on a Thursday afternoon and questioned them on Friday. By Saturday morning the defense lawyers were in court requesting permission to see the limousine in order to verify that the witnesses could peer through the darkened windows. On Sunday they called Garrison and informed him of the new development. They could not have moved much faster without a general practice of disclosing every possible lead to the prosecution. And if they had to do that, there would not be much left, as Judge Sullivan later wrote in dissent on the court of appeals, of the lawyers' "ethical duty" to their client: "Defense counsel is not required to, and may not ethically, assist the prosecution in its collection of evidence, case preparation, and trial presentation."[14] So far as one can tell, the trial judge ruled against the defense because she was irritated that on Saturday morning when the defense requested to see the limousine, they did not disclose the possibility of new witnesses.[15] A missed beat brought a possibly innocent defendant that much closer to conviction.

What the lawyers do, therefore, shapes the trial. The Indiana "rape-shield" statute prohibits the use of the alleged victim's prior sexual history except in specified situations. Yet prosecutor Greg Garrison brought Desiree Washington's sexual behavior to the forefront by portraying her as a "good Christian girl" different from the chorus line eager to accept a sexual date with Mike Tyson. The defense responded that the prosecution had thus "opened the door." They "should not be able to shut it in the defendant's face."[16] In many courts in the United States, this would have been a compelling argument of fair play. It did not carry the debate in this case, at least under the pressures of the new political trial.

Greg Garrison drove his advantage to the extreme. He even sought to mock the nature of criminal defense by reading critical language from a Supreme Court opinion to the jury. In a dissenting opinion, Supreme Court Justice Byron White had once allowed himself to opine on the nature of the adversary system. He distinguished between the commitment of prosecutors to search for the truth and the duty of defense counsel to defend the interests of their clients, regardless of the truth. And he went on: "If [defense counsel] can confuse a witness, even a truthful one, or make him appear at a disadvantage, unsure, or indecisive, that will be his normal course." Garrison read this passage to the jury in order to portray himself as the one party in the trial who could be trusted. His apology for his maneuver was that he was merely arguing the law to the jury, and that he was allowed to do so under the Indiana constitution. Yet a dissenting opinion is not law. And even if it were, Justice White's reflections are dictum—irrelevant to the legal issue in the case. For technical reasons, however, the court of appeals refused to consider the prejudicial impact of the prosecutor's posturing before the jury.

The prosecutor's behavior in reading Justice White's opinion was untoward, because he was stepping out of his role. It was as though he were saying to the jury: "Believe me because I have a duty to pursue the truth; do not believe my opponent, because his duty is to confuse truthful witnesses." Prosecutors do have a duty to pursue the truth. But they may not proclaim their objectivity to the jury.

They may not represent that they personally believe that the defendant is guilty. Prosecutor and defense counsel appear in stylized performances. They are there to present a case. They are not quite like actors on a stage, but they are not simply individuals engaged in a personal argument. When they try to gain an edge by allowing personal opinion to break through or by commenting on their role, they violate the boundaries of the courtroom as a magic circle.

It is no accident that the Tyson trial brought to the fore so many conflicts at the boundary between fair play and zealous prosecution. The pressure of the new political trial drives the prosecution to seek a conviction, even at a high cost. I make no suggestion that Garrison had sold out to the demands of feminists to make an example of Mike Tyson. Yet there were factors that made the Indianapolis courtroom receptive to the political currents of the times. The prosecutor identified strongly with the "uncommon courage and commitment" of the alleged victim.[17] The trial judge, a former sex-crimes prosecutor, seemed to favor the state in every "discretionary ruling." This was a case that turned out to be more than one woman in conflict with one man. The movement to vindicate the dignity of women had encountered a high-profile defendant, with a reputation for womanizing, whose conviction could send a message to all men that "no means no."

When a case takes on these political overtones, when the drive toward conviction becomes a cause with mobilized partisans behind it, there is little to protect the accused but the procedural guarantees of the Bill of Rights. Those guarantees are the concrete embodiment of the American notion of a fair trial, and at their center lie the Fifth and Sixth Amendments. Thus we are led to assess the extent to which those Amendments have already swayed in the winds of the new political trial.

The Fifth Amendment

The Fifth and Sixth Amendments capture the paradox between fairness as a level playing field and fairness as solicitude for the accused. In general terms, the Sixth Amendment tries to achieve equality of arms at trial, and the Fifth seeks to cut back the weapons of the prosecution in order to protect the innocent. According to the Fifth Amendment:

1. No one shall be held for trial without being charged by a grand jury.[18]
2. No one shall be subject to double jeopardy, which means roughly that no one shall be tried twice for the same crime.[19]
3. No one shall be forced to incriminate himself.[20]

These three principles limit the power of the prosecution. These are things the state may not do. It may not bring a person to trial without first testing the charge before a group of lay people called the grand jury. It may not prosecute someone twice for the same offense, and it may not compel incriminating testimony. The purpose of these restrictions is not to empower David, but to restrain Goliath. This is fairness as solicitude for the accused—innocent until proven guilty.

The provision concerning the grand jury vests in lay people the power to check the initiatives of government. Prosecutors cannot decide by themselves, at least in serious cases, to bring someone to trial, subject him to a devastating assault on his reputation, and inflict upon him the risk of a criminal conviction. When the people say no, as did the first grand jury in the prosecution of Bernhard Goetz in January 1985, the prosecution falters. It cannot proceed to trial, however convinced it may be of the guilt of the accused. This kind of lay control on the power of the state is unknown outside the English-speaking world. It reflects an Anglo-American approach to the design of a fair trial.

We should not forget that these provisions were originally designed to apply just to the federal government. Most provisions protecting the accused have become applicable to the states as elements of due process under the Fourteenth Amendment. But the grand jury is an exception. This lay filter of the prosecution's power is not so fundamental that it is thought to be necessary for a fair trial.[21] This explains why the state of Florida, among others, does not always employ grand juries as the first stage of prosecution. In the William Kennedy Smith trial, for example, the prosecution filed charges directly, without convening a committee of lay people to pass on the charges. Thus the accused was spared a temptation to clear himself early in the process. Had a grand jury convened, Smith might have seen an advantage in testifying, in which case he would have presented a version of the alleged rape that could later be used to search for inconsistencies in his testimony at trial. As the grand jury was used in the Tyson trial, only the defendant suffered. He had committed himself to a story that later came back to haunt him at trial. Even an innocent defendant can be hoist on his own petty inconsistencies.

Grand juries sometimes have the effect of insulating prosecutors from political responsibility. This was the case in the early stages of the Rodney King proceedings when a California grand jury decided not to indict any of the 20 plus officers who stood at the scene of the beating and refused to intervene. So far as they indirectly rendered aid and support, the bystanders were liable in principle as accomplices in the beating, but the "people," probably under prosecutorial influence, decided to limit the charge to the four most prominent participants. If this was a political decision, it would have been better for the District Attorney to assume responsibility for the decision himself. Grand jury proceedings cut like a two-edged sword. They work sometimes to the advantage of one side, sometimes to the advantage of the other.

The rule against double jeopardy appears to be a strong protection against harassing suspects with multiple proceedings. The principle is that once the prosecution brings an accused to trial, it crosses a one-way border. If the jury is empaneled and sworn, the fate of the accused must be resolved. There are some exceptions to this principle, as, for example, when the jury cannot reach a unanimous verdict one way or the other. So it was with the juries that first heard the evidence against the Menendez brothers. Both juries deadlocked between those who wanted the leniency of a manslaughter conviction and those who knew murder when they "saw" it. Also, merely going before a grand jury does not create "jeopardy." If one grand jury refuses to indict, as in the Goetz case, the prosecution can claim new evidence and convene a second grand jury that might be more favorable to its arguments.

The principle of double jeopardy kicks in, generally, after the jury is empowered to decide the defendant's fate. The trial judge may not decide, mid-trial, that the prosecution has done a sloppy job preparing for trial, that the trial should be suspended, and that the prosecution should be given an additional opportunity to collect evidence against the accused. The idea of a "day in court" is basic to our tradition. And once the day begins, it is not over until a decision is reached, the jury is deadlocked, or some other intervening factors necessitate a mistrial.

In the European inquisitorial tradition, which has survived in the former Communist legal systems, trial judges can hear the evidence, decide there is insufficient proof of guilt, and remand the case back to the prosecution. The fate of the accused remains on hold. Keeping the accused dangling this way offends the American sense of fair play. After the game begins, you do not call "time out" for further training.

The federal prosecution of the four Los Angeles police officers struck many lay observers as a violation of the principle of double jeopardy. Powell, Koon, Briseno, and Wind were found not guilty in the state trial. How could they be charged again and thus "be twice put in jeopardy of life or limb"? After the federal grand jury returned the indictments, the National Board of the ACLU—no friend of the police—condemned the federal intervention as a violation of the Fifth Amendment.[22] Columnist William Safire came to the same conclusion.[23] Once around the track, they said, should be enough: The Constitution prohibits a federal retrial for the same beating. The Los Angeles chapter of the ACLU felt betrayed. How could the national board not understand the necessities of the situation? To paraphrase Stacey Koon, observers in the East did not understand "the truth of the society" that had to prosecute "in order to protect itself."[24]

The official answer to the puzzle of double jeopardy requires some imagination. You have to pretend that we live in a federation of states, each state being independent and sovereign in its borders. The federal government stands above all 50 sovereign states as an independent sovereign. State crimes injure a community defined by the state, and federal crimes injure the federal version of the same people. Two sovereigns, two crimes. This might be a good argument if we lived in a loose federation like the European Community. European lawyers can readily imagine a crime against the entire European Community that would be distinct from a crime, say, against the Spanish government. But this is where the argument for federal power in the United States gets turned on its head. A federal government ready to intervene to correct injustices in the state courts is not exactly the loosely joined European confederation. The single nation that the United States has become can no longer pretend to be a sovereign entity removed from the individual states. Yet for purposes of the double-jeopardy clause, this is precisely the pretense that permits the second prosecution.

This official dogma of dual sovereignty should not be taken too seriously. It is a good example of technical reasoning in the law that masks the arguments that do the scoring. The real explanation for this exception to the double-jeopardy clause lies in a curious feature of criminal trials. We do not allow prosecutors to appeal jury verdicts of not guilty. Every country in Continental Europe permits the prosecution to appeal as a way of correcting wayward verdicts for the accused. Even former English colonies—those like Israel that never had the jury system—permit the prosecution to appeal. Yet we insist that if the jury speaks for the accused, its voice is final. Rendering justice to both sides requires some accommodation, some compensation to the prosecution. The necessary compensation, I submit, is permitting the federal government to prosecute for a violation of civil rights in the aftermath of a state jury acquittal.

Yet we are far from recognizing that the federal government should prosecute for a deprivation of civil rights in every case in which a defendant has been unjustly acquitted. Witness the prolonged debate about federal intervention in the Yankel Rosenbaum case. Historical factors shaped this intervention and limited it to cases in which the state has acted (police brutality) or perhaps to crimes that occur on the public streets (Rosenbaum). Crimes that occur between private individuals on private property are excluded (Meir Kahane, Kennedy Smith). Yet it seems that the public aspects of the slaying of Harvey Milk and George Moscone are sufficient to have warranted a civil-rights action, and that theoretical prospect, whether technical arguments would bring the case under the statute or not, should give us pause. It does indeed seem to exemplify the wrong of double jeopardy for the State to proceed a second time against a murder suspect after one jury has found him or her guilty of manslaughter. Under the language and theory of the civil-rights statutes, however, nothing should turn on whether the accused is acquitted or convicted at the state level.

We rest uneasy, then, with this theory that federal civil rights action is a fair form of prosecutorial appeal. It may be a necessity in extreme cases in which state courts turn their backs on worthy victims. Yet it is an institution responsive to political pressure. Threatening to riot, as in Los Angeles in 1992, generates the pressure of the streets. Lobbying the attorney general, as did activist Jews in 1993, expresses the leverage of the polls. This is not exactly the rule of law. The occasional surrogate appeal of civil-rights actions provides an unprincipled way of muddling through a weakness in our legal system. It releases the tensions generated by the new political trial.

The third provision of the Fifth Amendment expresses a peculiarly American concern for the accused. Of course, the state must be able to prosecute crime, but it cannot secure a conviction by forcing the defendant to confess her guilt or to testify against herself. The Constitution does not stand opposed to voluntary confessions; it even recognizes the possibility of convicting for treason "on Confession in open Court."[25] The Fifth Amendment zeroes in on "compelling" self-incrimination as an evil of an overbearing state. At an earlier stage in European procedure, prior to the French revolution, compelling confessions was a normal practice. When officials were convinced that the accused was guilty but the legally required form of proof was lacking, they had to proceed, with torture if necessary, to secure a confession. The prohibition against involuntary self-incrimination, then, protects the individual against the tyrannical power of officials who are privately convinced of the need for a conviction. Here we detect the efforts of Americans to distinguish themselves from Europeans and their characteristic mode of trial.

As Justice Frankfurter once expressed the identity of the American legal system,

> ours is an accusatorial and not an inquisitorial system—a
> system in which the State must establish guilt by evidence
> independently and freely secured and may not by its own
> coercion prove its charge against an accused out of his own
> mouth.[26]

The point on which Frankfurter's reasoning turned is that we are not like *them*—those inquisitorially-minded Europeans who are presumably willing to secure confessions at any cost. One wonders, then, about the confessions secured from Lemrick Nelson. He was sitting alone, a 16-year-old, in an interrogation room. The record of the confession lies exclusively in the fallible memory of the two police officers who, one by one, listened to him speak. We should not feel comfortable saying that Nelson voluntarily incriminated himself, simply because the officers testified under oath that they informed him of his right to remain silent and his right to have a lawyer present and that he thereupon waived his rights. In fact, these procedures depend entirely on the good faith and integrity of the police officers. They come perilously close to the authoritarian methods that Justice Frankfurter condemned.

Strictly speaking, the Constitution does not forbid forcing a suspect to talk. It only forbids using coerced words to gain a criminal conviction. There are two well-known ways of compelling testimony. One is to grant immunity to the witness against the subsequent use of his statements in a criminal trial. Thus the prosecution granted immunity to Troy Canty and James Ramseur, two of the young men Goetz shot in the subway, in order to induce them to testify. Both testified that they had had no intention of robbing the defendant Goetz. The other way of producing involuntary testimony is to threaten the witness with dismissal from employment if he or she does not participate in an on-the-job investigation. If this kind of implicit coercion takes place—if, perhaps, the police department puts its employees to the choice between dismissal and testifying about the conduct of their colleagues—the government cannot subsequently use the coerced testimony.[27] The police department can use it, however, because its disciplinary proceedings are not criminal in nature. But so far as criminal prosecutors are concerned, the coerced testimony is tainted. More significantly, all evidence derived from these coerced statements, such as testimony influenced by them, is inadmissible in a criminal trial.

Whenever a departmental inquiry produces coerced statements of this sort and others are exposed to the statement, therefore, the argument of tainted evidence haunts the trial. Any witness who might have derived his testimony from the coerced source becomes questionable. The specter of a turnaround on appeal for using improperly influenced testimony looms larger after Oliver North won reversal on this ground.[28] After the beating of Rodney King, the Internal Affairs Division of the LAPD conducted its own investigation. Officer Powell and Sergeant Koon gave statements after being advised that their refusal to do so could lead to dismissal. The hearing created a virus that could infect the entire trial. The government would have to rely on testimony unaffected by their coerced statements.

The mere existence of these coerced statements and the access of other police officers to them generated the possibility of a reversal after the federal conviction of Powell and Koon. On appeal they relied on claims that both Sergeant Conta's expert testimony and Officer Briseno's testimony in state court reflected the influence of the coerced testimony. It was a difficult claim to make stick, because Briseno had testified not on the basis of the other officers' testimony but as a percipient witness to the beating.

The use of a videotape of Briseno's testimony in state court particularly irked the defense. Breaking ranks, he was willing to criticize Officer Powell as being "out of control." Charged only with one stomp to King's back, Briseno appeared at the state trial to be trying to save himself at the expense of the others. In a gesture of solidarity, he decided not to testify at all in the federal trial. This was, of course, his right under the Fifth Amendment. No criminal defendant need take the stand and testify.

In Briseno's situation, we had the added twist that his state court testimony had been recorded on videotape. Technology brings with it new problems of fairness. In principle, there is no problem in introducing the defendant's voluntary testimony from a prior proceeding. If a voluntary confession is admissible against him, so is his public testimony. Yet exhibiting Briseno's testimony on a large screen seemed to nullify his constitutional right to remain silent. The defense objected as well on the grounds of "sandbagging." The prosecution did not seek to use the tape in the presentation of its case but merely as evidence to rebut the defense's position. Because Briseno had not testified, the defense argued, there was nothing to rebut. Judge Davies ruled against the defense on this point, but nonetheless induced the parties to negotiate about the portions of the state testimony that would be aired in the federal trial. In the end, they decided not to show the segment containing Briseno's statement that Powell was "out of control." Yet there remained many passages on the large screen in which Briseno made clear that he could not comprehend why the others had responded so violently.

These, then, are the restrictions on the state's power that express solicitude for the accused. The most powerful of these restrictions, particularly as used against state officials, is the modern interpretation of the privilege against self-incrimination. In every case in which a governmental agency has sought to clean its own house, its investigations have yielded coerced statements that lurk in the shadows of the trial. These statements can reassert themselves on appeal as the best possible grounds for a surprise reversal.

The Sixth Amendment

The Sixth Amendment, devoted to the "rights" of the accused "in all criminal prosecutions," seeks to equalize the power of the prosecution and the defense. The Amendment secures to each criminally accused the right:

1. to a "speedy and public trial"
2. to trial by jury
3. to have "an impartial jury"
4. to be tried "in the State or district wherein the crime shall have been committed"
5. "to be informed of the nature and cause of the accusation"
6. to be "confronted with the witnesses against him"
7. to have "compulsory process for obtaining witnesses in his favor"
8. "to have the Assistance of Counsel for his defence."

According to the common opinion of lawyers, the Sixth Amendment vests these rights only in the accused—not in the prosecution, not in the victim, not in the community. But if we take a close look, we note that in fact the prosecution—also known as the state or the People—enjoys them as well, at least in general terms. Negotiations between the prosecution and the defense shape the progress of a criminal case. Both sides appear in court to argue for and against continuances and other delays. In this sense both sides enjoy a right to a speedy trial. The prosecution also has the right to an impartial jury so far as it enjoys virtually the same power to challenge jurors for cause and without cause (peremptorily) as does the defense. It prosecutes in the district where the crime was committed. And of course the state need not be informed of the charges against the accused, for it draws up these charges. The prosecution also enjoys compulsory process to subpoena witnesses and present its case. As a matter of custom and practice, lawyers for the state enjoy full rights of cross-examination, and thus they have the capacity to confront the witnesses for the accused. By definition, because the prosecutor is a lawyer, the People have the assistance of counsel.

Thus the state has all the powers that the Amendment confers upon the accused, with the possible exception of items 2 and 4: the right to a jury trial and the right to have the case heard in the place where the crime was committed. In fact, the prosecution does enjoy something like a right to a jury trial—although this may come as a surprise to many lawyers. The defendant may waive the jury trial but the prosecution may object and block the waiver, thus ensuring trial by jury.[29] As a matter of constitutional right, then, the prosecution may insist on trial by jury.

This right, however, is not readily asserted. A prosecutor might well want to insist on a jury trial even if the defendant wants to proceed before a single judge. The judge could well be more inclined toward acquittal in certain kinds of cases than would a jury of lay people. But short-term tactical decisions are not always feasible. I recall a rape prosecution that I handled during my brief career as a prosecutor. The case was to come before a judge who, as everyone in the office knew, had a particular aversion toward convicting defendants charged with sex offenses. Of course, the defense wanted to waive the jury trial and proceed before the judge. As the deputy district attorney in charge of the case, I wanted to insist on a jury trial. When the higher-ups in the office got wind of my plan, they said no. "Don't insult the judge," they said. "We have to go before him every day. If one of our deputies shows that he has no confidence in him, that will hurt us in more cases than this isolated rape case."

There is an important point in this little vignette. To exercise your rights forcefully, you must be assured that there will be no indirect retaliation, no hidden price for claiming what should be yours. Defense counsel's insisting on a jury trial is understood as the normal course of events. But if a prosecutor insists on the same point, the move is treated as deviant, as an insult to the judge. Retaliation may well follow.

Grounding Justice

Of the rights protected by the Sixth Amendment, only one has received an interpretation that goes far beyond the text of the amendment. The Bill of Rights properly recognizes a right to a trial by an impartial jury, but nowhere specifies how far the courts should go to ensure that the men and women sitting in the jury box are indeed impartial. Yet the courts have recognized the constitutional necessity of changing the location of a trial if necessary to improve the chances of impartiality. Thus we find convictions reversed because a state court declined to "change the venue" of the trial to a different county within the state. The argument is that passionate feelings about a crime can make it impossible for the defendant to receive a fair trial where the deed was allegedly done.

The spirit of the Sixth Amendment runs contrary to changing venue just because of intense local publicity and concern. Federal trials should take place "in the State or district wherein the crime shall have been committed." This language of the Sixth Amendment expresses a policy of grounding trials in the soil from which they spring. In keeping with this principle, the trial of the police officers who beat Rodney King should have occurred in the locale, the county, of the beating. This policy of localization does not find its warrant in home town jurors' knowing more about the crime. Too much supposed familiarity can sometimes lead to bias. The point is rather that local communities have an interest in adjudicating responsibility for crimes that rent the internal bonds of cooperation and solidarity. The beating of Rodney King is an event that touched a tender nerve in Los Angeles. For that reason alone, the affected population, expressing itself through a jury, should have confronted the 56 baton blows to King's body and tried to reach a just verdict.

Solicitude for the accused officers, however, prompted an appellate court to order a change of venue. The judges were concerned that excessive publicity in Los Angeles County would make it impossible for the defendants to receive a fair trial on their home grounds. Of all the decisions that went awry, this one survives as a glaring mistake. And the error went beyond trial Judge Weisberg's choosing Simi Valley, a suburban community with a small black population. The problem was misconceiving the connection between geography and justice. The decision to relocate the trial prevented the residents of Los Angeles, people of all ethnicities, to resolve their own conflicts.

Sending the case to another county with an equivalent proportion of African-Americans would hardly have been better. The issue was not simply whether blacks would have a voice in the trial and whether there might be more of them available as potential jurors. The crime occurred specifically to and among the people of Los Angeles, white, Latino, and Jewish as well as black. It was *their* case—not the case of their counterparts in other communities. In the 1993 trial of police officer William Lozano, a Latino charged with killing an African-American, a Florida judge made the mistake of scouring the state for a community that would contain the proper mixture of people resembling the victim as well as the defendant. An Orlando jury of three whites, two Hispanics, and one black acquitted Lozano of a killing that occurred in Miami.[30] Does the racial balance matter if the people come from a different city? And was it the right balance? Unfortunately, we have no theoretically sound basis for knowing whether the balance was right or wrong. After all, what counts? The representation of the defendant or of the victim? Nonetheless, many voices have come forward in the aftermath of the Simi Valley trial to urge changes of venue only to counties whose ethnic composition is analogous to that of the place of the crime.

A better solution would be to return to the text of the amendment and *abolish changes of venue*. Trials should take place not only in the "state or district" but in the county where the crime occurred. The only reason we now permit changes of venue, I submit, is that we misunderstand the defendant's right to a fair trial by an impartial jury. A sound connection between geography and justice would acknowledge the right of the people to work through their own experience with crime, to find their own impartial citizens for the jury, and to protect sitting juries from conduct by counsel and the press that might generate an unfair advantage for one side.

It is worth recalling the general principle in private international law (sometimes called "conflicts of law") permitting trials wherever the parties are found. A dispute about contracts, torts, or property can be tried any place in the world. A court in Europe will apply U.S. law if that is what the rules require. But there are two notable exceptions: divorce and crime. If a married couple lives in one state, they cannot get the courts of another state or country to grant them a divorce. In the days before easy divorce, many couples went to Nevada for a weekend of gambling, sun, and a quicky divorce. The trick was that Nevada permitted couples to establish legal residence faster than they could elsewhere. Behind this easily circumvented residency rule lies an important principle: The community where a couple lives has a legitimate concern about the survival of the marriage and the family it represents. Therefore, only that community should be able to grant a divorce and terminate a marriage.

The more serious and unmanipulable version of the same principle limits the mobility of criminal cases. Criminal prosecution must take place where the crime occurs (or, in exceptional situations, in the place to which the victim or the defendant is connected by citizenship). It is unthinkable that a French court would prosecute a German for a crime committed in Italy against an Italian. It is equally beyond the realm of the possible for California to prosecute a New Yorker for a crime committed in New York. It does not matter if the suspect is arrested in California and all the witnesses live in California. The crime cannot be abstracted from the soil on which it occurred, transported, and then replanted in a different locale. One could describe this almost mystical connection in sociological terms:

When a shocking crime occurs, a community reaction of
outrage and public protest often follows. . . . Thereafter the
open processes of justice serve an important prophylactic
purpose, providing an outlet for community concern, hostility,
and emotion.[31]

This language is cited in a daring precedent in which the
Supreme Court held that despite the concurrence of prosecution and
defense, criminal trials must remain open to the public. The Justices'
arguments reflect concern about the First Amendment rights of the
press, but even more basically they ground the duty to keep the trial
public in the right of the people:

Looking back, we see that when the ancient "town meeting"
form of trial became too cumbersome, 12 members of the
community were delegated to act as its surrogates, but the
community did not surrender its right to observe the conduct
of trials.[32]

The mandate to open the trial to the public (absent special
concerns about fragile witnesses) "inheres in the very nature of a
criminal trial under our system of justice."[33] At least this has been
true since the abolition of the Star Chamber in England in 1641. It
matters not whether the prosecution and the defense want a private
trial. The people as whole—not just the press—enjoy this right to
their trials. For the Justices of the Supreme Court, this bold recognition of a public claim lay embedded in an obvious historical truth.

If the people of Los Angeles had a right to be present at the trial
of the four alleged abusers of Rodney King, they also had a right to
have the trial remain present among them. They did not simply have
the right to witness trials that happened to take place in their courthouse. Nor would *any* group of observers provide a sufficient safe-
guard against the chicanery to which closed doors are prone. The
public that matters is the public that experiences the crime. It was
their trial. They not only had a right to be there. They had a right that

the trial be among them, involving them, and expressing their best efforts to come to a just resolution of the conflict.

The democratic principles of local autonomy and community participation militate against changes of venue. One wonders, then, how the courts ever came to the conclusion that the right to fair trial required a change of venue from one county to another. The Sixth Amendment, as applied to the states, has never mandated a transfer from one state to another. But it is nonetheless questionable to force local communities to give up their "crimes" and allow them to be tried elsewhere in the same state.

The leading decisions on changes of venue as a constitutional matter arise from the abundant anxieties that surround death-penalty cases. In a 1961 case that originated in rural Indiana, the local prosecutor released a press statement saying that the suspect had confessed to six murders.[34] The local newspapers pressed the suspect's guilt on their readers. Accordingly, with a small local pool of jurors, it was difficult to find candidates who had not made up their minds. The case went to trial with 8 of 12 jurors saying they would try to be impartial even though they thought the defendant was guilty. The Supreme Court reversal of the ensuing conviction saved the defendant from a death sentence.

Capital cases undoubtedly fall into a special category. In the 1960s and 1970s, when a majority of the Court strongly opposed the death penalty, we find cases of reversal for failure to grant a request for change of venue. Reflecting back on those cases from another time and another sensibility, we can observe the change of venue as a last-ditch solution to two recurrent problems: First, prior to the institutionalization in 1966 of the *Miranda* warnings, the police could more easily secure confessions, and the prosecution was much less responsible in advertising its evidence in the press. Changing the venue was a corrective for a prosecution too eager to demonstrate the results of its investigation. Second, when the local newspapers were willing to convict someone in print prior to trial, it appeared that the impact might be purely local. Changing the venue expressed the hope of finding uncontaminated minds.[35]

Reporters today are as willing as ever to indict and convict Dan White, the four L.A. police officers, El Sayyid Nosair, Lemrick Nelson, to turn the tables on accuser Patricia Bowman, and to rake Mike Tyson over the coals. Yet they are less likely to secure the cooperation of prosecutors willing, as they once were, to broadcast confessions prior to trial or to manipulate the media in an effort to influence the jury. A widespread contemporary complaint is that the media have fallen prey to staging and posturing not by prosecutors but by defense counsel.[36]

In addition, in an era of nationwide supermarket tabloids and CNN, the notion of securing a jury unaffected by publicity seems fanciful. The residents of Simi Valley knew every bit as much about the Rodney King affair as did the denizens of downtown Los Angeles. Moving the case to another county hardly increases the likelihood of finding jurors indifferent to the passions stirred by the crime. Changing the venue of the trial is but a crutch better left untouched. In a large urban area, as in New York, Los Angeles, or Miami, there are ample ways of securing a large and diverse jury pool. Judges can use questionnaires and interviews, as they did in the Bernhard Goetz case and in the federal trial of the L.A. police officers, to winnow the venire down to those who can serve without bias. It is also the court's responsibility to discipline prosecutors and defense counsel who try to win in the media before the trial begins. And trial judges must use their formidable contempt powers to prevent the press, during sensitive trials, from infiltrating the jury room and interfering with the process of impartial deliberation. These are means more effective and less violative of democratic principles than the dislodging of cases from the communities that should decide them.

We are so inclined to think about the rights of the accused that we insufficiently heed the interests and the rights of the people to decide cases that rupture their communal life. Yet the Bill of Rights, properly understood, would protect their right as well as the defendant's right to a fair trial by an impartial jury. The community has a stake in resolving guilt for the crimes that disturb its peace. It has a claim not only to determine the liability of a suspected offender but to participate in the vindication of the men and women who suffer deprivations of their dignity and equality as citizens.

Postscript: The appeal in the federal Rodney King proceedings provides a case study in interpretation of the Fifth Amendment. The two convicted officers, Koon and Powell, claimed that their conviction violated the Privilege against Self-Incrimination. Why? Because they had to testify, for fear of losing their jobs, in an Internal Affairs hearing of the LAPD. In this sense, their testimony was coerced. The government could not use that testimony in federal court. Nor could they use any testimony that could be causally traced to the coerced testimony. The government had to prove that the testimony of their witnesses, particularly Briseno and Conta, did not derive from the tainted evidence. The appellate court held that it was sufficient to show that the evidence derived from an independent source—such as seeing the events first-hand or on tape. After analyzing the sources of Briseno's and Conta's testimony, the court concluded the government met its burden of proof.

The Fifth Amendment double jeopardy clause reentered the case by a curious means. First, the defendants sought to revive the argument that federal prosecution violated the clause, but the judges rejected the claim. Further, the prosecution objected to Judge Davies' attempt to justify the 30-month sentence, a substantially lower penalty than required by the Federal Guidelines, on grounds of (almost) double jeopardy. Judge Davies reasoned that the trial suffered "the specter of unfairness," namely the second prosecution after the first acquittal. This was a form of fuzzy logic haunting the trial. Judge Davies had reservations about the legal analysis of double jeopardy and attempted to say something like: the law is only 70% correct and I will make up the difference by lowering the punishment. The court of appeals would have none of this fuzzy splitting of the sentence. They ruled that the residual image of unfairness had no bearing on the gravity of the offense or on the culpability of the offender. It was a mistake for Judge Davies to think that it was relevant. On the basis of these arguments and others, the court of appeals affirmed the convictions and recommended a higher sentence on reconsideration by the trial court.

The O.J. Simpson proceedings confirmed some of the arguments on pages 169–74 against changing venue in search of jurors unaffected by publicity. Though no trial in recent memory has gained more publicity, the defense did not seek to remove the trial from Los Angeles County.

CHAPTER SIX

Victims at the Center

"The best index to a person's character is . . . how
he treats people who can't fight back."
—*Abigail Van Buren from her column "Dear Abby."*

TRUE, THE PEOPLE AFFECTED BY A CRIME HAVE A RIGHT TO ADJU-
dicate the guilt or innocence of the suspected offender. But who are
those people? In one sense they are the entire population in the locale
touched by the unnerving event. In another sense they are the special
groups—the gays, blacks, Jews, women—who see the wrong as a
personal assault against them. They are *Las Madres* marching in
Plaza de Mayo demanding prosecution of the police who kidnapped
their children. They are the Japanese who are disturbed because a
Louisiana court refused to convict an American homeowner who
killed a young Japanese exchange student, a seeming intruder on
Halloween, who did not understand the command "Freeze." They
are all the middle-class citizens, all the people who play by the rules,
who are disturbed by leniency for Lorena Bobbitt, or Damian
Williams, or Erik Menendez. When criminals are no longer punished for their crimes, the people's sense of harmony goes askew. The
criminal's wrong is compounded by official cowardice.

A criminal judgment carries a message. Convictions communicate condemnation. The message of condemnation carries a stigma,

sometimes more, sometimes less. The criminal is branded, in degrees, as a wrongdoer and a threat to society. Leniency toward the defendant testifies to the opposite: The wrong committed against this victim is not as heinous as the same act visited upon the average person. This is the way the gay community in San Francisco interpreted the manslaughter conviction of Dan White. The jury seemed to declare Harvey Milk as less worthy than straight San Franciscans. And non-enforcement or a seemingly unjustified acquittal conveys the most radical point of all: Victims like Rodney King, Meir Kahane, and Yankel Rosenbaum have no value at all.

Of course, leniency on the part of the jury need not imply a lesser wrong. Acting in good faith, the jury might mitigate the alleged crime or acquit altogether for a mélange of reasons that underlie a verdict "not guilty." For one, the 12 men and women might have reasonable doubts about whether the defendant committed the crime at all. This was presumably the case in the unexpected responses of the Kahane and Rosenbaum juries. Also, understanding the special circumstances of the case, the jurors might concur that the conduct was justified and for that reason was not a wrong to the victim. This would be the case if they thought that the victim was the aggressor and that the defendant had responded in reasonable self-defense, or if they thought that the alleged victim had consented (in a rape case). There are undoubtedly some cases bordering on justification where the jury senses that the defendant's violence was a fit response to a pattern of evil conduct by the victim.

In a totally distinct way of thinking about the circumstances of the crime, the jury might believe that the conduct was wrong, that the victim's rights were violated, but that the defendant is not personally to blame for the violation. This inference about blamelessness would follow from the defendant's having a good excuse, either full or partial, for committing the wrong charged against him. Apart from the Kahane and Rosenbaum cases, virtually all those we have considered have been instances of excuse. There was no doubt that Dan White had killed Milk and Moscone. No one would have dreamt of justifying the act. The only problem was whether in view of the stress of the moment Dan White was fully to blame for the cold-blooded killings. The defense of diminished capacity makes no claim about the rectitude of the action; the claim is merely that in view of his mental condition the culprit should be found guilty of the lesser offense of manslaughter. Of course, the gay community could read the verdict as a judgment about the worthiness of a gay victim. The question is whether we can improve the message conveyed by jury verdicts so that the public can better understand the grounds for classifying a homicide as either murder or manslaughter.

In our earlier discussion of rape cases, we noted the conflicting objectives of laying down a rule and resolving a dispute about an incident of alleged sexual coercion. The rule for the future specifies the rights and duties of the parties in potential conflict. A breach of the rule "no means no" violates the rights of someone who has asserted her interest in bodily autonomy. It does not follow, however, that every violation spells criminal liability. The possibility of a reasonable mistake opens a window of divergence between violation and guilt, between wrongdoing and culpability. The violator might have a good excuse for unwittingly acting in disregard of the victim's rights: He did not know and could not fairly have been expected to know that he was violating her preference not to engage in sex.

Similarly, there is no doubt that Dan White violated Harvey Milk's right to life; the killing reeked of wrong and contempt for human life. Yet one could imagine circumstances of psychological abnormality—apparently not present in the actual case—in which the offender was not to blame in the same way as a fully self-actuating killer. In other words, the act of killing and the violation of the victim's rights can be separated from the circumstances that drive a person to engage in evil. Whether an offender is excused or partly excused need not reflect ill on the status and dignity of the victim.

The way the system works now, however, there is no way of knowing whether a verdict of "not guilty" represents a judgment that the victim was not worthy of protection or whether despite the violation of the victim's rights the offender could not be fairly blamed for the apparent evil. The jury in the Dan White case (or at least many of the jurors) might have thought that shooting a gay man is, as one observer put it, "doing a service to society."[1] Or the dominant sentiment might have been: This is a horrible killing, Milk and Moscone have our full sympathy, but it does not follow that we hold a sick man fully accountable for his criminal deeds.

Reforming the Verdict

A step in the right direction would be to induce juries to clarify their grounds for acquittal. My recommendation, therefore, is that in every case the jury should first decide whether the act itself is a violation of the victim's rights and therefore criminal, and second whether the defendant is accountable for the criminal act. If this reform had been in place, the jury in the Dan White case would have had to decide first whether the act was a *violation* of the victim's right to life, and second whether White was fully accountable or *guilty* for the killing. The best way for a jury to express this judgment would be to have the option of three verdicts: fully guilty, partially guilty, and not guilty. Fully guilty would be equivalent to a verdict of murder, and partially guilty, equivalent to a verdict of manslaughter. If the issues had been so framed and decided and then properly reported in the press, we would not have encountered the widespread resentment that the White jury had convicted on a lesser charge as a result of its low estimation of gay life.[2]

This system of staggered verdicts would have had a salutary effect on the first Menendez proceeding in 1993. The jury would have been put to the test first of determining that the killing was criminal—a violation of the parents' right to life. It would have had to confront all the innuendos of the defense and popular opinion that the killing was not really criminal—or not fully criminal—because Jose and Kitty had got what they deserved. Once that issue was settled, the jury could have turned to the question of whether the brothers were fully or only partially accountable for the criminal killing. They would be partially accountable and guilty only of manslaughter if the jury believed that they had acted without malice in the good-faith belief that their lives were in imminent danger. Earlier I explained why I think that this legal principle was misunderstood in the first prosecution. It bears not on the criminality of the killing—the wrongfulness of violating the parents' rights—but on the degree of the defendants' guilt or accountability for the killing. They would be less guilty—indeed guilty only of manslaughter under California law—if they had acted in a good faith (but perhaps unreasonable) fear of an objectively imminent attack by their parents.

There is no need to claim too much for this proposed reform. The gay community in San Francisco might not have believed the jurors no matter what they said. A judgment about the degree of Dan White's guilt could be misunderstood as a judgment about the moral worth of a gay victim. Regardless of the court's best efforts at clarity, some people might have thought the issue in the Menendez case was whether "a history of child molestation can justify parricide."[3] The notion of justification, properly understood, bears not on the relative accountability of the defendants but on the rightness or wrongness of the action. These kinds of misunderstandings may be inevitable. Yet there is every reason to think that structuring the verdict would be a step in the direction of clearer communication about what is at stake when a jury decides. If the public could better understand the distinction between the victim's rights and the defendant's guilt, the two-stage verdict would reconcile the conflicting objectives of respecting the rights both of victims and of defendants.

This proposal could become reality simply by adapting techniques and institutions already in place. Many states already employ the two-stage verdict, at least implicitly. Their system of pleas and verdicts distinguishes between "not guilty" and "not guilty by reason of insanity." The latter implies that the act committed by the insane person is still wrongful or criminal. A defendant acquitted after the finding that he committed a criminal act is more likely to be held for psychiatric examination; if he is still dangerous, he will be detained in a hospital-with-bars for compulsory treatment. My proposal requires merely that this procedure be generalized to include all grounds of full or partial excuse. All excuses—insanity, duress, personal necessity, reasonable mistake—have the effect of denying the defendant's guilt or accountability without casting doubt on whether the act was a violation of the victim's rights.

The system I am proposing has already established itself in civil cases. A good example is the approach of Judge Abraham Sofaer in the 1985 civil suit of General Ariel Sharon against *Time* magazine. The magazine had published allegedly defamatory statements about Sharon's role in the Sabra and Shatila massacres of Palestinian prisoners in the fall of 1982. Under the law as it had evolved up to that time, however, merely proving that a published statement was false and harmful to the plaintiff's reputation was not sufficient to recover monetary damages. In addition, the plaintiff had to prove that the defendant magazine had recklessly disregarded the falsity of what it had published. This is the standard imposed by the Supreme Court in cases, such as this one, in which the plaintiff is a public figure. "Reckless disregard" requires more than negligence or carelessness by a reporter in checking sources. The plaintiff had to prove that "a person or persons at Time, Inc. knew that the defamatory statement was false or had serious doubts as to its truth." This is called in the law "actual malice."

The normal way to try these cases is to condition the entire lawsuit on the question of liability. The plaintiff must establish all the premises (a defamatory publication, falsity, and actual malice) in order to gain a victory. Anything short of liability is a total loss. Judge Sofaer broke from this pattern of high-stakes gambling by introducing an alternative, verdict-by-verdict game plan. The jury would first address a series of questions bearing on the violation of Sharon's right to have his reputation reflect his actual merits. If the magazine published demonstrably false statements implying Sharon's deceit in his conduct of the war, there would be no doubt it had violated his rights. And the jury found that it was so. Sharon won the first battle of the trial.

But later, when the jurors' attention shifted to the defendant's malice, they found Sharon's proof wanting. There was insufficient evidence that *Time*'s chief reporter had actually known that Sharon's allegedly direct encouragement of the massacres was false. Nonetheless, the jurors issued an informal statement criticizing the reporter, David Halevy, for having acted negligently. Financially, the outcome of the trial was a victory for *Time*, which escaped a costly judgment of liability. Yet Sharon had won too. He proved the falsehood, rescued his reputation, and saved his political career. As he said after the final verdict:

> I came here to prove that *Time* magazine lied. We managed to prove there was a clear defamation. We came over here to prove that they have done it with negligence and with carelessness. Altogether, I feel that we have achieved what brought us here to this country."[4]

This single case experience bears several important lessons. If it was valuable to give Sharon the opportunity to establish the violation of his rights apart from the defendant's liability, it would be valuable in many criminal cases to afford the same option to the victim, his family, or the people who identify closely with him. This could be done by instituting the procedure of a preliminary verdict that the act was a criminal violation of the victim's rights. Also, the Sharon experience demonstrates that many people sue in order primarily to recover their reputation, their dignity, or their sense of self-esteem after an experience of victimization. The money they might recover is secondary. Surely, in criminal cases, where the victim does not gain tangibly from the defendant's suffering in prison, the thrust toward the victim's self-vindication should lie at the core of the process.

In the new political trials that we have surveyed, the victim's community does indeed seek vindication of its worth under the criminal law. In the Dan White case, gays sought to establish primarily that killing one of them was the same wrong as killing a "straight" person. Whether Dan White languished in jail for a longer or a shorter period does not speak directly to that question. The victim's community would have achieved its end if at the first stage of its deliberations the jury had to decide, separately, whether the killings of Milk and Moscone were criminal acts. It would have been impossible for a self-respecting group of citizens to come back with the inconsistent verdicts that killing Moscone but not Milk was criminal. After rendering this verdict, the jury would retire again to determine whether the defendant was personally fully guilty, partially guilty, or not guilty of each of these two criminal acts. Again, I think it would have been impossible for the jurors blatantly to discriminate between the two victims. They might have come back with the ultimate conclusion of partial guilt (manslaughter), but they might well have seen that this verdict made little sense against Moscone and have concluded that White was fully guilty of killing him (murder). If that had happened, then elementary consistency—more obvious when the verdicts are broken down into distinct stages—would have required the same verdict about the killing of Harvey Milk.

The two-stage verdict would focus the jury's deliberations on the right issues in rape cases. The first question should be whether the woman had experienced coerced intercourse. Whether the jury believes this to be true beyond a reasonable doubt depends largely on how much it credits her version of the events. The Indiana jury would have believed Desiree Washington, but the Florida jury might have had doubts about whether Patricia Bowman experienced intercourse against her will. Having rendered a judgment that the victim was raped, the jury would retire to determine whether the defendant was accountable—that is, was fairly to blame—for the infliction of involuntary intercourse. Tyson argued that he was not to blame because he was reasonably mistaken about Washington's consent.

In a separate stage of the Tyson deliberations, the jury would have considered whether this alleged excuse was sound. These are the two halves of every case of disputed date rape. They correspond to the distinction discussed earlier between establishing the rules that should govern future sexual interactions between men and women (or between homosexuals) and the determination whether an alleged offender is indeed guilty for an incident that occurred in the past.

The question whether Desiree Washington had been victimized turns not only on whether the jury believes her story but on a particular vision of the respect due to women who say no. Whether Tyson is guilty depends not on the way she saw the matter but on the way he perceived the interaction and whether this perception measured up to the criteria of reasonableness—what we can fairly expect of men under the particular circumstances.

If the questions had been framed this way, the Indiana jury might still have decided that Tyson's mistake was unreasonable and that he was therefore guilty of rape. At least, under the two-stage verdict, informed by all the relevant evidence, Tyson would have had a fair trial. As it was, the Indiana court eliminated the second stage of the inquiry. It assumed that if the victim had experienced intercourse against her will, then Tyson was guilty. It collapsed two stages of inquiry, two perspectives on the problem, into one.

There may have been many gays who believed in 1979 that the only test of Harvey Milk's value was the sentence that Dan White received. And there may have been many women who identified with Desiree Washington and believed in 1992 that the only way she could be vindicated was for Tyson to suffer. Statistics on these matters are hard to come by. But one thing we do know: A heavy penalty is not enough to satisfy the public's urge to see the victim validated in a criminal judgment. That El Sayyid Nosair received a heavy penalty for offenses incidental to the killing of Meir Kahane did not satisfy Kahane's people, who saw the acquittal on the main count as an expression of contempt toward a Jewish victim. If it is not imposed for the right reason, the penalty is not enough. And if a verdict validating the worth of the victim is forthcoming, the penalty might not be so important.

The test for the procedure I am proposing would be whether it would have made a difference in the first Rodney King trial in Simi Valley. The first question put to the jury would have been whether the police officers had violated King's rights by using objectively unreasonable and excessive force against a surrounded suspect. If the jury had answered yes to that question, the beating would have been identified and condemned as unlawful. The remaining question for the jury to consider would have been whether Powell, Koon, Briseno, and Wind were responsible, each of them or all of them, for the unlawful beating. The primary excuse in the officers' case was analogous to Tyson's claim: They were reasonably mistaken about whether King was armed and dangerous. If King had been armed, if he was on the verge of a serious attack against the officers, the use of force probably would have been justified. But King was not armed, and most people do not believe that the officers were in actual danger. Nonetheless, the perspective of men and women in blue might have been different. The officers might have been reasonably mistaken about the threat that King posed. The jury should have had the opportunity to consider that question separately from the issue of whether the beating was objectively unlawful and a violation of the victim's rights.

The most one could say on behalf of the four Los Angeles police defendants is that they were reasonably mistaken about the need for 56 baton blows to King's body. This is the point, I believe, that defenders of the verdict have in mind. Yet that point gets lost in the general verdict of not guilty, a verdict that is easily interpreted by African-Americans as a pejorative judgment about the dignity and value of men like Rodney King. The question is whether those who are so inclined to read a verdict of not guilty would think differently of an outcome like the Sharon/*Time* compromise. If the jury had concluded that the beating was unlawful but that the officers were reasonably mistaken and therefore not liable, there might not have occurred the same reaction of contempt for the entire legal system.

I am inclined to think, therefore, that the two-stage verdict would have made a difference. A finding that the beating was objectively unlawful would have validated King's moral and legal position and in addition would have provided him with a powerful legal basis for bringing a tort action for monetary damages against the officers. Civil courts should accept the verdict of an unlawful beating as determinative of that issue in the private action; and because the standards for proving fault are lower in civil than in criminal litiga-tion, King would have been in a solid position to demand a high monetary settlement. A verdict of unlawful police action would also establish a clear rule for the future. The legal system would be on record as saying: This simply does not go. Even if these four had been acquitted, the entire police force would be properly warned that in the future they could be held liable. If all these aspects of the proceeding had been properly explained in the media, the full signifi-cance of a verdict of unlawful police action could well have assuaged the need for self-vindication in the victim's community.

I make no claim that the officers were reasonably mistaken about the danger latent in King's failure to act submissively. Nor do I have convictions about whether Tyson was reasonably mistaken about Washington's attitude toward sexual relations. I am on the fence as well about whether Bernhard Goetz reasonably believed that he was about to be attacked by the four youths who surrounded him on the New York subway. My only claim is that a jury should focus on the issue of reasonable mistake in isolation from efforts by the defense to secure an acquittal by depreciating the victim.

In cases that pose the problem of mistaken self-defense—the King beating, the Goetz shooting, many claims by battered wives—a serious problem stands in the way of the procedural reform I advance here. Most criminal lawyers and judges would find it difficult to comprehend the difference between a use of force that violated the victim's rights and the defendant's responsibility for the violation. This distinction might be clear in rape cases; we recognize the difference between actual consent and mistakenly perceived consent. The distinction is just as basic between real self-defense, based on an actual attack, and mistaken self-defense, based on a perceived attack. German, Russian, Japanese, Latin American—all these legal sys-tems regard this distinction as fundamental. Yet virtually all the statutory approaches to self-defense in the English-speaking world confound the difference. American lawyers would typically respond: If the defendant reasonably believes that she is about to be attacked, then her use of force is always real self-defense; it does not matter whether she is actually being attacked or not.

But it does matter—from the victim's point of view. If there is an actual attack and the defendant responds with appropriate force, then it would be difficult to brand the use of force as a violation of the victim's rights. It is, after all, his attack that triggers the response. It makes all the difference in the world, therefore, whether Rodney King really was about to attack the officers, as they claimed, or whether he was innocent of aggression and aggressive designs. If the jury found the latter, it would be difficult to avoid the conclusion that the beating was an objectively unlawful police response. Yet if the jury found that the police reasonably believed they were in danger (or had reasonable doubts on this issue), it could properly acquit the officers of responsibility and liability for violating King's rights.

These are elementary distinctions that make sense in most parts of the world. That Americans resist them, that they cling to statutory formulations adopted in ignorance, speaks ill both of the legal profession and the teachers who bear responsibility for educating lawyers in concepts and structures that facilitate the aims of justice. The reigning ideas in this area of the law still confound and confuse American legislators and judges. There is much work to be done in reforming the way lawyers think about self-defense before they can grasp that the use of force might violate the victim's rights without entailing the defendant's responsibility. Only when that distinction becomes instinctive in the thinking of American lawyers, as it is abroad, will we have a chance of fairly resolving the conflicts that define so many criminal trials.

The Victim's Role from Charging to Sentencing

The victims' rights movement in the United States is a compendium of diverse political agendas. A large segment of the movement seeks to protect all victims, present as well as future, by combating crime as effectively as possible. That can be done, this group reasons, by making it easier to convict suspected criminals. Constitutional developments under the Warren Court, particularly in the late 1950s and 1960s, reflected solicitude for criminal defendants. To counteract this libertarian swing, the advocates of crime control and law and order remind us that the victim is the other side of the equation. As defendants have rights under liberal interpretations of the Fourth, Fifth, and Sixth Amendments, potential victims also have the right to security in their homes, safety on the streets, and confidence in the marketplace. That all citizens have these rights in some general sense is undoubtedly true. It is not clear, however, that facilitating convictions against particular suspects will redound to the benefit of ordinary people properly disturbed by the scourge of crime.

This anti-defendant aspect of the victims' rights movement has become dated. It had an impact on the passage of Proposition Eight in California in the aftermath of the Dan White trial. Yet it is not prominent on the political agenda today. The Supreme Court has become more conservative and has pruned back the protections once extolled as the flowering of the Bill of Rights. And yet crime continues to increase and undermine the quality of American life. The level of suspicion and distrust has risen to the point that middle-class citizens arm themselves, wire their homes and cars with the latest technology, keep their children on tight leashes, and minimize contact with strangers who could turn out to be dangerous. In this climate of fear, one could hardly expect a reduction in crime just by making it easier to interrogate a suspect or to use unconstitutionally seized evidence.

Much of the movement has turned, therefore, to treating crime victims as we treat the victims of natural disasters. We should spread the cost by ensuring governmental compensation for those whose lives are disrupted by violent crime. Omitted from the current political focus is the kind of victim participation in the processes of justice that could alleviate the dangers posed by the new political trials from the prosecution of Dan White to the acquittal of Lemrick Nelson. The purpose of "victim participation" is to restore the dignity of the victim and all those affected by the crime. It is expressed in questions about such matters as the control of the victim over plea-bargaining, the role of the victim at trial, and the place of the victim's sentiments in determining a just punishment. The challenge in all these areas is to find a way to vindicate the position of the victim without compromising the rights of the criminal defendant.

The current state of the victims' rights movement is revealed in a model statute called the Uniform Victims of Crime Act, which the American Bar Association (ABA) has adopted and recommended for passage throughout the country. Significantly, the ABA adopted this model statute at its 1992 summer meeting in San Francisco, the same meeting at which it adopted a task-force report designed to respond to the Los Angeles riots several months before. The timing seems a pure coincidence, for there is no apparent connection between the ABA's perception of victims' rights and the task force's sense of what went wrong in the Simi Valley trial.

Most of the Uniform Victims of Crime Act is devoted to securing compensation from the state and reparation from the defendant for the harm inflicted. A small portion of the Act is addressed to issues of victim participation. In its provisions on this score, the ABA draft takes three significant stands, explicitly and implicitly, on what the victim should be able to do to influence plea-bargaining, the course of the trial, and the determination of the sentence after conviction. I disagree with all three positions.

Plea-bargaining. In a case that arose in Brooklyn, two Israeli parents had sent their 13-year-old son Shai to a Hasidic rabbi, Shlomo Helbrans, to train Shai for his bar mitzvah.[5] The boy disappeared for two years. When he surfaced in the spring of 1993, he wore Hasidic clothes and displayed other signs of religious commitment. He denounced his parents as irreligious. When the parents complained, Brooklyn District Attorney Charles E. Hynes charged the rabbi with kidnapping. It was clear that the boy had acquired his new orientation while living under the rabbi's close tutelage. Then the plea bargaining began and the politics of a private community seeped through the public walls of the People's representative. Hynes was then considering running for attorney general. He listens to his constituents. (He finished third in the September 1994 primary.)

In the end, the D.A.'s office agreed to a plea bargain that would let the rabbi off on a reduced charge: five years' probation and 250 hours of community service. Justice Thaddeus E. Owens agreed. The parents had no say in the matter. *Their* complaint had become public property. Only after it had been settled were they informed of the outcome.

Though roughly 90% of all cases are disposed of consensually, without trial, there is something unseemly about the prosecution's trading a lower charge in return for the defendant's cooperating and waiving his right to trial. The very idea that the authorities cut special deals with particular defendants offends the rule of law. Many legal systems on the Continent, Germany most strongly, have long rejected this kind of discretionary justice as "opportunism." German lawyers refer to American-style discretionary justice as the *Opportunitätsprinzip* (principle of expediency) as opposed to the *Legalitätsprinzip* (principle of legality), which demands prosecution according to the extent of the perceived legal violation. Even-handed justice under the law should mean that everyone receives the same treatment: no leniency for those who promise something in return. In recent years, however, even the Germans have admitted plea-bargaining at the edges of their system. The pressure of the case load in contemporary criminal courts overwhelms the usual protestations of principle.

In the American system, plea-bargaining seems to be inevitable. If all those who now plead guilty insisted on a jury trial, the system would collapse under the burden. But if plea-bargaining is a necessary part of the American landscape, it should be conducted fairly, with due consideration of the victim whose complaint initiates the action.

The ABA's model statute recognizes this problem and requires prosecutors "to the extent practicable" to "confer with a victim" before agreeing to a plea bargain.[6] Yet it does not require them to defer to the victim's wishes, and it prescribes no legal consequences for ignoring the victim altogether, as Charles Hynes' office did in the case of the alleged kidnapping by the Brooklyn rabbi. The statute merely exhorts prosecutors to pay more attention to victims in an effort to generate "greater victim satisfaction."[7] In the view of the ABA, victims have no right to veto a plea bargain because prosecutors should be free to act in the "interests of the State."[8]

There is something wrong in this exaggeration of undefined "interests of the State." What is, after all, so important that the prosecution has no time to confer with victims or to consider deferring to their interests? If the victim and the defendant have reached a personal reconciliation about a relatively unserious offense, then perhaps there is no state interest in insisting on conviction and punishment. The interests of the state often reduce to the immediate needs of the prosecutor's office for witnesses willing to turn "state's evidence" and testify, in return for reduced charges, against other members of a criminal plot. Or, as in the case of the rabbi's alleged kidnapping, the state's interest may become equivalent to the prosecutor's personal political needs. The standard is simply too vague to provide victims protection against unjust manipulation.

Justice Owens must also have sensed that there was something untoward about a plea bargain that ran roughshod over the victim's sensibilities. He first accepted the guilty plea and then, after publicity broke in the case, he scheduled another hearing and insisted that the case go forward.[9] In July 1994, Rabbi Helbrans withdrew his plea of guilty to a lesser charge and prepared to go to trial on charges of kidnapping. Whatever the outcome of the prosecution, this case illustrates the dangers of allowing prosecutors to make backroom deals.

Treating prosecutors as the bearers of the state's interest correlates with a particular view of why the state punishes criminals. Thinking of the state's role as engineering public safety by punishing some and perhaps all offenders supports the ABA's way of thinking about the prosecutorial option to confer with victims. If the practice of punishing criminals focuses exclusively on avoiding future crime, the victim falls out of consideration—except as an irritating source of discontent. This approach toward punishment is generally called "social control" or "general deterrence." The thrust of the victims' rights movement has been to call into question social engineering as the aim of the criminal law. It is better to keep our sights limited, to think small, and not to lose concern for the concrete suffering that produces the prosecution in the first place. A criminal trial is primarily an occasion not for shaping the future but for coming to grips with the past. This is a position for which I must, in due course, provide more compelling arguments.

But if we do keep our focus on the crime and the victim, then it seems plausible to give the victim or a homicide victim's next of kin stronger powers than those recognized in the ABA draft. I would go so far as to vest in the victim (or the homicide equivalent) the power to approve or disapprove of any plea bargain. The presumption should be that the prosecution will enforce the law as written and as interpreted in the courts. Any deviation from this standard should meet with the approval of all parties involved—the court, the prosecution, the defendant, and the victim. Of all these parties, only the victim is treated as below the threshold of procedural empowerment—as someone whose objections carry no legal weight. It is hard to know why this is so, but as we turn to the trial phase of the prosecution we gather a clue from an intriguing dissonance between the structure of criminal trials in Continental Europe and their structure in the English-speaking world.

The Victim at Trial. We should recall one of the striking anomalies in the Simi Valley trial against the four L.A. police officers. The world's best-known victim of the 1990s, Rodney King, did not appear in his own trial. Prosecutor Terry White determined King's role in his own drama. White decided that the risks of cross-examination, particularly about King's criminal record, outweighed the tactical advantages of the jury's hearing directly from the man who felt the blunt edge of the baton. This may have been a bad tactical decision, as King's effective testimony in the subsequent federal trial seemed to prove. More significantly, denying King the right to present his version of the events to the jury was the clearest way of saying that it was not King's case at all. He was merely a conduit of proof that the prosecution, the People, could use or not use, as it saw fit.

European trials have a different structure. The injured party may join the criminal proceedings as a participant with rights of his own. According to the German Code of Criminal Procedure, any victim of a crime to the person or to property (plus assorted other offenses) may join the proceeding as a private prosecutor.[10] His purpose is jointly to pursue his civil remedy for damages against the defendant and to further the criminal prosecution. He can call witnesses and, like other participants in the trial, formulate questions for the judge to ask the witness. The only apparent restriction on the private plaintiff at trial is that he must rely on a lawyer for certain purposes, such as to examine the file, or dossier, prepared by the prosecutor on the basis of the pre-trial investigation[11] or to formulate legal challenges to the trial judgment.[12] These are reasonable restrictions designed to facilitate victim participation in a way consistent with efficient and businesslike proceedings.

Giving the victim a similar role in American trials is apparently unthinkable. The ABA's model statute, the Uniform Victims of Crime Act, ignores the topic, as does the literature on victims' rights. We should inquire why it would be so subversive to allow the victim to play a role comparable to that of the criminal defendant. After all, a criminal defendant can defend himself *pro se* (by himself, with a fool for a client, as the saying goes) or appear as co-counsel for herself, as did Angela Davis in 1972. Why should it be so unusual to contemplate Rodney King as co-prosecutor, appearing alongside Terry White? If Rodney King's inexperience in court is the problem, we should follow the German example and require him to appear via a lawyer as intermediary. King's own lawyer would obviously call him as a witness, if that is what King wanted.

There are various ways that a victim like Rodney King might appear in a criminal trial that centered on his own victimization. He might appear himself and make an unsworn opening statement, precisely as the prosecutor and the defense lawyer make opening statements to the jury. Or he might accomplish the same end through a lawyer. He might appear personally during the trial just to pose questions to the witnesses. Or he might accomplish that too through a lawyer. None of these modes of appearance would shock a European lawyer, but they are, I am sure, profoundly disturbing to lawyers trained in the adversary system.

The key feature of European criminal trials is that the judge is fully in charge of the proceedings. He reads the dossier prior to trial, calls the witnesses, filters the questions formulated by the parties, and keeps the official record of the trial. At the end, he alone decides the facts and interprets the law, though in more serious cases he is assisted by lay persons called assessors. His single judgment combines the questions of guilt and of sentencing in one stroke. The European judge is not as powerful as the inquisitors of the past who combined prosecutorial and judging functions in one role. Yet he is definitely at the center of a wheel of justice with many spokes. There is no conceptual problem in allocating one of those spokes to the victim.

The structure of the Anglo-American system resembles not so much a wheel as a seesaw operated by two lawyers. They are alternatively in control; sometimes one is flying high, sometimes the other. The judge and the jury are merely the audience to their self-directed act. The style of Edward Rappaport, the judge in the Yankel Rosenbaum case, was objectionable largely because he tried to run the trial as a European judge would. His most objectionable move—announcing that several police officers had to return to court to clarify their testimony—would not have been so egregious a mistake coming from a French or a German judge. But then again, in trials on the Continent the judge need not worry about unduly influencing a jury, for he is judge and jury (or a major part of the jury) wrapped into one.

With the prosecution and the defense in control of the adversary trial, it is not easy to crack their bipolar power. Introducing the victim as another prosecutor would seem like having two pitchers throwing possible strikes at the batter. It would disrupt a game that everyone is now comfortable with—everyone, that is, except the victims who are excluded. Recall how disturbed prosecutor Greg Garrison was at the prospect of late-appearing witnesses testifying for the defense and breaking the pace he had set for the prosecution's case. A victim playing an independent role at a trial Garrison had orchestrated would introduce an unwelcome chord.

Nonetheless, we should be willing to think about the unfamiliar. It would matter greatly to many victims if they could play some active role at trial. It would have mattered to Rodney King, and to Norman Rosenbaum, Yankel's articulate brother. It might have mattered greatly to Patricia Bowman, who enjoyed, at best, a distant relationship with the prosecutor of her accused, William Kennedy Smith. Admittedly, there may be many trials, perhaps the vast majority, in which the victims are comfortable under the tutelage of prosecutors—like Garrison or Clymer and Kowalski—who identify closely with their interests.

What kind of role might the victim play? At first I thought it would make sense to permit the victim to appear and make an unsworn statement, precisely as the defendant, so far as he represents himself, can make an unsworn statement on his own behalf. In this way, the victim could function as a co-prosecutor. The advantage of being able to make an unsworn statement, of course, is that the victim would not be subject to cross-examination. It would give him an opportunity to address the jury without risking the embarrassment of a searching critique of both the story and his possible motives for lying. It is not clear, however, whether investing this privilege in the victim would withstand an attack based on the defendant's Sixth Amendment right to confront and cross-examine the witnesses against him. The victim as co-prosecutor would not technically be a witness against the defendant, but the functional impact of even an unsworn statement on the jury would be at least as strong as a witness's testimony. I am afraid that the confrontation clause—a guarantee not found in European procedures—entrenches the adversary system so deeply that no niche is left for the victim to gain a foothold as a co-prosecutor in the trial.

The most we could do under the Constitution would be to permit the victim, acting alone or through an attorney, to ask questions of both the prosecution witnesses and the defense witnesses. Rodney King could have appeared at the Simi Valley trial, at his own discretion, at least to ask the defendants: "Did you really think that I was a threat to you?" Bringing him into the trial to that extent would vindicate his status as a citizen. He should have the power if not to make a statement without being subject to cross-examination, at least to ask a question without personal risk. Of course, the questions themselves may subtly convey a message to the jury. This form of undercover communication goes on all the time. Defense counsel are masters at asking questions that carry snide insinuations. In the course of the Yankel Rosenbaum trial, Arthur Lewis typically ended his cross-examination with a throwaway statement or question designed to discredit the witness. Recall his comment at the end of his cross-examination of black officer Robert Lewis, "You were used again."

We generally assume that the judge's instructions not to treat questions as evidence protects the jury against undue influence from wildcat remarks. Judges could impose stricter discipline on the victim and insist on questions put in proper form. If necessary, the court could require that the victim be represented by counsel. As an extreme measure against the risk of sneaking in an unsworn statement in the guise of asking a question, the judge could require that the victim's questions first be submitted in writing.

This recommendation is not as novel as it seems. In the prosecution of El Sayyid Nosair for the killing of Meir Kahane, the judge recognized the extraordinary possibility of allowing the members of the jury to ask questions if they first submitted them in writing. If jurors can break into the bipolar control of prosecutors and defense counsel over the pace of the trial, so too can those who have a particular stake in the verdict. The promise of permitting the victim's participation is not only that an additional perspective will come to bear on the jury's fact-finding, but that the victim will receive moral recognition in the very act of asking questions.

The Victim at Sentencing. One of the curiosities of the American victims' rights movement is that it balks at strong measures to empower the victim at the pre-trial and trial phases and then abandons all restraint on the victim's input at the time of sentencing. If the jury finds the defendant guilty, then the victim comes into his own. The ABA's model statute recognizes the right to offer a "victim-impact statement" between the jury's verdict and judge's determination of the sentence:

> [T]he court shall permit the victim to present a victim-impact statement concerning the effects of the crime on the victim, the circumstances surrounding the crime, the manner in which it was perpetrated, and the victim's opinion regarding the appropriate sentence.[13]

This enhanced role of the victim is possible at sentencing because the unsworn testimony of literally everybody is admissible at a sentencing hearing. The ordinary rules of evidence are suspended. The adversary process is put in abeyance. In reaching a decision on the proper sentence, the judge allows everyone in the community to express their opinion about the need for punishment, for mercy, for setting an example, or for sparing the defendant the corrosive effects of confinement. If total strangers are free to express themselves at this time, then all those who are affected by the crime should have a chance to put in their "two cents' worth."

Yet there is a danger that informal testimonials by the angry and aggrieved could generate excessive sentences serving primarily the need for revenge. This problem comes into relief in the Supreme Court's jurisprudence on using "victim impact statements" in hearings to determine the applicability of the death sentence. Typically, in a separate phase of a homicide trial, the jury (in some states, the judge) must decide whether the killing warrants capital punishment. During this phase, witnesses may be called to inform the jury about the degree of suffering experienced by the victim's family. In *Payne v. Tennessee*, recently decided by the Supreme Court,[14] the defendant was convicted of a particularly brutal murder of a mother and her infant daughter in the presence of her three-year-old son Nicholas. The state called the victim's grandmother to testify about the impact of the incident on the little boy. She testified that the boy continued to cry for his dead mother and sister. In his argument for the death penalty, the prosecutor concluded:

> Somewhere down the road Nicholas is going to grow up, hopefully. He's going to want to know what happened. And he is going to know what happened to his baby sister and his mother. He is going to want to know what type of justice was done. He is going to want to know what happened. With your verdict, you will provide the answer.[15]

Previous decisions of the Court had held that it was constitutionally impermissible to make precisely this argument.[16] Relying on evidence seemingly unrelated to the defendant's blameworthiness created an unacceptable risk, under the cruel and unusual punishment clause of the Eighth Amendment, "of the arbitrary imposition of the death penalty."[17] The role of the victim in capital sentencing was, in the past, subject to careful scrutiny and tight discipline because the Supreme Court was anxious about the constitutionality of the death penalty. Yet by 1991, with the appointment of a more staunchly conservative Court, capital punishment seemed relatively safe from constitutional attack and the Court undertook to reexamine precedents, such as those related to the role of the victim, designed to minimize the risk of "arbitrary" sentencing.

The Justices in the *Payne* case all accepted the principle that capital sentencing should be based on the blameworthiness of the defendant. That is a sound principle for all criminal cases, but one that seems compelling to the Court only when the stakes are life and death. The argument against the victim's relevance in assessing blameworthiness is based on the sound point that in many cases the offender has no knowledge at the time of the act of the victim's personal qualities, of his or her family situation, or of the long-range impact of the crime. The offender should be prosecuted for the murder pure and simple and not held accountable for events beyond the formula under which the homicide is prosecuted. The moral character of the victim, whether good or bad, should be irrelevant. If we genuinely respect human life, the murder is just as heinous whether a three-year-old boy survives a homicidal assault on the family or not. The offender is not accountable, not blameworthy, for things of which he or she is faultlessly ignorant.

Justice Souter responded to this objection by arguing that when conceived more abstractly, the victim's characteristics are indeed attributable to the defendant's knowledge: "[H]arm to some group of survivors is a consequence of a successful homicidal act so foreseeable as to be virtually inevitable."[18] In the end, six Justices were persuaded that it was fair to consider the impact of the crime on poor Nicholas. But should the sensibilities of a little boy, as perceived and reported by his grandmother, determine our criterion of justice? There is little warrant for projecting an untutored lust for the death penalty onto the sensibilities of a child. Why, after all, should young Nicholas grow up and feel that if Payne merely received a long prison sentence, justice was not done? The standard for rectifying his sense of deprivation and victimization must be resolved by appealing not to a personalized need for justice but to a collective judgment about just punishment. Suppose Payne had killed the mother and daughter in an automobile accident induced by drinking? Would we still be inclined to attribute to little Nicholas the sense that capital punishment was the only just response? However justice in punishment is understood, it should not be reduced to a matter of providing satisfaction—or compensation—to the victims.

Some people would maintain that just punishment is indeed a form of compensation to the victim. If it is, we should apply the rule that the courts use in civil actions for damages: The defendant "takes the victim as he finds him." If the victim has some peculiarity—the eggshell skull is the classroom example—the defendant must pay for extraordinary, even unforeseeable harm resulting from the accident. Once liability attaches, the defendant pays whatever is necessary to make the particular victim whole again. But in the traditional quest for a mode of punishment that fits the crime, the "crime" is always understood as a generalized wrong, not as a wrong to the particular victim. A theft is a theft, regardless of how rich or poor the deprived owner might be. A murder is a murder, regardless of how large or small a family the decedent might have. The peculiarities of the victim count for everything in determining the proper amount of compensation for personal injury. But they should not count in determining the gravity and proper punishment for a criminal act.

Raskolnikov kills an old woman to take her money. Should it matter that she has no friends, no family? She lives alone and no one notices that she is no longer there. The murder is just as heinous, as any man with a conscience comes to discover. It is wrong, still arguably unconstitutional, to punish a man more severely just because the victim turns out to leave behind a little Nicholas who will miss him. The older law was right.[19] But by confounding compensation and punishment, the Supreme Court came to the unfortunate conclusion that the victim's sensibility should influence the jury's judgment in a death-penalty case.

Punishment as Solidarity with Victims

One lesson to be drawn from these disputes about the victim's role at various phases of the trial is that so much turns on our rationale for punishment. If we think of punishment primarily as a social measure, inflicted by the People for the future security of the people, then the public prosecutor emerges as the primary player in the trial. The people are represented in the prosecutor's office. The victim is left on the margins of the trial. If we think of punishment as a form of compensation for the wrong done, then the person to whom the compensation is owed, namely the victim, comes center stage.

My own view about punishment is that neither of these views is correct. Punishment is neither a means of engineering public safety nor a mode of compensation. Police on the beat do a better job of deterring crime than sentences declared from the bench. And private lawsuits, victim against injurer, are the right way to bring about compensation. Many people have argued that punishment should rehabilitate the *offender* and reintegrate him or her into society. Too often ignored is the function of punishment in reintegrating the *victim* back into society. The work of the philosopher Immanuel Kant is the closest we come in the literature to a proper view of punishment as an act of justice that serves the goal of vindicating the dignity of the victim.[20]

Kant defends punishment simply as a just response to a criminal degradation of another human being. He rejects punishment as a means of deterrence or social control, for making an example of offenders degrades them by treating them as a means to an end. He applauds the biblical formula of "an eye for eye, a tooth for a tooth";[21] in its metaphoric way, this *lex talionis* expresses a principle of equality between offender and victim. By insisting on equality as the guiding principle of punishment, Kant brings the victim to the center of our concerns.

Kant defends punishment as the first duty of social organizations. He imagines that a society is about to disband, but it has a problem: There are still murderers, condemned to die, languishing in prison. What should it do about them? Kant insists that the murderers should be executed "so that each has done to him what his deeds deserve and blood guilt does not cling to the people for not having insisted upon this punishment."[22] Executing them seems to be pointless, because no good could possibly follow. This is precisely Kant's point.

The notion of a society's disbanding should be treated as a thought-experiment, very much like the idea of a society's coming together in a social contract. Neither of these events ever occurred in history, but they are useful constructs for testing our intuitions about the conditions of a just social order. Further, the biblical reference to blood guilt is highly suggestive. It brings to bear an ancient rationale of biblical culture that a manslayer acquires control over the victim's blood; the slayer has to be executed in order to release the blood, permitting it to return to God as in the case of a natural death.[23] Failure to execute the murderer means that the rest of society, charged with this function, becomes responsible for preventing the release of the victim's blood.

Whatever the metaphysics of gaining and releasing control of blood, the point relevant today is that the failure to punish renders the rest of society, those charged with a duty to punish, complicitous in the original crime. As those who "stood idly by"[24] in biblical times were charged with blood guilt, today we see the failure to punish as a form of complicity that falls on those who abandon the victim to his or her "private" tragedy.

A primary function of punishment, then, is to express solidarity with the victim. It is a way of saying to the victim and his or her family: "You are not alone. We stand with you, against the criminal." The idea of dominance expressed in gaining control over the victim's blood remains with us, in other forms, today. Criminal conduct establishes the dominance of the criminal over the victim and, in the case of homicide, over the victim's family. This is obvious in some crimes, such as rape, mugging, and burglary, where victims typically fear a repeat attack by the criminal. It is also true in blackmail, where the offender induces services or money in return for silence and is in a position to return at any time and demand additional payments. Instilling fear and this form of subservience is a mode of gaining dominance. Punishment counteracts domination by reducing the criminal to the position of the victim. When the criminal suffers as the victim suffered, equality between the two is reestablished.

The failure to punish implies continuity of the criminal's dominance over the victim. When society fails to punish, it becomes complicitous in this state of subservience and dominance. The existence of the institution of punishment creates an opportunity to counteract the criminal's achieving dominance over the victim. The failure to use the institution, the passively standing by when there is an opportunity to act, provides the foundation for shared responsibility. Admittedly, this rationale for punishment hardly works to justify the institution of punishment at the outset. Something like Kant's argument of equality is necessary to justify punishment as a matter of principle. Once the institution is in place, however, once a tradition of punishing crime takes hold, it acquires a logic of its own. The practice of punishing crime provides an opportunity for the victim's co-citizens to express solidarity and to counteract the state of inequality induced by the crime. If they willfully refuse to invoke the traditional response, they disassociate themselves from the victim. Abandoned, left alone, the victim readily feels betrayed by the system.

The connection between punishment and solidarity has become apparent in the last few decades in the numerous countries that have overcome dictatorial regimes and have begun the transition to democracy. The first notable example was Argentina, which in the mid-1980s began a program of prosecuting the generals who were responsible for mass disappearances in the period of the military junta. The victims' families themselves—led by *Las Madres*—insisted on prosecution as a means of vindicating their dignity as citizens. The terror of the refusal to prosecute became clear when one victim, who thought there would never be prosecution of those who kidnapped and tortured his children, committed suicide in Buenos Aires. Since the shift of government from Presidents Alfonsin to Menem, the leaders of the military junta have been pardoned.[25] Those connected to the victims must endure the sight of those responsible for their suffering now leading the good life as free citizens.

The transition to democracy in Eastern Europe has led to repeated demands to punish the leaders of the Communist governments that were responsible for evil deeds ranging from encouraging Soviet intervention in Budapest in 1956 and Prague in 1968 to shooting escaping East German citizens in the 1980s. Technical problems, such as the statute of limitations, prevent many of these prosecutions. Yet the Germans have been insistent about prosecuting border guards for killings at the frontier between East and West, and the Hungarians seem resolute about prosecuting former Communists who committed the most egregious crimes, particularly in the aftermath of the abortive 1956 revolution.

The American version of these same concerns is the series of trials in which gays, blacks, Jews, and women have expected solidarity from the rest of society. It is not only the particular victims or their friends or next of kin who demand that we stand by them. An entire class or group or gender exacts identification with their victimization. If we refuse to respond justly to the gays in San Francisco, the blacks in Los Angeles, the Jews in New York, and the female victims in rape trials everywhere, we become complicitous in the crimes committed against them. We testify to not caring, to being indifferent to their suffering. And when we turn our backs, we begin to participate in the crime. We compound the original suffering with the victim's indignity in being abandoned. We have no choice but to inflict punishment on those who deserve it.

Postscript: In initially sentencing Sergeant Koon and Officer Powell, Judge Davies relied on a provision in the Federal Sentencing Guidelines that permits a lower sentence if the victim's wrongful conduct has "contributed significantly to provoking the offense behavior." Judge Davies cited wrongful behavior by Rodney King, including fleeing arrest, refusing to cooperate, and attempting to escape on foot, and concluded that this behavior was "the initial provocation for the subsequent course of events." Even though the officers eventually crossed the line of legality and used excessive force, King was, in Judge Davies' view, somehow responsible for his own fate.

In its decision announced August 19, 1994, the court of appeals recognized the difficulty of drawing the line between the lawful and the unlawful use of the police baton. The three judges concluded:

> The slenderness of the line . . . is a reason for victims, and for society, to be especially concerned. It cannot at the same time be a reason to partially excuse those who transgress.

The only time that the victim's misconduct should reduce the sentence, the court concluded, is when it is so immediate and provocative that it lessens the officers' blameworthiness for the offense. The proper analogy is to conduct in the "heat of the moment" as in a "crime of passion." Police officers, whose job it is to apprehend uncooperative suspects, might be able to invoke this ground for mitigation in some extreme cases, but, the court concluded, this was not one of them.

In Baton Rouge, Louisiana, victims invoked another classic remedy for rectifying a mistaken judgment by a trial jury. The parents of Yoshihiro Hattori, the exchange student killed when he failed to "freeze," sued the homeowner Rodney Peairs who shot and killed their son, allegedly in self-defense. On September 15, 1994, the trial court, hearing the case without a jury, found the defendant civilly liable for wrongful death and fined him $650,000. The verdict made headlines in Japan.

CHAPTER SEVEN

Justice by the People

"I do not know whether the jury is useful to those
who have lawsuits, but I am certain that it is
highly beneficial to those who judge them. . . . It is
the most efficacious means for the education of
the people which society can employ."
—*Alexis de Tocqueville, 1835.*[1]

THE COMMUNITY IS IN THE COURTROOM. THEY SIT IN THE GAL-
leries observing and participating vicariously in judging the fate of
the defendant and the victim. More critically, the jury of 12 lay
people (or sometimes six) center the trial. They are off to the side of
the courtroom, and they speak only under exceptional circumstances. Yet they are the focal point of the lawyers' rhetorical appeals.
In their lay wisdom, they express solidarity with the victim, bring
compassion for a defendant trapped by difficult circumstances, and
deliver the people's vision of justice.

There could be no more powerful expression of democracy.
Those who otherwise hold little power decide whether Dan White
is guilty of murder or manslaughter, whether the four Los Angeles
police officers are guilty of using excessive force, whether the
alleged assassins of Meir Kahane and Yankel Rosenbaum are
guilty as charged, and whether William Kennedy Smith and
Mike Tyson improperly misread signals saying no to sex. With

the people as our judges, we get the kind of criminal justice we deserve.

No government can implement a program that the members of the jury resist. The legislature can pass laws prohibiting physicians from assisting others in dying. But if a jury of lay people is unwilling to convict Jack Kevorkian, the legislation is no more than spiritless words.[2] The English chose not to export the jury system along with the common law to colonies such as India, Cyprus, and Palestine. They reserved means to circumvent the authority of local American juries in cases of smuggling—critical to the New England economy—and killings charged against British officers. The Declaration of Independence complains of "depriving us in many cases, of the benefits of trial by jury." The colonial authorities knew that the popular will was likely to resist official efforts to enforce the occupier's law. The jury represents a great danger to a morality imposed from above, indeed to any governing authority that is out of touch with popular sensibilities.

Yet this power to nullify the law is a two-edged sword. The local community can undermine the piety of those enforcing official morality, but for every case of Jack Kevorkian there are the deviations of failed prosecutions against the four Los Angeles police officers, Lemrick Nelson, and El Sayyid Nosair. For every piece of legislation out of touch with popular sentiment and properly nullified in the jury, there are cases where wayward juries fall prey to prejudice and lawless disobedience.

Juries and American Justice

Faith in the jury system turns largely on national identity. Most Europeans are convinced that professional judges are in a better position to weigh the evidence dispassionately and to apply the law objectively than are untrained lay people. For the sake of democratic input, Europeans are happy to include lay assessors as participants in the judging process, but these assessors deliberate together with professional judges. European lawyers are appalled by the common law practice of turning over total authority to a group of novices. They find it hard to believe that the law can prevail in the face of unfounded acquittals of the sort we have observed in this survey. Yet it is difficult to persuade an American, a Canadian, an Englishman, an Australian, or a New Zealander that in criminal cases we should abandon lay judgment and surrender our liberty to the power of judges appointed by the ruling political party. For reasons of cost and convenience, the English-speaking world—with the exception of the Constitution-bound United States—has turned against the jury in civil cases. Yet in the core arena of criminal justice, the heirs of the English common law have remained faithful to justice by jury.

That European judges sometimes function as the henchmen of political regimes explains, in part, why they enjoy so much less authority and prestige than do judges in the common law tradition. Goethe's poetic and politically astute couplet resonates in the European mind: *"Anstatt Richter und Henker, brauchen wir Dichter und Denker."* (Instead of judges and hangmen, we need poets and thinkers.) The hands of common law judges remain unsullied by the imperative of convicting offenders; they are not grouped with "hangmen" as the bearers of state oppression. As Tocqueville comments, "[I]n no country are the judges so powerful as where the people share their privileges."[3] Because the judges remain above partisan law enforcement, they enjoy the respect that accrues to men and women who stay above the fray.

The issue is not fairness to the defendant. Professional judges are capable of appreciating the arguments for the defense and expressing compassion for defendants caught in the maelstrom of circumstance. In a classic empirical study conducted in the 1960s, Harry Kalven, Jr. and Hans Zeisel established that the disparities between the jury's judgment and the professional assessment are less dramatic than we would expect: judges and juries agree with each other 75% of the time.[4] For pessimists, this may mean that the glass is empty one-fourth of the time. But the correlation on the whole supports the good judgment of common people, of judges, or of both.

In routine, apolitical cases, we do not need popular control over the government. Faith in the jury expresses concern about protecting dissidents in extraordinary, politically charged cases. And more deeply, the jury expresses a certain conception of democratically sound methods of conviction and acquittal. With the jury in charge, the resolution of criminal disputes springs not from "judges and hangmen" but from the people as the fount of democratic legitimacy.

How the people came to this authority remains obscure. Historians concur that the precursor of the contemporary petit (or trial) jury is the presentment jury, which consisted of 12 people from the local unit of government called "the hundred." Their function was to charge the accused with a crime on the basis of their personal knowledge of the crime and the offender's participation. The suspect's guilt or innocence was probed by a superstitious means of fathoming divine judgment. As the biblical story relies on throwing lots to determine whether the endangered sailors should throw Jonah overboard, the early common law relied on proof by oath-taking or, when that failed, on trial by ordeal or battle.[5] In the Ordeal of Hot Iron, the accused carried a heated iron nine feet; his hands were bandaged for three nights and then examined. If the wounds had healed, he was innocent; if not, his fate testified to the just decision.

A major transformation occurred some time before the end of the 14th century when those in authority began to ask the presentment jury for a verdict on the suspect's guilt or innocence. A probable inducement for this change was that in 1215 Pope Innocent III prohibited priests from participating in the ordeal. Efforts to fathom the supernatural began to lose their spell, and thus was born, gradually, the practice of secular fact-finding. Henceforth human beings would decide for themselves, without resorting to divine signs, whether a suspect was guilty or not.

The year 1215 was eventful not only in Rome but at Runnymede. King John conceded in the Magna Carta that "no free man" shall suffer loss of liberty except "by the lawful judgment of his peers." The notion of judgment by one's peers has become part of the lore of the jury trial, though in fact the term does not appear in the U.S.

Constitution and it has no particular meaning except the "equals" of "free men." At the time of King John, there were two ways that peers could protect the liberties of the elite. The same group of peers functioned, in inquisitorial style, both as accusers and ultimate judges of the facts. By the 16th century, the accusing function became localized in the grand jury, recognized later in the Fifth Amendment, and the judging function in the petit or trial jury, entrenched for criminal cases in the Sixth Amendment and for civil cases in the Seventh Amendment.

More mysterious than this natural division of function, however, was the evolution of the jury from a group of citizens who had personal knowledge of the crime and its circumstances to a group of local denizens who were supposed to be neutral, impartial, and willing to decide solely on the basis of the evidence presented at trial. Legal historians still ponder how these transformations came about. All we know is that at some vaguely defined point about four centuries ago, we found ourselves with an impartial trial jury, consisting of 12 persons, which was called upon to decide guilt or innocence, unanimously, on the basis of the information and evidence the lawyers presented at trial.

It seems as though we always knew what the common law jury was and how it functioned. But many of these assumptions have recently come under scrutiny. To save time and money, a handful of states have begun experimenting with juries smaller than the traditional number of 12. Thus we find the Kennedy Smith trial taking place before a Florida jury of six. The constitutionality of this innovation in jury size came before the Supreme Court for the first time in 1970. The Justices had to decide whether the traditional number of 12 was of the essence of the jury or merely an accidental feature of lay power in criminal trials. The Court concluded that the drafters of the Sixth Amendment had no particular number in mind when they sought to guarantee "trial by an impartial jury." If the function of the jury is to "prevent oppression by the Government,"[6] a jury of six appeared to be the functional equivalent of a jury of 12. Both resulted "in the interposition between the accused and his accuser of the common sense judgment of a group of laymen."[7] "And, certainly the reliability of the jury as a fact finder hardly seems likely to be a function of its size."[8] There might even be some advantages for the defense in a smaller group: After all, fewer votes are needed for a finding of not guilty.

The logic of these arguments left a residue of anxiety in the legal profession. The Court ignored the possibility that 400 years of history could forge a conceptual link between "trial by jury" and certain particular features the jury might display.[9] The fear in the early 1970s was that the argument of functional equivalence could lead to juries even smaller than six. After all, five, four, or even three lay people provide a buffer against "oppression by the Government." These speculations came to rest in 1978 when the Court resisted an effort by Georgia to convict a suspected pornographer with a jury of five.[10]

The Court carefully evaluated a large number of jury studies stimulated by the 1970 decision permitting a reduction in jury size. Simulated studies of jury deliberation indicated that when jury size declines, the risk of convicting an innocent person increases. It is also the case, however, that the smaller the jury, the lower the risk that the guilty will escape conviction. Reducing the number of persons deliberating, therefore, pits a bad marginal change (convicting the innocent) against a desirable one (convicting the guilty).[11] Significantly, the Court approved as "not unreasonable" a research design that weighted the evil of convicting the innocent as ten times worse than letting the guilty go free.[12] And on that basis the researchers concluded that a jury of five would be less than optimal.[13] This is one of the few times that an argument from the social sciences actually determined the outcome of a constitutional dispute. It is important to note, however, that the social scientists bet on a particular conception of fair trial that stacks the deck in favor of the defendant.

The 1970s reexamination of the jury encompassed challenges to the traditional rule of unanimity. Once the size was open to question, the requirement of unanimity began to crumble. In 1972 the Court approved a Louisiana rule that permitted a conviction on the basis of

9 votes to 3,[14] and an Oregon conviction based on a 10-to-2 vote.[15] After these dispiriting decisions, it was not clear whether any aspects of the jury at common law remained sacred. The Court rekindled some faith in the stability of the system when later in the decade it ruled that a six-person jury must adhere to the rule of unanimity.[16] These disputes have come to an end without any firm resolution of the required voting rules in juries larger than six.

These debates about the optimal size of juries preceded by several years the preoccupation in the 1980s and early 1990s with the fair representation of the victim's and the defendant's community on the jury. A jury of six in Simi Valley would have halved the possibility of securing African-American representation. A smaller jury in Manhattan might not even have generated the problem of keeping Leona Kaplan on the jury that decided whether Nosair killed Kahane. In an era when the primary concern is finding a way to diversify the ethnic composition of juries, the appeal of smaller numbers is less compelling.

The new wave of interest in non-discrimination and fair representation began in 1986 when the Court ruled, by a strong majority of seven to two, that the prosecution could not use its peremptory challenges to dismiss blacks on racial grounds. The prosecutor in this case had dismissed four African-Americans without any apparent rationale except the likelihood that because of their race they would sympathize with a black defendant. When a pattern of discrimination emerges, the Court held, "the burden shifts to the State to come forward with a neutral explanation for challenging black jurors."[17] The Court reaffirmed the long-standing principle that "a defendant has no right to a 'petit jury composed in whole or in part of persons of his own race.' "[18] Recognized as the *Batson* principle, the Court's holding prohibited prosecutorial discrimination that could adversely affect a defendant's chances for a fair trial. Justice Marshall wrote a concurring opinion arguing that the vice was not only discrimination but the very existence of peremptory challenges.[19] Yet peremptory challenges and the *Batson* principle prohibiting discrimination in their use have gained general acceptance.

The *Batson* restriction on peremptory challenges left in its wake a nagging problem. If the prosecution could not discriminate on the basis of race, did that mean the defense could not do so either? In the trial of Dan White and the Simi Valley trial of the four Los Angeles police officers, the defense was able de facto to use its challenges to exclude jurors who because of sexual orientation or race were likely to empathize with the victim. In their *Batson* opinions, both Justice Marshall and the two dissenters anticipated the problem of applying the principle of non-discrimination to the defense.[20] For the dissenters, this intrusion on the options of the defense was an argument against entering the field altogether. For Marshall, the limitations on the defense would be a blessing; reflecting our schizophrenic attitude toward the notion of fair trial, Marshall shifted from protecting the accused to balancing the scales with the prosecution. "Our criminal justice system," he argued, quoting 19th-century language, " 'requires not only freedom from any bias against the accused, but also from any prejudice against his prosecution. Between him and the state the scales are to be evenly held.' "[21] The paradox of fairness reasserts itself. When the issue is the optimal size of juries, the Court reasons that convicting the innocent is ten times worse than acquitting the guilty. When the question is discrimination in jury selection, the scales of justice should be evenly balanced.

The problem of discrimination by the defense reached the Supreme Court in the winter of 1992. In a case structurally similar to the trial then gearing up in Los Angeles—a white defendant charged with assaulting black victims—the prosecution sought a pre-trial order preventing the defense from using peremptory challenges on the basis of race. In the particular county in Georgia, 43% of the population was African-American. A non-discriminatory selection of the jury would have practically assured the participation of some black jurors. Of course, the defense would have preferred an all-white jury that might sympathize with a white man engaged in a racially motivated assault. The problem for the Court and for the legal profession was to find a principle for fairly restricting the options of the defense to select the most sympathetic jury it could find.

Under Justice Marshall's conception of a fair trial, the proper way to apply the *Batson* principle to the defense would have been: The prosecution (or the victim) has the right not to suffer discrimination by the defense that could adversely affect its chances for a fair trial leading to a conviction. Alas, the courts are still reluctant to affirm that either the prosecution or the victim has rights that are parallel to the defendant's rights. Whether the scales of justice should be evenly held or not, lawyers assume that only the defendant (and in some instances, the public as a whole) should enjoy constitutional rights.[22] Or so it seemed, circa 1990.

In the first few years of the decade, as juries were voting for acquittal in the cases of Meir Kahane and Rodney King, the Court's thinking underwent a transformation. In 1986 the Court was clearly focused on discriminatory action by the prosecutor as a denial of equal protection to a black defendant. But the use of the equal protection clause invited a shift in focus to new victims of discrimination in the use of peremptory challenges. The harm accrued neither to the defendant nor to the prosecution, but—of all people—to the jurors who could not serve. The Court—or at least its majority— reconceptualized jury service from a duty of citizenship to a right of participation. Being denied this right on grounds of race or gender began to appear comparable to denial of the right to vote. In an important transition case, the Court commented, "Indeed, with the exception of voting, for most citizens the honor and privilege of jury duty is their most significant opportunity to participate in the democratic process."[23] The upshot of this reorientation was the Supreme Court's holding in 1992 that the defense could not inflict this harm on potential African-American jurors by excluding them solely on the grounds of their race.[24]

There were some thorny legal problems that stood in the way of this reconceptualization of the jury. The most interesting derived from the language of the Fourteenth Amendment: "No state shall . . . deny to any person within its jurisdiction the equal Protection of the laws." The prohibition against discrimination applies only to the state and its agents. How could one say that defense counsel, doing her best to resist the state's effort to convict her client, was acting as an agent of the state?[25] Writing for a slim majority of five, Justice Blackmun constructed a plausible argument to show that when defense lawyers pick a jury they contribute to the exercise of state power; if there is discrimination in the selection of the jury, then they participate in an act of government that violates the jury candidates' right to equal treatment. It would be startling to insist that defense lawyers working with the levers of state power are merely private agents who should be able to claim immunity from constitutional principles.

More interesting than this technical debate is the way the excluded jurors became profiled as the victims of discrimination. When statutes prevented African-Americans from serving on juries, the Court could readily surmise that the

> very fact that colored people are singled out and expressly denied all rights to participate in the administration of the law . . . though they are citizens, and may be in other respects fully qualified, is practically a brand upon them . . . an assertion of their inferiority. . . .[26]

When the Court wrote this language in 1879, it had no trouble invalidating the statute that prohibited "colored people" from serving on juries. But the primary focus of the decision was that the defendant, an African-American, was denied equal protection because he would invariably be judged by a jury that would very likely include men who would be hostile to his race. Significantly, the Court had no problem with another provision of the statute, which excluded women from jury service. The Justices presumably felt that though whites could not always be fair in judging blacks accused of crime, men could be fair as well as protective in judging women.

In 1992 Justice Blackmun referred back to this language from the 1879 decision and misleadingly characterized its import as "recogniz[ing] that denying a person participation in jury service on account of his race unconstitutionally discriminates against the excluded juror."[27] There is a world of difference between excluding all blacks from the administration of justice simply because they were former slaves and challenging particular blacks on the ground that they are likely to be sympathetic with the victim. It is hard to see how using peremptory strikes as a strategic matter is "an assertion of their inferiority." There is hardly a "brand" upon someone who is suspected of being sympathetic to other members of his race, ethnic group, or gender.

Yet this is criminal justice, 1990s style. It would have been much more sensible to recognize the victim as the bearer of the right to a jury selected without ethnic factors stacked against him. But "anti-discrimination" sells better than "victims' rights." The Justices prefer to think that excluding jurors on the basis of race runs parallel to the brand of inferiority imposed when an entire group is excluded, wholesale. There is little coherence, however, in the claim that the excluded juror is the victim with a right to complain. No group has a right to serve in any particular case. And no defendant has a "right to a 'petit jury composed in whole or in part of persons of his own race.' "[28] It is hard to know, then, without a particularized right to serve, when or why an excluded juror has suffered victimization.

The new philosophy of jury selection became more transparent in April 1994, when the Court ruled that neither prosecution nor defense could exclude men or women from a jury solely on the basis of their gender.[29] In a suit to establish the defendant's paternity and obligation to pay child support, the prosecution used 9 of its 10 peremptory challenges to remove male jurors. Its assumption was that women would be more likely to impose liability for child support. The defense engaged in the reverse tactic—excluding the female candidates. Because there were more women in the pool, however, the jury consisted only of females, and they found the defendant liable. On appeal to the Supreme Court, six Justices upheld the defendant's complaint that the prosecution had engaged in unconstitutional discrimination.

The opinion contains only a passing reference to the harm that gender discrimination caused the male defendant in this case. The Justices devote all their rhetorical energy to a recitation of discriminatory practices toward women in the past. It is true that women gained the right to vote and to participate in juries later than did African-American men. It took the Nineteenth Amendment in 1920 to universalize the suffrage, and as of 1947, 16 states still denied women the right to jury service. This discrimination, the Court reasoned, was based on "stereotypical presumptions" about the competence and biases of women. These assumptions about men and women and their propensity "reflect and reinforce patterns of historical discrimination."[30] If lawyers rely on their intuitions about men and women, they supposedly reinforce the historical pattern of discrimination against women.

It is understandable, then, that the Court said almost nothing about whether it was fair to the defendant in this particular case to be tried by an all female jury. Implying that a female jury would be partial to a female complainant would reinforce the stereotype that women think differently from men about certain issues. To avoid this tempting (and in my view reasonable) conclusion, the Court had to indulge in the assumption that the state had violated the constitutional rights of the men who were excluded from serving on the jury. It is unclear why this defendant, if he had received a fair and impartial trial, should secure a reversal of the judgment against him just because the rights of some other unnamed men were violated.

Curiously, in this line of cases, the most conservative Justices— Scalia, Rehnquist, Thomas, and O'Connor—end up in the role of the defendant's champion. Those accused of crime should be able to maximize their options of a verdict in their favor by striking whomever they wish. These same Justices would vote, in the typical case, to curtail the rights of the accused. Yet in the hierarchy of values in the 1990s, liberals and conservatives gravitate toward unfamiliar positions. For liberals, the imperative to extend equal protection to disadvantaged groups trumps the rights of criminal defendants. It is more important to root out stereotypes about women and ethnic groups than it is to protect the traditional options of the accused. For conservatives, the historically rooted conception of a fair trial does not surrender to the new ideology that seeks to ban "stereotypical presumptions that reflect and reinforce patterns of historical discrimination."[31]

Many feminists, building on Carol Gilligan's work, argue that one should expect men and women to think differently about a wide range of issues.[32] They would not be at all surprised by the breakdown of the hung jury in the 1993 trial of Erik Menendez. Six women accepted Erik's tale of abuse and voted for manslaughter. The six men held out for the more severe verdict of murder. Prosecutors could well sense a female tendency toward leniency but not be able to justify a challenge for cause. Or the defense could intuit a male bias toward severity but not be able to satisfy the judge that this was the case. Greg Garrison, Mike Tyson's prosecutor, was convinced that in rape cases women tend to blame the victim and therefore are inclined to find the accused not guilty.[33] According to some recent simulation studies, however, young university women may be more likely than men to convict in rape cases.[34] There is nothing about these patterns or lawyerly intuitions that brand either men or women as inferior. There is nothing that could perpetuate "historic patterns of discrimination." Yet the Constitution now forbids lawyers from acting on what they experience as true—namely, that sometimes men and women think differently about crime and punishment.

A deep paradox runs through the Supreme Court's jurisprudence on jury selection. If stereotypical assumptions about racial, ethnic, and gender leanings are taboo, why should we be inclined to think that there was something wrong about a jury without African-Americans judging the fate of Rodney King's complaint, or juries without gays hearing the case of Harvey Milk's assassin? Why was it so painful in the Nosair trial for the prosecution to lose Leona Kaplan? Of course, might come the reply, sophisticated people pay no attention to these stereotypes of ethnic sympathy, but common people do. A verdict that issues from a homogeneous jury, one that is different from either the victim or the defendant, is less likely to gain community support. If this is true, then picking a jury should attend as well to these community sensibilities. And in the real world, apparently less politically correct than the current majority of the Supreme Court, no one would be dismayed if 12 women sympathized with the plight of an unmarried mother seeking child support.

The paradoxes thicken when we turn to other groups that suffer discrimination in jury selection merely on the basis of who they are. Does the new jurisprudence of equality extend to Jews and to gays? In May 1994 the Court refused to hear an appeal from a Minnesota decision permitting prosecutorial discrimination on the basis of religion. The prosecutor had dismissed a prospective juror who professed to be a Jehovah's Witness. She explained her decision as flowing from her experience that members of this sect were "reluctant to exercise authority over their fellow human beings."[35] Her thinking obviously leveled all Jehovah's Witnesses to the same stereotype, and yet for the Minnesota Supreme Court that was all right. The U.S. Supreme Court shied away from the case presumably because the Justices could hardly agree on which stereotypes are so offensive as to be unconstitutional and which are not.

There is ample case law prohibiting explicit discrimination in the selection of those included in the venire or pool from which the jury is chosen.[36] A law that prohibited gays, blacks, Jews, or women from being in the pool would encounter swift judicial nullification. Yet between the pool and the inner 12, there's many a slip. The right to the former becomes a chance at the latter. And as we move from candidacy to election, the law of discrimination becomes distorted. In the end, we have only two clear rules against discrimination in jury selection. Neither side may discriminate on the basis of race, and neither side may discriminate on the basis of gender. If this is all a fractured Court can do, then we will be treated to debates in the lower courts about whether for these purposes Hispanics are a race or an ethnic group and whether Jews are a race, a religion, or something else (shades of the Third Reich!). Debates about the boundaries of "race" as a category hardly befit a modern legal system.

This is just the entry into the thicket. How do we apply the Supreme Court's teachings to gays? If the Dan White case were to occur today, could defense counsel exclude all gays from the jury?

My sense of justice recoils at the thought. Are stereotypical assumptions about gays any less objectionable than those about women? Yet I doubt that the court will favor gays as it has set its canon against gender stereotypes. If we must live with current judicial biases, we will witness the decline of a great legal system into the arbitrary allocation of protection from cultural stereotypes.

We are in this unhappy state because we are unsure what we are trying to accomplish by eliminating discrimination in jury selection. The Court cannot correct the way the masses of people think about gays, Jews, the old, the young, men, or women. We cannot achieve impartial juries by pretending there are no cultural differences that can, imperceptibly, spin a juror's judgment in a particular direction. Yet the rationale for promoting minority-group representation in jury deliberation should not be based on how they will vote or how they will argue in the jury room. We should be concerned rather to guard against prejudiced comments in the deliberations.

Anna Deavere Smith reports a post-verdict interview with Maria, the black postal worker who sat on the federal Rodney King jury.[37] Maria discloses that when the jurors came down for breakfast in the hotel where they were sequestered, some of them would say, in effect, "It's a shame to spend so much money on the likes of that man." Maria properly sensed that this not so veiled derision of Rodney King could make a difference in the deliberations, and she protested. She put an end to it. She objected as a black woman and halted the slide toward what she perceived as slurs based on race and class. The same might be expected of a gay man who heard fellow jurors make snide comments about Harvey Milk's immoral "lifestyle." Or Jews who heard comments about how people like Kahane and Rosenbaum always stick together. The presence of minority members on the jury tends to keep the argument closer to the merits of the case; and jurors who regard racial slurs as taboo in speech may be inclined to vote as they speak.

On the whole, we do better to resist the anti-stereotype preaching of the Supreme Court and to support programs that recognize differences among cultural groups and thus seek to increase class and ethnic diversity on juries. If this is the goal, then the way to get there may not be to impose haphazard restrictions on the use of peremptory challenges but to consider eliminating peremptories altogether. This was Justice Marshall's position in *Batson*, and it may eventually prove to be the wiser course.

The problem is whether we should eliminate peremptory challenges or merely reduce their number to, say, three for each side. The disadvantage of these challenges, for which no reason need be given, is that they provide a cover for biased generalizations about how particular groups of citizens are likely to think. A large number of peremptories reduces the diversity of the jury: Both sides eliminate the groups that, as a statistical matter, are likely to be sympathetic to their case. But the retention of some peremptories may be necessary to ensure a fair trial for both the defense and the prosecution. The value of the jury, particularly for the defense, is that it infuses lay power into the determination of guilt. That power would be compromised if judges alone could decide when jurors were biased—that is, subject to challenge for cause. There may be many situations when defense counsel sense danger but they cannot persuade a judge that they are right. This is most often the case if the accused and the judge themselves come from different subcultures. The availability of peremptory challenges means that the lawyers, not just the judges, have their say about who makes the ultimate decision of guilt or innocence.[38]

Also, it is not clear that a judicial decision or a statute could effectively do away with peremptory challenges. The English tried to eliminate peremptories by the prosecution, but the courts devised a surrogate called "standing down" the candidate for the jury. If the prosecution objected to a juror, it could force him or her to "stand down"—precisely as if he or she were being removed on a peremptory challenge. Also, if peremptories were officially banned, the criteria for a challenge on the basis of cause would invariably be diluted. If the defense in the Nosair case could not have used a peremptory challenge against Leona Kaplan, for example, the court would have had to apply a more expansive conception of bias based on personal acquaintance with the parties. The better solution, then, would be legislation at the federal and state levels to limit the number of peremptory challenges to no more than three. A limited number of strikes-without-reasons would protect the interests of the defendant and of the victim without significantly affecting the demographic diversity of the jury.

Other measures are necessary as well to promote better representation of diverse groups on criminal juries. One of the complaints frequently aired after the acquittal in the Yankel Rosenbaum trial is that not enough middle-class Jews make themselves available for jury service in Brooklyn. The problem is a general one. About five million people are called to jury service every year in the United States; two million respond by appearing in court. Of these, about half actually serve. This rate of 40% response is remarkable in light of the financial loss to jurors who are self-employed.[39] The task is not only to make lists of those summoned more inclusive but to make the sacrifice in time and money palatable for more citizens.

A high-level panel in New York recently recommended a range of reforms, including providing more amenities for jurors and raising jury compensation from the paltry $15.00 to the federal level of $40.00 per day. Instead of an obligatory two weeks, frequently wasted in waiting, citizens would serve one day or one trial; they would be guaranteed dismissal if they were not seated on the first day.[40] The juror rolls should be drawn from not only motor vehicle, tax, and voting lists but, in the name of class diversity, from welfare and unemployment files as well. All these efforts are designed to maximize the participation of citizens in self-government, of experiencing firsthand the institution that Tocqueville regarded as the great medium of educating all classes in doing equity and judging one's neighbor as one would be judged oneself.[41]

The Implications of the Jury System

The best way to understand the American jury is to think of the lay people, so empowered, as akin to child emperors. They enjoy far more power than they have been trained to exercise. They can defeat a legislative decision to punish assisting suicide. They can find the four Los Angeles police officers not guilty—with unforeseen but disastrous consequences for the city in the distant smog. Indeed jurors in the common law tradition have far more power than do the professionally trained judges in Continental European courts. But as with child emperors, the dependent officials of the court seek to channel the jurors' authority.

Courts try to guide the mind of the jurors by keeping them insulated from the media. It would never occur to a European judge not to trust herself to read the local papers during a politically sensitive trial, but American jurors are routinely instructed to tune out all outside influences. They must keep their impressions of the evidence limited to what they hear in court. They should not expose themselves to newspapers or television news; they should not discuss the case with family members. My impression is that on the whole jurors follow these instructions. In particularly sensitive cases, they are sequestered, which means that during their deliberations or during the whole trial they live together, cut off from unsupervised contact with the rest of the world. In the federal prosecution of the four Los Angeles police officers, Judge Davies sequestered the jury for the entire trial and kept their names and addresses confidential. New York State now requires mandatory sequestration of all felony juries, but only during the process of deliberating a verdict.

The power of the jury is expressed in the nominal finality of an acquittal. While all the decisions of European judges—for or against the defendant—are subject to appeal, a common law jury's finding of not guilty purports to be the end of the matter. This is the principle of asymmetric appeal that has played such a critical part in the new political trials. A state jury's having the final word in rendering a verdict of not guilty explains why the federal government has felt compelled to prosecute those who seem to have been unjustly acquitted in a state court. Instead of an appeal from the verdict in Simi Valley, we get a new trial, in downtown Los Angeles, for the violation of Rodney King's civil rights. Instead of appealing the acquittal in the trial of Meir Kahane's alleged assassin, the federal government indicts Nosair and several other suspected terrorists in a prosecution for a pattern of terrorist activities under the federal anti-racketeering statute. These federal remedies would hardly be necessary—at least in these cases—if appeals were possible from state-court acquittals.

The system of one-sided appeal has also inhibited the judicial reform of pro-defendant jury instructions, such as the anachronistic rule permitting juries to infer consent to intercourse from the fact that the complaining witness had engaged in "unchaste" sex in the past. Trial judges were reluctant to change this practice for fear of making a ruling adverse to the defense, subject, in the event of a conviction, to reversal on appeal. If they adhered to the old rule, giving an undeserved edge to the defense, they ran no risk of professional embarrassment. If the defense won, the prosecution could not appeal, and therefore the only recourse of women's groups seeking reform of the law was legislation mandating the elimination of outdated assumptions about sexual experience.

The mind of the jury is channeled to flow in paths laid out as reasonable and plausible under the rules of evidence. Consider the two controversial items that might have been decisive in the rape trials of Smith and Tyson, one in each case. In the first, the trial judge excluded the testimony of the three witnesses who would have testified about Smith's having imposed or sought to impose his sexual will in the past. In the second, the judge excluded the testimony of three witnesses who would have said under oath that they saw Tyson and Washington necking a half hour before the sexual confrontation in Tyson's room. In both cases, the judges ruled out of fear that the jurors would be tempted to draw an improper inference that could have decided the case. In the Smith case, the inference would have been: If he did it in the past, he is likely to have done it this time. In the Tyson case, the inference would have been: If they were "all over each other" in the car, they were likely to have consented in bed. European judges would allow themselves to make these inferences but would accord them only the weight they warranted. The fear in common law jury trials is that the jury will run with an inference that is barely suggested in the facts.

Any time a remark by the defendant might be too provocative, too inflammatory, a veil of silence insulates the jury. In racially sensitive cases, this rule cuts deep. The Goetz jury was not allowed to hear, for example, that prior to the shooting, Goetz was heard to say at a meeting of his neighborhood association, "The only way to clean up [14th Street] is to get rid of the spics and niggers."[42] For similar reasons, the second Rodney King jury did not learn that shortly before the Rodney King beating, Officer Powell had described a domestic dispute between African-Americans as akin to "Gorillas in the Mist." Had they heard these statements, the respective juries might have had a different take on the racial dimension in the cases before them. But for fear of exaggerated jury response, the evidence is laundered. The mind of the jury is disciplined by judicially imposed ignorance.

The channeling of the jury's thinking occurs as well in the separation of fact-finding on guilt and innocence from the sentencing phase of the trial. Civil juries decide both the question of liability and the amount of damages. This means that if they have doubts about, say, the degree of the defendant's fault in a negligence case, they can readily compromise by rendering a lower damage award. Criminal juries could conceivably engage in the same kind of negotiations if they had the capacity to decide the number of years convicted defendants must serve in jail. Yet by common agreement in the common law tradition, juries do not have the power to render sentences. This authority is reserved to judges alone. Significantly, the jury is not informed about the gravity of the charges and how serious it would be to convict on one rather than on another. The temptation to compromise is limited to convicting for some alleged crimes and not others. This leads to seemingly illogical verdicts, such as the failure to convict El Sayyid Nosair for killing Meir Kahane but finding him guilty of assault against two bystanders in the same outburst of violence. In capital cases, juries typically do have the power to decide the fate of a convicted murderer, but the practice of rendering the sentence in a separate verdict insulates the deliberations about guilt from the temptations of compromise.

The surprising fact is that Continental European courts function without distinguishing between the phases of guilt and of sentencing. Both are lumped together in one determination of fact and law. This interweaving of two questions—responsibility for the crime and society's response to the crime—leads to one of the most disquieting features of the civilian trial. As the trial begins, Continental judges interrogate the defendant about his person: name, residence, occupation, marital status, and, believe it or not, prior criminal record! If the American mind recoils at these potentially prejudicial questions, recall that in the formerly Communist countries the judges would ask the defendant not only to identify his nationality (not exactly a break for Gypsies and Jews) but to state his *partijnost'*, that is, disclose whether he was a member of the Communist Party. Posing these questions at the outset of the trial was conceivable only on the assumption that judges are so well trained that they are not likely to be biased against a criminal defendant on the basis of a prior record, national identity, or political affiliation. In the common law tradition, one would never assume that lay juries could assimilate all this information and render an unbiased, undistorted judgment.

As an unexpected benefit, the jury system liberates defense lawyers to be far more aggressive and zealous in their advocacy than one can expect from Continental European defense lawyers. The reason is simple. European lawyers must constantly ingratiate themselves with the judge, who serves both as fact-finder and interpreter of the law. If the lawyer argues too vigorously about a point of law, the judge can retaliate against her in making the low-visibility findings of fact. Alienating the judge means losing the trial. Common law defense lawyers can go much further in their arguments on points of law with the judge. First, those arguments take place outside the hearing range of the jury, and therefore no matter how obnoxious the lawyers become they do not risk losing votes on the jury. Second, if they do alienate the judge, they risk little and defense counsel may even gain if they drive the judge into making a prejudicial ruling on a question of law. This undoubtedly is the strategy plied by aggressive lawyers like William Kunstler defending El Sayyid Nosair or Arthur Lewis on behalf of Lemrick Nelson. If the judge makes a mistake, after all, the defense acquires a good ground for appellate reversal.

The jury system expresses the ethos of a culture that believes in the anti-authoritarian virtues of decentralized power. In the European inquisitorial tradition, the powers of investigation, interrogation, and fact-finding are concentrated in the judicial arm of the trial. But as we accept the division of governmental functions among the three branches, we subscribe to a similar division of authority among judge, jury, and lawyers. Each "branch" of the trial has its functions and is limited by the authority of the others. The jury receives its information from the lawyers and learns its law from the judge. The judge filters the information presented to the jurors and instructs them on the law, but she has no power to overturn a verdict of not guilty. The lawyers present evidence and argue vigorously to the jury; they watch the judge for error and note grounds for appeal; but the judge retains the power to regulate trial demeanor and even to punish lawyers if they become unruly.

Against the backdrop of these distinct functions in the common law trial, we turn to questions of possible reform. How might it be possible to better protect the integrity of the jury and at the same time improve its reliability and performance?

The Integrity of the Jury

We think of the jury as an unprogrammed and largely unpredictable infusion of common sense into criminal trials. For the jury to preserve its role as an independent, democratic voice, it must function autonomously. The jurors cannot be subject to influence from the media; they should not receive signals from the judge about the better way to decide; they should not be subject to manipulation by the lawyers. Of the forms of intrusive pressure that we should seek to contain, I shall mention two, one that could have had a destructive impact in the trials we have surveyed but did not, and one that did contribute to denials of justice.

In these trials with gays, blacks, Jews, and women as victims, defense lawyers won some surprising victories. The reduced verdict for Dan White, the first acquittal for the LAPD officers, the acquittals of Nosair and Nelson, the acquittal of Smith, the hung jury in the Menendez case—these victories display defense lawyers at their vigorous best. In many of these cases, we might well believe that the verdict was contrary both to the evidence and to the demands of justice. Yet in none of them did the lawyers appeal to the juries to exercise their innate power to acquit in the face of the evidence and regardless of the judge's instructions.

This power—sometimes called the power of jury nullification— has played a major role in profiling the jury as a political institution that protects the people from the possibility of official oppression. It is associated with pre-revolutionary resistance to laws imposed on Americans by a Parliament across the seas. It bespeaks a capacity to do justice when the law is unjust. When the 18th century law of libel turned a blind eye to the truth as a defense, the jury recognized nonetheless that those who speak the truth should not suffer liability; thus they acquitted John Peter Zenger of charges of seditious libel. The jury has this power, but by and large jurors do not know it. Lawyers are no longer allowed to appeal explicitly to the legitimacy of nullification. And yet somehow, in the cases under discussion, defense lawyers got their juries to do their bidding, to rise up in power against the evidence and the law. They did all this without ever voicing in court the ultimate power of the jury to decide in favor of innocence regardless of either the facts or the law.

In contrast to the lawyers' subtle use of the rapier, the expert witnesses—from the Dan White to the Menendez cases—brought to bear a club of "scientific truth." Expert witnesses are allowed to opine on matters ranging from the defendant's psychological well-being to the general impact of child molestation only because they have access to a special brand of knowledge that is generally accepted as true. They have qualifications that enable them to testify about these truths even when they have no particular knowledge about the defendant or the alleged crime. An underlying theme of these new political trials is the abuse of this expert authority. Another way to think of this recurrent problem is in the idiom of the jury's autonomy and independence.

The jury relies on the common sense of everyman and everyman. The expert speaks in the voice of an objective truth available only to the initiated. The interweaving of these two worlds threatens the autonomy of common-sense judgments about such questions as whether individuals acted with malice and premeditation, whether the police beat a man unreasonably, and whether "getting caught up in a riot" undermines personal responsibility. The great debate in the aftermath of the Dan White verdict about psychiatrists in the courtroom was in effect a debate about the autonomy of the jury. Would ordinary people, relying on their personal moral experience, make the decision about whether a killing was murder or manslaughter? Or would science preempt the question and force its own mode of classifying crime on the minds of the jurors? In the early 1980s the tide seemed to be running in favor of the ordinary citizen's moral judgment.

The anti-expertise movement never sought to limit the information the jury might receive and assimilate into its judgment. There was a never any doubt about whether experts should be able to testify about the statistical results of DNA blood testing, as they did in the Yankel Rosenbaum slaying. The problem has always been imperialistic expertise: the intrusion of expert opinion into matters that should be reserved to the moral judgment of the jury. This is the form of expertise that has generated arguments against the personal moral responsibility of those who kill and beat defenseless victims.

The lawyers for the four LAPD defendants built their case on expert opinion as a means of weaning the jurors from their instinctive condemnation of police brutality. Expertise has its own way of looking at things. As the psychiatrists in the Dan White case shifted attention from the assassination of two political enemies to matters of diet and depression, the use-of-force experts in Simi Valley taught the court that the better way to look at the video was frame by frame. Violent swings became stationary poses. King's every movement was instinct with danger. The question was no longer what did happen but what could have happened. The fear that King might get up and go on the offensive became near-reality.

The still-motion analysis of the videotape, frame by frame, prompted the jurors to distrust their reactions to life at ordinary speed. Reading the tape in his own way, the defense expert Sergeant Charles Duke generated the intellectual foundation for the argument that every one of the 56 blows was defensive in nature. Each and every blow could be pitched to some gesture of the man on the ground, and each of these gestures could be understood as aggressive or "threatening." The state prosecutors failed to neutralize Duke; their sole expert, Michael Bostic, was castigated as a desk man without adequate experience on the street. In the same way that the prosecution lost the battle of the experts in the killing of Harvey Milk and George Moscone, they lost the first skirmish over the beating of Rodney King.

The simple truth is that experts have no particular knowledge or wisdom on the question whether it is reasonable under the law to beat a man while he is down or on the question whether blows to the head are within the law or without. They have even less to say about the legal issue of reasonable force than psychiatrists have to offer about the legal questions of malice, premeditation, and deliberation. To get our bearings about the role of experts in cases of allegedly justified violence, think about the trial of Bernhard Goetz. Here was another instance of seeming overreaction. A 37-year-old, slimly built white male encounters four black youths in the subway. One asks him for five dollars, another moves toward him. He responds by pulling out a concealed .38 Smith & Wesson and firing five shots, injuring all four. The question in his case, as well as in the Simi Valley trial, was whether the use of force was reasonably necessary under the circumstances. Goetz's lawyers tried to introduce other subway riders, also once mugged like Goetz himself, who would testify about what they thought was a reasonable reaction to the kind of confrontation that led to the shooting of the four blacks. The judge sensibly said no: the question of reasonable force is for the jury, not for experts. There is no experience, no scientific evidence, that can resolve the moral question whether it is right or wrong to use force to avert an attack or to subdue a criminal suspect.

The experts defend their role in police-brutality trials by drawing an analogy between medical malpractice and police malpractice cases. There is definitely a need in medical malpractice cases for experts to inform the civil jury about the customary standard of care in particular medical specialties and in particular communities. The customary practice of physicians informs, though it does not determine, litigation about whether a physician treated a patient negligently. There might be analogous questions in lawsuits for negligent conduct against a police officer, who, let us say, carried his gun in a way that led to an accidental firing and killing. On this issue, experts might well testify about the way police officers ordinarily carry their guns under particular circumstances.[43] But this is not the type of factual question that Commander Bostic and Sergeants Duke and Conta addressed in their testimony. They did not speak about what police officers ordinarily do on the streets. They appeared as experts on the internal policy of the Los Angeles Police Department, a policy that expressed itself in the police manual and in the oral tradition of instruction to police officers.

Neither of these topics—what police ordinarily do and the way the police manual is taught—has any bearing on whether the police behaved reasonably in administering 56 baton blows to Rodney King's body. The customs of police on the street differ in many respects from the customs of the medical profession. First, in the latter case, the patient enters into a contract for services with the physician. The patient is entitled to expect, as an implied term in the contractual relationship, that the physician will provide care at least as good as that which is customary and normal in the particular context. Citizens do not enter into contracts with the police. Their legitimate expectations are based not on the way the police ordinarily behave (which might be systemically illegal) but on what the law requires. True, if the suit is for negligently firing a police revolver, the customary norms of safety might have some bearing on the issue of negligence. But the action against the four LAPD officers was not for negligence. It was for the willful beating of a citizen in violation of his constitutional rights. Thus, even if the use-of-force experts had something to say about how the police ordinarily behave when they stop motorists or when an African-American shows them disrespect, it would have been interesting but not relevant to the jury's task.

As interpreters of official police policy, the experts have their own implicit agenda. With the collusion of the judge and the prosecution, they established the principle that the police have a primary duty to conform their conduct to departmental rules. This may be true—so far as the department is concerned. But it is not true under the law. The police behave criminally—either under the state or federal charges—as the jury applies not the departmental regulations but the law of the jurisdiction. The impact of expert testimony, as I argued earlier, is to reinforce the notion of an autonomous police department responsible primarily to itself.[44]

These use-of-force experts should never have been allowed to intrude upon the jury's judgment by pawning off their opinions as scientific expertise. What we learned in pruning back the influence of psychiatrists in criminal trials should have applied to them as well. So far as I know, no one—and in particular no member of the bar—has condemned the appearance of experts in cases of police brutality. We have come to realize that insanity as well as malice and premeditation are legal and moral questions; doctors should not be able to shape the jury's judgment with imperial claims of expertise. One can only wonder why we have not applied the same principle to the police. In the wake of the Dan White trial, Californians began to speak of victims and their rights. Now, a little more than a decade later, they seem to have forgotten that other forms of expertise can also claim its victims.

The travesty of expertise in the Rodney King case has repeated itself in other trials that raise borderline questions of moral responsibility. In the Reginald Denny beating case, a UCLA psychologist, Armando Torres Morales, testified about his theory of "riot contagion," which, in his view, undermined Damian Williams' capacity to intend evil when he lifted a fire extinguisher and threw it at Denny. According to Morales, riots sweep people up and eliminate their capacity to act responsibly. The prosecution called other experts to counter this parody of scientific thinking. But to little avail. The jury had one expert who legitimated an apparent desire to be lenient: it acquitted Williams on the most serious charges of attempted murder and aggravated mayhem and convicted him of simple mayhem. In an interview after the trial, the expert Morales confided in a journalist: "There is no right, no wrong, but rather a different perspective of reality."[45] Of course, if it is only a matter of personal perspective and inclination, one wonders why Morales should have been allowed to influence the jury with his peculiar brand of moral indifference.

Expert testimony is now reaching comic proportions. In the first Menendez trial, Ann Burgess, a professor of nursing from the University of Pennsylvania, offered her "scientific" opinion that research on snails could explain why the brothers killed. She reportedly claimed that Erik and Lyle killed their parents "in a reaction of fearful, almost primordial survival."[46] She offered the general conclusion that child abuse had led to the "rewiring" of Erik's brain, leaving him "highly sensitive to imminent violence."[47] If the stakes were not so high, Burgess's pretentious babble would simply be laughable. But there is a serious risk that when an expert takes the stand, recites her qualifications, and the judge "qualifies" her as someone who can speak with authority, she can influence a jury's deliberations. The consequences are comic and tragic at the same time.

Now one might react to this trend by saying simply that jurors are smart enough not to pay heed to the 1990s version of the "junk food" defense. But jury deliberations generate highly complex interactions, and a "scientific" opinion validated as legitimate at trial can feed inclinations toward leniency. Interestingly, all the "junk science" that comes forward serves only the side of the defense. In no case under review do we find the prosecution calling experts to demonstrate that the accused was really more evil than the facts suggest. The only way to restore balance in the trial, therefore, is for trial judges to prohibit experts from testifying about moral issues that are appropriately left to the jury's shared sense of right and wrong.

My proposal, then, is to enforce stricter limits on expert testimony. Judges should not allow the expression of opinions when their primary purpose is not to supply information but to offer a "perspective" on the defendant's moral responsibility. The Federal Rules of Evidence suggest the right standard. Rule 704(b) prohibits experts from testifying about whether a defendant "did or did not have the mental state or condition constituting an element of the crime charged or of a defense thereto." If that standard were applied in cases like the Dan White case, the psychiatrists could not have testified about whether the defendant had acted with malice or premeditation, for these are "states of mind" as that term is ordinarily understood in the law. Similarly, the issues of intention and culpability in the prosecution of the four LAPD defendants, Damian Williams, and the Menendez brothers should be beyond the competence of the experts. The principle is on the books, at least for federal trials. The state courts should adopt the same standard in the interest of furthering jury autonomy over questions of moral responsibility.

Understandably, judges are fearful of reversal if they restrict the right of the defense to present its case. And the vague standard I have proposed would probably not prevent Morales and Burgess from offering the jury their supposedly scientific wisdom about riot contagion and the rewiring of the brain. Yet there is no way to restore moral coherence to the criminal law without carrying through the program that reformers initiated after the Dan White decision. In the early 1980s, the victims' rights movement found an easy target: the defense of diminished responsibility. They thought that if they abolished that defense, they would solve the problem. But this abolition offered no salvation from the original sin—namely, imperial expert testimony that displaces the moral judgment of the jury. If we believe in the jury and the common sense of the ordinary citizen, we must protect the jury from the intimidations of pseudo-science. Getting strict with experts might help, but one fears that exhortation would not go far enough.

Toward an Interactive Jury

The answer may lie not in seeking to protect the jury from imperial experts but in making the jury a more active participant in the trial. We should follow up on an opening that developed in the trial of El Sayyid Nosair in Justice Alvin Schlesinger's Manhattan courtroom. In a surprise to court observers, the jurors wanted to ask questions of the witnesses. Justice Schlesinger recognized in principle that they should be able to do so but required that they first submit the questions, in writing, to him. The procedure he improvised resembles the way lawyers pose questions in the standard Continental European trial; the lawyers channel their questions through the judge to the witness. The principle that jurors may ask questions, even if routed via the bench, provides an opening for additional impulses from the jury in the unfolding of the trial.

To understand why this input from the jury is imperative, we should review some of the curiosities in the deliberative process that we have learned from interviews with jurors after unexpected verdicts of not guilty. As revealed in the jurors' reasoning in the Kahane and Rosenbaum cases, a process of amateur sleuthing often takes hold. The jurors rely on rules of thumb that the lawyers and judge never anticipate. The Kahane jurors made much of the absence of a witness who saw both Nosair shooting and Kahane being hit. It was not enough in their minds that someone saw Nosair holding the gun a split second after the shots rang out. Yet the weight of this particular item of evidence is left to the jurors' untutored experience. Similarly, the Rosenbaum jurors bet their credibility chips on the peripheral fact that the officer testifying had put in for a commendation for his role in apprehending Lemrick Nelson. They made the unexpected assumption that officers might lie to protect their previous statements in applications for departmental recognition. These are modes of reasoning—central to the outcome of jury deliberations—that fall outside jury instructions.

There is no way that lawyers can address reasoning of this sort, whether for or against the defense, unless they become aware of the jury's hunches and reservations while the trial is still in progress. If the jurors come forth with questions revealing their hunches about supposed gaps in the evidence or the likelihood that some witnesses and not others are telling the truth, the lawyers can address these issues and help steer the jurors' thinking toward more rational rules of thumb. The resulting interaction would not compromise the jury's integrity but only improve its deliberations.

Lawyers apparently need feedback from juries on the verge of deliberation. They are often out of touch with the propensity of the jurors to value non-legal factors such as the defendant's good motive. The deliberations in the Kevorkian prosecution illustrate the centrality of motive in the jurors' judgment of guilt. The State of Michigan charged Jack Kevorkian with assisting in the suicide of a terminally ill man suffering from Lou Gehrig's disease. Kevorkian placed a mask over the man's face and the man pulled a string, which released poisonous carbon monoxide. The applicable, recently enacted statute recognized an exception for physicians who cause death though their "intent is to relieve pain or discomfort." All lawyers generally mean by "intent" is the immediate aim or objective of the action. But many members of the jury apparently thought that the motive to help patients by ending their life was the same as an intent to relieve pain. One juror said, "He convinced us that he was not a murderer, that he was really trying to help people out, and I can't see anything wrong with it."[48] Another said, "I believe he did this to relieve this man's pain and suffering."[49] In short, if Kevorkian had had good motives, he could not have the intent of a criminal.

The central importance of motive helps explain the Manhattan jury's failing to convict El Sayyid Nosair of the assassination of Meir Kahane. The jurors complained that the prosecutor failed to account for Nosair's motive. William Greenbaum wanted to steer clear of Middle East politics. If jurors are going to convict, they expect the narrative of the crime to make sense to them. They must be able to integrate the events into their views of how and why people do as they do. "Normal people do not commit murder," as defense counsel Douglas Schmidt argued to the jury in the Dan White case. Or, as Leslie Abrahmson put it on behalf of the Menendez brothers, "Good parents do not get shotgunned by their kids. Period." If the "kids" do kill or try to kill, they must either be crazy or have a good motive.

It is not clear that jurors asking questions will mention these logical tangents that become evident only when they sit down to deliberate. And even then, as Rodney King juror Maria revealed to Anna Deavere Smith, it may take several days for them to work through their own psychological associations with the trial before they turn systematically to the evidence.[50] Once this process begins, the lawyers are excluded. But the judge need not be.

The judge remains in contact with the jurors throughout the deliberative process. They can send the judge notes with questions. The judge responds by calling the jurors into open court and reading back testimony or instructions on the law. Judges should encourage this interaction by making his or her advice available on tangential matters of law, such as whether the police officers in the Nelson case could be liable for perjury if they stuck to a false story in their applications for commendation. We do not allow our judges to summarize the evidence, as do English judges when they instruct the jury. But perhaps we should reconsider this practice and allow judges to err on the side of greater personal input in the deliberation process. This, of course, is a practice fraught with danger, as we noticed when Justice Rappaport intervened and expressed skepticism about several witnesses against Lemrick Nelson.

The one area where we can safely encourage greater judicial interaction with the jury is the stage of instructions on the law prior to the onset of deliberations. There is little doubt our present practices in this regard are a farce. The instructions, filled with boilerplate from manuals of standard instructions, drone on for hours and days. As Jerome Frank wrote years ago:

> Time and money are consumed in debating the precise words which the judge may address to the jury, although everyone who stops to see and think knows that those words might as well be spoken in a foreign language.[51]

On the whole, juries do their best to translate these instructions into lay English and to follow them. Of course, they cannot be faulted for not fathoming the distinctions among four different kinds of criminal homicide or keeping the five elements of assault in their minds. Yet the normal reaction of citizens called to public service is to act in good faith, follow the rules, and protect themselves from criticism after they reach a decision. Typically, after an unpopular verdict, as in the cases of Rodney King, Yankel Rosenbaum, and Meir Kahane, the jurors will tell the press that they followed the instructions and simply tendered reasonable doubts about the defendant's guilt.

To achieve greater comprehension by the jury, judges should experiment with less formal modes of instruction. They should encourage jurors to ask questions as the elements reel off and the legal options pile up. Judges could signal the elements that are particularly relevant by pausing to invite questions. They could sound jurors out about whether the legal jargon made any sense. These easy ways of communicating are what one expects from proceedings that are, as Tocqueville said, "the most efficacious means for the education of the people which society can employ."[52]

Postscript: Describing the kind of jury that he desired in the O.J. Simpson case, politically incorrect lawyer Robert Shapiro said that he desired a mixed race, all female jury. Why all female? Shapiro is quoted in *The New York Times Magazine* (September 11, 1994) as saying that "Frankly, I think women are more intuitive." Apparently, he has not gotten the message that the Supreme Court frowns on gender stereotypes.

CHAPTER EIGHT

Ten Solutions

THE CRIMINAL TRIAL HAS BECOME THE MOST VISIBLE MEANS OF addressing aggression from one community into another. As between straights and gays in San Francisco, between blacks and Koreans in Los Angeles, among Jews and blacks and Muslims in New York, between men and women on dates and in the home, aggression threatens more than the particular victim. Crime has a special meaning when it occurs at the interface of subcultures. An entire group of Americans identifies with the flesh-and-blood victim. Criminal courts have become the medium of doing justice for these groups as well as for individuals. And when the criminal trial fails, as it has in San Francisco, Los Angeles, and New York, something like war breaks out on the streets.

In concentrating primarily on four groups of Americans in the shadows—gays, blacks, Jews, and women—I have allowed events to be my teacher. I have followed the trials and the riots and the marches that have made obvious the new form of community involvement in criminal justice. Of course, I am mindful of neglecting two large groups of hyphenated Americans: Hispanic-Americans and Asian-Americans. It is hard to know whether Jose Menendez should be cast primarily as a Cuban or as a parent. Perhaps I should have paid more attention to the killing of Chinese-American Vincent

Chin in Detroit.[1] The trial of Latino police officer William Lozano for killing two African-Americans provides rich material.[2] My study is limited in many respects. Its purpose is not to exhaust the field but to rely on specific cases to illustrate the problems that affect all Americans who have suffered discrimination.

Against the background of these trials, I suggest ten principles for bringing justice both to victims and to defendants. Nothing in the solutions I propose detracts from the rights or the recognized guarantees protecting criminal defendants. We can improve the participation of the victim without rolling back the liberal constitutional gains of the last several decades. These, then, are my proposed solutions, organized as a code for easy reference.

Solution One:
Think of Every Case as a New Political Trial

The new political trial, as defined in the Introduction, expresses the grass-roots passions of groups who identify with victims. The implicit threat of civil disturbance sometimes awakens the courts and the public to deeper sensibilities of justice. The outrage over the Dan White verdict in California leads to a voters' initiative that abolishes the defense of diminished responsibility. Mindful of the despair and excessive violence produced by the Simi Valley verdict, the federal court in Los Angeles pays greater attention to the rights and interests of Rodney King as a person and as a symbol of social conflict. After the Jewish community in New York joins in organized protest and lobbying in Washington, the Justice Department convenes a grand jury to investigate the murder of Yankel Rosenbaum. After years of organized feminist protests against date rape, an Indianapolis prosecutor and judge display great zeal to convict Mike Tyson of rape. In all these cases, the victims come center stage. After several centuries of neglect, the victims have reclaimed their rightful place in American criminal trials.

This is no apology for violence. To the contrary. The best way to avoid violence in the future is for all courts, in all cases, to act as though the victims were organized and demonstrating outside the courthouse doors. Consider for a moment the systematic attack on the character of Jose and Kitty Menendez in the first trial of Lyle and Erik for murdering them. A quirk in California law, the doctrine of imperfect self-defense, together with an expansive interpretation of this doctrine, permitted the defense to manufacture an attack on the victims' character. Jose supposedly engaged in years of sexual abuse of his boys, and this abuse rendered the brothers' alleged fears plausible. The parents, of course, were not at the trial to defend themselves. They enjoyed no presumption of innocence. Everything that called into question their character, no matter how private or personal, was admissible.

Imagine if they had been victims in a rape trial and the defendant had tried to impugn their character with similar allegations of sexual misconduct. Rape-shield laws would have protected them against defense counsel who sought to defend their clients by convicting the victim. But women have organized to protect their character as complaining witnesses in rape cases. Parents have not organized, presumably because the evil represented by the Menendez killing is so mercifully rare. Yet the judge should have treated the parent-victims as though they represented a political force and warranted full protection at trial. Judge Weisberg could easily have justified the conclusion that the inquiry about parental sexual abuse was simply irrelevant and prejudicial.

The same could be said of male victims in battered-woman self-defense cases. Women are well organized to protest their victim-hood. Men are not. When Lorena Bobbitt went on trial for having cut off her husband's penis, she claimed that she had been abused. The Ecuadoran National Feminist Association voiced support for Lorena, by birth one of their own. They reportedly threatened to castrate 100 American men if Lorena was convicted and sent to prison.[3] Many American women demonstrated on behalf of Lorena, right or wrong.

No one marched for John Wayne Bobbitt. Men felt threatened

by the specter of castrating women, and as individuals they spoke out on talk shows. But they did not assert themselves as an organized group of victims. Yet the court should have done it for them. In the trial against Lorena, it should have protected the interests of John as victim, and in the trial against John for marital sexual abuse it should have protected the interests of Lorena as victim. Perhaps they both deserved conviction. As it was, both juries concluded that each had suffered enough and turned their backs on the entire affair.

The Bobbitt trials illustrate the tactic of competing for the status of victim. When John and Lorena were on trial as defendants, both tried to portray themselves as the real victims of the conflict. This typifies the battered-woman syndrome and the battered-boys syndrome in the Menendez trial. When a guilty defendant can portray himself or herself as the real victim, the trial loses its moral bearings. The value of protecting the victim becomes perverted into a claim for leniency, thus violating the rights of another victim.

This was the tactic favored by the defense of Damian Williams for violent assault in the bloody aftermath of the Simi Valley verdict. In the beginning, no one took seriously their argument that they were the victims of racism, riot contagion, and other forces beyond their control. Somehow, however, they managed to profile themselves as the beneficiaries of the political forces behind Rodney King. Lost in the process were the rights of Reginald Denny and all the truck drivers, all the working-class people, all the Caucasians who might have identified with him. The jury may well have feared a renewal of violence in reaching its compromise verdict of acquitting Williams of the most serious charges of aggravated mayhem and attempted murder. If so, one senses the dangers of perversion in the new sensitivity to victims.

There is nothing wrong with the word "political" so far as it signifies an organized effort to be taken seriously. A fine line separates the virtue of attending to the interests and needs of victims, on the one hand, and the political intimidation of juries, on the other. Intimidation follows from getting confused between the victim in particular cases and the defendants pretending they are victims because they belong to an oppressed group.

The only solution to this manipulation of victimhood is to intensify the focus on the trial at hand. Every time a guilty defendant can claim to be the real victim, another suffering human being is ignored. The way to achieve the proper emphasis on the actual victim in the trial itself and in the press is to keep the evidentiary lens narrowly focused. The broader social struggle between battered women and abusive men, between African-Americans and abusive police, should be beyond the scope of trials like those of Lorena Bobbitt and Damian Williams. The only way to protect victims in the long run is to keep our sights on who, in every trial, is the real victim. Judges must resist the efforts to broaden the inquiry by introducing past patterns of abuse. They must focus on the actual conduct of those accused and leave out of consideration the "social forces" that may have led them to act the way they did.

If judges think of every trial as an example of the new political trial, they will remain sensitive to the real victims—the Menendez parents, Reginald Denny viciously assaulted on April 29, 1992, each of the Bobbitts in the trial of the other, men whose wives kill them when they are asleep, and all the other victims in the routine cases that never make the news reports. Also, importantly, the lessons learned from high profile cases should lead to an across-the-board reform in all criminal trials. To those reforms, we now turn.

Solution Two: Divide the Verdict into Two Stages

The most intriguing lesson to be learned from both the Dan White and the Simi Valley cases is that verdicts of mitigation or of not guilty often communicate the wrong message. In the minds of the victim's community, they imply that the jury thought ill of the victim—that Harvey Milk and Rodney King were unworthy of the law's full response. In both cases, a less insulting message is camouflaged by the catch-all phrase: not guilty. There are in fact two legitimate tracks for finding a defendant not guilty or for mitigating the crime. One track begins with the victim. In a case of self-defense, for example, a decision that the use of force is justifiable means that because the victim was the aggressor his rights were not violated. So far as the defendant in a rape case argues consent, he rests his defense on what the victim did, namely that she actually consented to intercourse. In these cases of justification based on the victim's conduct, the appropriate verdict is "no violation" of the victim's rights.

The other track leads to the defendant. The four Los Angeles police officers built their cases on their subjective perceptions of necessity. They acted reasonably, they claimed, in interpreting King's conduct as threatening. Thus one track puts the victim's rights into question; the other track concedes a violation of those rights but argues that solicitude and compassion for a morally innocent defendant requires an acquittal.

These two distinct tracks leading to acquittal should generate two distinct verdicts. If the jury finds "no violation," the trial is over. If it finds that the defendant has violated the victim's rights, it should say so clearly and directly and then turn to the question whether the defendant is guilty or accountable for the violation. In many of the cases under study, the jury's verdict of not guilty would have translated, under my proposal, to a first verdict of violation, followed by an acquittal or mitigation on the issue of personal guilt or responsibility.

There is ample precedent for this innovation in criminal procedure. Many jurisdictions recognize a separate verdict of not guilty by reason of insanity. My proposal requires merely an extension of this separate verdict to include all conditions for excusing or mitigating the crime, namely diminished capacity, reasonable mistake, duress, as well as insanity. Claims of justification, such as consent, self-defense, and lesser evils, would bear on whether there is a violation of the victim's rights. A justified action is not a violation.

The prosecutions in which the bifurcated verdict would have made a difference include Dan White, the four Los Angeles police officers, Bernhard Goetz, William Kennedy Smith, and Mike Tyson. In the Smith trial, it would have been important to know whether the jurors acquitted because they had doubts about whether Patricia Bowman consented or whether they thought that Smith acted under a reasonably mistaken impression about her consent. These two distinct issues are typically run together, with unfair consequences for the defense.

The virtue of the bifurcated verdict is that it enables both sides to emerge from the trial with some recognition of their rights. Even if a conviction is not possible, the victim can have the consolation that a jury found that his or her rights were violated, a verdict that could be useful in a subsequent action for civil damages. Even if the defendant suffers this loss, there remains hope for acquittal based on a personal excuse. The bifurcated verdict, then, is a way of doing justice to both sides.

Solution Three:
Reallocate the Victim's Power from Sentencing to Plea-bargaining

Under the current state of the law, the victim has the greatest power at the stage where he or she least deserves and needs it—at sentencing. As a structural matter, the system can tolerate victim input at the time of sentencing, for at that stage everything is admissible. Everyone in town has a say about what should be done with a convicted felon. The victim too might as well fuel the public's lust for vengeance or promote the virtue of forgiveness. It would be a mistake, however, to privilege this input from the victim and treat it as critical to a proper level of punishment.

Punishment responds to the wrong the offender commits, but not to the particular wrong as measured by victims willing to testify. Killing a homeless beggar is as great a wrong as depriving a family of a loved one. Or at least that is what we have always assumed about homicide. It hardly makes sense to think of life as sacred if its value is a function of how much others love or need the person killed. That the victim is a human being is sufficient to determine the evil of killing. Thus the suffering of the survivors hardly seems the right basis for determining, say, whether the death penalty is justified.[4]

The power that could make a difference in the life of victims lies not at the end of the process but at the beginning. In contrast to England, the United States no longer permits private prosecutions. The police and the public prosecutor gain control over the case and from the outset regard it as their own. They dispose of it at will. The American Bar Association proposes that prosecutors confer and hear the victim out "to the extent practicable," but that does not go far enough. At the stage of plea-bargaining, the victim should be regarded as a party whose consent should be necessary to short-circuit the trial process. Recognizing this power of the victim would unquestionably compromise the options of prosecutors, and for that reason they would likely oppose it. But bringing the victim into the limelight would bring new legitimacy to the occasionally shady practice of plea-bargaining.

Bringing the victim in from the cold might reorient plea-bargaining in a direction that many German reformers have urged.[5] German scholars would like to see the criminal process serve the goal of reconciliation between offender and victim. If the victim must sign off on every plea bargain, prosecutors would have an incentive to create a mood between victims and offenders that would facilitate understanding between them. Under these circumstances, the victim would have a less urgent need for vindication at a public trial; there would be no reason to object to the offender's pleading guilty to a lesser charge. By gaining control over the wrong that has occurred to him, the victim would have greater hope of reestablishing his position as a person secure in his rights, and from this position of strength he could approach the offender with a less compelling need for vengeance.

Solution Four:
Give the Victim a Role at Trial

Once we recognize the critical importance of criminal trials in reintegrating the victim into society, we cannot tolerate the occasional alienation of the victim from the adversarial criminal trial. Prosecutors represent the people or the public at large, and therefore they feel justified in downplaying the importance of the person or family (of a deceased) that has suffered most. A startling example of this indifference is Rodney King's silence during the Simi Valley trial. The man whose beating defined the charges watched the trial from his living room. Prosecutor Terry White refused to call him, for fear of damaging the supposedly incontrovertible proof provided by the videotape. When King finally testified at the federal trial, we could grasp the human dimension of the drama. He turned out not to have the menacing demeanor that everyone expected. He provided new evidence (they called me "niggah"); he explained his desire to escape the beating to offset the allegation that he was charging Officer Powell. Without King on the stand, the trial would have lacked important information. Without the victim's voice, the trial could hardly claim to bring about a vindication of the victim as a full-status citizen.

In every homicide case, we encounter an analogous problem. The people most affected by the death, the next of kin, are silent at trial. Because he was not a witness, Norman Rosenbaum, Yankel's brother, could only watch the trial patiently from the audience. He could criticize the process, attack the verdict, but he could not participate in rendering justice. This need not be our reality. Continental European trials permit the victim or the victim's family to appear as a party to the proceeding. We resist this innovation because we assume that the prosecution and the defense have a monopoly as the official parties in dispute. Yet it would hardly do violence to the adversary system to permit some modification of the strict bipolar model.

It might be desirable, in principle, to permit the victim to make an unsworn statement at the outset of the trial. The accused can appear as a lawyer, so why should the victim not be able to appear as a co-prosecutor? There are, however, important disanalogies between the victim and the defendant. The accused understandably seeks to avoid conviction and therefore, as his own lawyer, might say anything to further his case. When the victim speaks, however, he or she appears not in the semi-theatrical role of lawyer, not as a player in the drama, but as a real person seemingly speaking the truth. We do not allow the prosecution or the defense to depart from their roles and speak, as it were, in their true voice. Greg Garrison could not tell the Tyson jury that he personally believed that Tyson was guilty. Similarly, it would be at odds with the rules of the game to let the victim deliver a statement without being sworn as a witness and facing cross-examination.

The better approach would be to permit the victim or the next of kin, either in person or through a lawyer, to appear in the trial to ask questions of the witnesses. It is not clear how many victims would do this rather than entrust the case to the prosecutor. The privilege would probably be exercised in rare cases, only where the prosecutor fails to gain the victim's confidence. In the atypical case where the victim wants to intervene, it would be better to allow the third voice at trial rather than freeze out the party for whom the proceedings may carry greater positive meaning than for anyone else.

Solution Five:
Establish Diverse Juries

There is no more disputed question today than our assumptions guiding jury selection. In the last eight years, the Supreme Court has developed a partial set of principles on permissible discrimination in the use of peremptory challenges; a new patchwork of rules governs when prosecutors and defense counsel can exclude candidates for the jury without giving reasons. Neither side may remove African-Americans without providing a race-neutral reason; neither side may exclude men or women without a satisfactory gender-neutral reason. Yet the new policy against discrimination is not likely to protect gays, immigrants, Jews, Asians, Catholics, the young, or the old. Blacks and women are singled out for special treatment, and no one quite knows why.

The Supreme Court may preach as it may, but we cannot banish cultural stereotypes from our thinking. Nor can the public. The only way we can ameliorate the dissonance that arose in cases like Harvey Milk, Rodney King, and Yankel Rosenbaum is to encourage the kind of diversity in jury selection that presupposes rough-and-ready judgments about cultural and class differences. For the sake of justice and for community acceptance of the verdict, it would surely have been better to have gay representation on Milk's jury, blacks involved in judging King's complaint, and some Jews hearing the evidence on the slaying of Rosenbaum. Yet there is no way to write a rule of law that would demand victim representation on the jury. It would be impossible to know which subcultures merited representation (orthodox Jews, Hasidic, Lubavitch?) and who counted as a qualified "representative." The most we can demand is a policy that increases the chances of a diversified jury that, as President Bill Clinton described his cabinet, "looks like America."

The great advantage of victim representation on the jury is not the resulting spin on the outcome but rather the inhibitory effect on the deliberations. With a gay, black, or Jew sitting in the jury room, the jurors are not likely to make comments that subtly reflect shared biases about these subcultures. The way to achieve this diversity is not to impose arbitrary rules on lawyers about when and why they can use their peremptory challenges. The Supreme Court's current policy represents a quest for fictitious homogeneity. It would be better to reduce the number of peremptories on each side sharply, say, to three or fewer, and to let lawyers use them as they see fit.

This is a modification of Justice Marshall's proposal in 1986 to abolish peremptories altogether. He would have been prepared to rule that the mere existence of prosecutorial peremptories was unconstitutional, and he would have "allow[ed] the States to eliminate the defendant's peremptories as well."[6] It would be difficult, however, to reach the conclusion that the Constitution permitted three and only three peremptories on each side. This is a change in the law that will depend on the initiative of state legislatures.

Solution Six:
Abolish Changes of Venue

The chronologically first wrong of the Simi Valley trial was changing the venue to a suburban community in the hope of finding a jury less biased by media reports of the beating and its aftermath. The wrong in sending the state prosecution to Simi Valley was not simply that there were no African-Americans to sit in judgment of the police; the wrong was rather that the community that gave rise to the dispute lost control over its outcome. To paraphrase the Declaration of Independence in the interests of victims, the community's grievance was against "transporting defendant beyond country lines to be tried on the basis of pretended defenses." There was considerable resistance to ratification of the 1787 Constitution because it referred ambiguously to jury trials without adequate recognition of local authority.[7] The response of the Sixth Amendment was to locate federal criminal trials "in the State or district wherein the crime shall have been committed." At the state level, the appropriate modification is that the trial must take place in the county where the crime was committed. As the public is entitled to access to criminal trials, local juries are entitled to sit in judgment of disputes that erupt within their community.

The policy of permitting changes of venue is, in effect, to accord the defense a wholesale peremptory challenge against the entire community.[8] The use of this wholesale peremptory in the Rodney King case obviously had discriminatory implications, but my case against changing venue goes beyond the issue of fair representation on juries. The wrong of depriving the community of the crime that occurs in its midst would have been just as great if the King case had gone to Oakland, a city with a racial demography comparable to that of Los Angeles. The crime and its implications were the affair not of Oakland but of Los Angeles.

Some lawyers might object to the seemingly mystical claim that the community "owns" the crime that occurs within its borders. The claim is no more mystical than the sensibilities of ordinary people who sense great injustice in not being able to sit in judgment about an event that has disturbed their tranquillity. If the event calls into question the entire pattern of race relations, there is a special urgency in the community's dealing with its own problem. The appellate court in Ventura County ordered the change of venue supposedly to achieve greater emotional distance from the conflict between the police and African-Americans in Los Angeles. The result was to substitute one set of passions for another, one set of interests for another. As with the quest for diversity in juries, it is better to stay at home and work to find a jury that is at once seemingly impartial but representative with a fair allocation of differing spins on the values at stake.

Abolishing the practice of changing venue requires changes at two levels of law-making. The Supreme Court should quietly abandon its precedents holding that the failure to relocate a trial can violate the defendant's Sixth Amendment right to a trial by an impartial jury. There has not been a new decision in this body of law since 1971.[9] This policy of benign neglect should continue.

Further, as a matter of state law, legislatures should repeal the provisions that permit transfers of cases from one county to another. Of course, in a high-profile case, where the media take sides, the problem remains of finding 12 jurors relatively uninfluenced by media propaganda. Yet in the era of CNN and Court TV, there are no high-profile cases that escape the notice of even the most remotely situated citizens. The best way to find impartial jurors is not to search for the ignorant and ill-informed but to find men and women who are capable of maintaining an open mind until they hear the evidence presented at trial. The screening of candidates with questionnaires and interviews worked well in the Goetz case and in the federal trial of the four LAPD defendants. It can work in all cases.

Solution Seven:
Establish an Interactive Jury

As they now function, jury trials display little capacity for self-correction and avoidance of irrational tangents. There is ample evidence that juries often go off on a logic of their own. The Rosenbaum jury assumed that police who apply for departmental recognition are probably lying. The Kahane jury assumed that unless there was an eyewitness to the shooting, there could be no proof beyond a reasonable doubt. The Goetz jury developed and applied a conception of intent as good-faith belief that the New York Court of Appeals had already dismissed as bad law.[10] The stories of wayward jury thinking are legion. Yet there is little thought about how to make the most of an institution that is ingrained in the American conception of justice.

Interaction between jurors and judge would enable jurors better to understand the instructions on the law. It is no secret that the current mode of guiding jury deliberations is not working. Judges should encourage jurors to ask questions and interact with them at the time they are trying to explain the law. We should also encourage jurors to ask questions of witnesses and of the lawyers. Though they typically do not know it, jurors have the innate power to do this now by putting their questions in writing and submitting them to the judge. Fostering this practice by advising jurors of this option would provide lawyers with some feedback about the way the jury was thinking. It would give them an option prior to the end of oral argument to address the jury's specific concerns. Nothing is gained by maintaining a wall of silence between the powers that decide and the agents of argument.

Solution Eight:
Psychiatric Experts Should Not Testify about Issues of Moral Responsibility

The problem of imperial expertise came to our attention in the Dan White case. The public was shocked by the jury's mitigating the double killing on the basis of diet or loss of sleep. The contemporary version of the same problem is the claim, heard in the Menendez case, that child abuse can lead to a "rewiring of the brain." The gay community in San Francisco perceived the reliance on pseudo-science as a problem of victims' rights, for the resulting verdict of manslaughter instead of murder communicated an ambiguous message. Reasonable observers could also understand the verdict to imply that the killing was less than fully wrong because the victim, Harvey Milk, was less worthy than a straight citizen.

When the voters in California adopted the Victims' Bill of Rights (Proposition 8) in 1982, they voted to abolish diminished capacity as a defense. That was their response to the injustice of the Dan White verdict. A similar correction would be possible in the Menendez debacle: The courts or the legislature could easily abolish the rule of imperfect self-defense that makes an unreasonable fear of attack relevant to the issue of malice. But these reforms miss the point. The deeper problem that cuts across these questions is that psychological expertise has gotten out of control.

The states should adopt a standard like that suggested in the Federal Rules of Evidence § 704(b), which prohibits experts from testifying about whether a defendant "did or did not have the mental state or condition constituting an element of the crime charged or of a defense thereto." This might be enough to prevent a witness like Ann Burgess from testifying that child abuse (unproven in the Menendez case) had led to the rewiring of Erik's brain or that "riot contagion" provides a defense for people who lose their heads when other people lose theirs. Yet a radical change of judicial attitude is probably required to restore moral culpability to its proper place in the criminal trial. The judges should simply become more restrictive about the kinds of expertise that could inform or advise the jury about matters relevant to their task of judging responsibility.

Solution Nine:
Experts in Police-Brutality Cases Should Not Testify about Departmental Policy

The Rodney King trial demonstrates the dangers of respecting the relevance of expert testimony. The problem was not pseudo-science but bad legal analysis. All sides to the dispute called experts to testify about the use-of-force policy of the Los Angeles Police Department. Everyone seemed to assume, without much discussion, that the policy—as opposed to the actual practice—of the department was relevant to whether the defendants intentionally violated King's constitutional rights. This was a false assumption that fostered the image of an autonomous police department governed by its own regulations. Victims have the right to see their charges litigated under federal law, not under departmental policy.

Experts play an important role in advising the jury about police techniques and actual practices. But departmental policies, as reflected in the police manual and training bulletins, tell us nothing of relevance to the question whether the police used excessive force and intentionally deprived King of his constitutional rights. These are questions of state and federal law, not of internal policy. Amazing as it may seem, both state and federal prosecutions took place on the assumption that this testimony did matter. No one asked why.

The simplest way to bring greater fairness to prosecutions for police brutality would be to restrict expert testimony to matters on which the experts have relevant expertise. They have nothing relevant to offer when they begin to argue, as did Sergeant Duke, that beating Rodney King was within the regulations of the department. Whether Duke was right or wrong, his testimony was irrelevant.

Solution Ten:
Toward Communitarian Punishment

The theme that runs through all these proposals is that we develop a new conception of why we prosecute and punish criminals. The standard debate on this subject fluctuates between grandiose ambitions of social engineering and abstract propositions about punishing simply for the sake of justice and, as the philosopher Hegel put it, vindicating right over wrong. The reforms I have urged express a more realistic purpose of punishment. The primary task of the criminal trial is neither to change society nor to rectify a metaphysical imbalance in the moral order. The purpose of the trial is to stand by the victim.

Crime has debilitating and demoralizing effects on those who become its prey. For a split second the world goes awry, the lives of people are changed forever. After a life-threatening burglary, a rape, a mugging, a killing in the family, it is not easy to come back and carry on with one's life. Shame in the looks of others leads to retreat. Fear of the offender makes one afraid to be alone. Of course money can help. Restitution and compensation are important, but they cannot so easily restore the dignity of those who have suffered arbitrary debasement.

The trial serves in large part to restore the victim as a self-respecting, functioning member of society. Punishing the offender, if he or she is guilty, may be part of that process of restoring the dignity of the victimized. But punishment is not always necessary. A simple jury verdict that the offender has violated the victim's rights goes a long way. And in cases of dubious responsibility it is far better to recognize this violation explicitly than to camouflage it beneath a verdict of not guilty. Our present system encourages victims to demand vengeance at the time of sentencing. It is far more important to bring to bear the energies of victims to the stage of plea-bargaining where they can insist on formal recognition of the wrong they feel or demand that the case go to trial. If the case goes to trial, the legal system should stand with the victim once more. As in Continental European legal systems, the victim should have a part to play at trial. At minimum, he or she should be able to ask questions of the witnesses. Most victims will not exercise this option. In view of their enhanced procedural power, victims will receive greater respect from prosecutors and presumably will trust the agents of the state to press their case for them.

Three reforms of the jury system will facilitate the public's expressing solidarity with victims. More diverse juries will increase the likelihood that the victim as well as the accused will find symbolic representation on the jury. If the victim is a member of a minority, the value of this representation is that it will inhibit derisive remarks about the kind of person the victim is. In view of the systematic effort to assault the character of victims like Rodney

King and the Menendez parents, this kind of protection in the jury room is necessary to a fair trial. Abolishing changes of venue will also increase the probability that victims will find a voice in the jury room of someone who is from the same locale and who can empathize with the victim's suffering. Promoting an interactive jury will lead juries to better, more just verdicts, serving the interest of both defense and the victim.

The two reforms in the use of expert witnesses will reduce the contemporary tendency of juries to acquit on the basis of pretended excuses. We must entrench the moral responsibility of the accused as the central question of the trial and not permit experts to distract jurors with false hypotheses about the way circumstances rob people of their responsibility. In police-brutality cases, we should no longer tolerate the spectacle of use-of-force experts converting the trial into an examination of internal police policy. Focusing on the right question will invariably assist victims by leading to the just condemnation of those who should be held accountable.

A just legal system must stand by its victims. We may neither deter future offenders, nor rehabilitate present inmates, nor achieve justice in the eyes of God. But by seeking to punish the guilty, we do not abandon the innocent who suffer. We do not become complicitous in the crimes committed against them. We seek justice not only for offenders but for all of us.

TIMELINE

THE CASE HISTORIES THAT INFORM THIS BOOK ARE ABSTRACTED from the give-and-take of daily events. Though they appear as distinct stories, they are in fact interwoven episodes in a single drama of justice that begins in 1978 and reaches a crescendo of intensity in the years 1989–1994. The chronology presented here shows the case histories as strands in a surge of trials that triggered popular identification with victims.

This chronological ordering includes some events not discussed in the book. They are included as suggestions of connections that the reader may draw if so inclined. I have my suspicions, say, about the link between the tendency of the press to credit the unproven charges leveled against Cardinal Bernadin and a parallel tendency to take seriously the Menendez brothers' tale of child abuse. But there is no way of knowing whether these events are but a historical coincidence or whether they reflect an underlying social trend. The temporal sequence is set forth here as an invitation to the reader's own perception of common themes.

1978–1987

November 27, 1978. Dan White shoots and kills George Moscone and Harvey Milk at San Francisco City Hall. About 25,000 mourners, many holding candles, assembled in front of City Hall.

May 1, 1979. The trial of Dan White begins; White pleads not guilty to all charges.

May 21, 1979. The jury finds White guilty of voluntary manslaughter. 5,000 gay men march from the Castro District to City Hall battling police, burning eight police cars, and smashing the doors of City Hall.

June 8, 1982. Californians adopt Proposition 8, the "Victims' Bill of Rights," by a popular vote of 56% to 44%. The initiative purports to abolish the defense of diminished capacity and plea-bargaining in cases of major felonies.

June 19, 1982. White autoworker Ronald Ebens attacks and kills Chinese-American Vincent Chin with a baseball bat in a barroom brawl in Highland Park, Michigan. Ebens reportedly thought that Chin was Japanese and was angry about competition from the Japanese automobile industry. Ebens pleads guilty to manslaughter and receives a sentence of probation. Asian-American activists protest the sentence.

January 6, 1984. Dan White is released from prison after serving less than five years in jail.

June 12, 1985. When her husband falls asleep, Judy Norman puts a gun to the back of his head and kills him.

October 22, 1985. Dan White commits suicide by inhaling carbon monoxide from his car's exhaust in his garage.

February 16, 1987. In Superior Court of Rutherford County, North Carolina, Judy Norman's trial for killing her husband begins.

March 3, 1987. The jury finds Judy Norman guilty of voluntary manslaughter.

March 5, 1987. Superior Court Judge John Gardner sentences Judy Norman to six years of incarceration for killing her husband.

May 1, 1987. After deliberating for about eight hours, a federal jury in Detroit of ten whites and two blacks acquits Ronald Ebens of violating the civil rights of Vincent Chin when he killed him with a baseball bat in a 1982 barroom fight.

1989

January 16. William Lozano, a Hispanic police officer in Miami, shoots and kills African-Americans Allan Blanchard and Clement Lloyd, who was riding a motorcycle allegedly in the direction of Lozano. Riots break out in Miami.

January 23. Lozano is charged with the manslaughter of Lloyd as well as of passenger Blanchard, who died the day after the shooting.

April 5. The Supreme Court of North Carolina affirms Judy Norman's conviction and sentence.

July 7. Governor James Martin commutes Judy Norman's sentence to the time she has already served.

August 18. Erik and Lyle Menendez drive to San Diego and purchase two shotguns.

August 20. While watching television in the library of their Beverly Hills mansion, Jose E. Menendez and his wife Kitty are riddled with 16 bullets from 12-gauge shotguns. The killers are their sons Lyle and Erik Menendez.

December 7. A six-person Florida jury of two blacks, one Hispanic, and three whites finds Officer Lozano guilty of two counts of manslaughter.

1990

March 26. Lyle and Erik Menendez are arraigned on first-degree murder charges for the homicide of their parents.

November 5. Rabbi Meir Kahane is shot and killed at the Marriot Hotel on Lexington Avenue in New York. The suspected assassin is El Sayyid Nosair.

November 20. Nosair is indicted on second-degree murder charges for the death of Kahane. Nosair is also charged with attempted murder of Carlos Acosta, a postal officer, as well as with assault, coercion, reckless endangerment, and unlawful possession of a weapon with intent to use.

November 21. Nosair pleads not guilty to all charges.

1991

March 3. Shortly after midnight, Rodney Glen King is stopped for speeding and is subsequently beaten by Los Angeles police officers.

March 15. Police Sergeant Stacey Koon and Officers Theodore Briseno, Laurence Powell, and Timothy Wind are indicted in connection with the Rodney King beating.

March 26. The four police officers plead not guilty.

March 30. Senator Edward M. Kennedy, his son Patrick, and his nephew William Kennedy Smith go to a Palm Beach bar, where Smith meets a young woman with whom he later has sexual intercourse on the beach.

April 1. The Palm Beach Police Department announces that a woman, later identified as Patricia Bowman, claims that she was raped at 4 A.M. on the beach at the Kennedy compound.

May 9. William Kennedy Smith is charged with sexual battery, Florida's equivalent to rape, and misdemeanor assault.

May 10. The grand jury decides not to indict the 19 police officers and two school security officials who were bystanders at the Rodney King beating.

June 25. The Florida Court of Appeal overturns the conviction of William Lozano for double manslaughter; the trial judge committed an error when he declined the defense motion for a change of venue.

July 18. At a beauty pageant in Indianapolis, Mike Tyson meets Desiree Washington and leaves with her hotel telephone number.

July 19. At 1:30 A.M., Tyson calls Washington. Later that night they engage in sexual intercourse in Tyson's hotel room.

July 22. Los Angeles Police Chief Daryl Gates announces his retirement.

July 23. The Court of Appeal in California reverses Judge Weisberg's denial of a change of venue and orders the trial of the four LAPD officers to be relocated outside Los Angeles County.

August 19. At the intersection of Utica Avenue and President Street in Crown Heights, Brooklyn, a car driven by Hasidic Jew Yosef Lifsh careens out of control and kills seven-year-old Gavin Cato; his younger cousin Angela suffers a broken leg. Three hours later, five blocks from the accident, a crowd of black youths stabs Yankel Rosenbaum, a Hasidic scholar from Australia.

August 20. In the early morning, Yankel Rosenbaum dies.

August 21. Lemrick Nelson is charged with second-degree murder in the death of Rosenbaum.

September 5. A New York grand jury decides not to indict driver Yosef Lifsh for Gavin Cato's death.

September 9. An Indiana grand jury indicts Mike Tyson for the rape of Desiree Washington.

September 11. Mike Tyson is arraigned on one count of rape, two counts of criminal deviate conduct, and one count of confinement. Mike Tyson pleads not guilty to all charges.

September 21. Television actress Roseanne Arnold announces, at a conference of over 1,000 incest survivors and therapists, that she has had reawakened memories of being sexually abused by both of her parents.

September 23. Professor Anita Hill of the University of Oklahoma Law School files a confidential statement with the Senate Judiciary Committee claiming that Supreme Court nominee Clarence Thomas had discussed pornographic movies with her and had repeatedly asked her for a date while they were working together at the Equal Employment Opportunity Commission ten years before.

October 12. The Senate Judiciary Committee commences hearings, before a live television audience, on allegations that Clarence Thomas behaved improperly toward Anita Hill.

October 15. At 2:02 A.M. the Senate Committee closes the hearings into Anita Hill's allegations against nominee Clarence Thomas. Later that night the full Senate votes to confirm Clarence Thomas's nomination to the Supreme Court.

November 18. Nosair's trial begins for the murder of Rabbi Kahane and other offenses.

November 26. Predominantly white Simi Valley is selected as the new venue for the trial of the four officers charged in the Rodney King beating.

December 2. Trial begins on rape charges against William Kennedy Smith. The proceedings, broadcast live on nationwide television, are said to be the most widely viewed in American history.

December 11. The jury deliberates only 77 minutes and finds William Kennedy Smith not guilty on both charges.

December 21. A Manhattan jury acquits Nosair of the murder of Kahane and the attempted murder of Carlos Acosta, the postal officer. The jury, however, finds Nosair guilty of possession of a weapon and of firing that weapon at Acosta and at Irving Franklin, a bystander.

December 30. Protesting the acquittal of Nosair, a hundred people march across the Brooklyn Bridge and demonstrate in front of police headquarters and the Criminal Court Building. Marchers also burn an effigy of Nosair in front of the Jacob K. Javits Federal Building.

1992

January 30. Mike Tyson's trial for the rape of Desiree Washington begins.

February 10. The Tyson trial ends and Judge Patricia Gifford directs the jury to retire and commence deliberations. After ten hours of deliberating, the jury returns a verdict of guilty on one count of rape and two counts of criminal deviate conduct.

March 4. The trial begins of the four L.A. police officers charged in the assault on Rodney King.

March 26. Judge Patricia Gifford sentences Tyson to ten years for each of the three felony convictions. Gifford adds that the sentences will run concurrently and that four years are suspended because of mitigating circumstances. Judge Gifford also levies a fine of $30,000.

April 2. Miami Judge W. Thomas Spencer rules that prior rioting in Miami requires a change of venue in the Lozano case; he relocates the case to Orlando.

April 23. The 12 Simi Valley jurors retire to deliberate on the charges against the four LAPD defendants.

April 29. On live television, the Simi Valley jury delivers its verdict: three of the officers are not guilty on all charges. The jury is hung on one charge of excessive force against Laurence Powell. Violence erupts in South Central Los Angeles. At the intersection of Florence and Normandy, a videotape captures Reginald Denny being dragged out of his truck and brutally beaten. Governor Pete Wilson calls in the National Guard.

April 30. Mayor Tom Bradley imposes a curfew on Los Angeles.

May 1. President George Bush declares Los Angeles a federal disaster area. 30,000 people march through Koreatown in solidarity with the Koreans who were singled out by the looters and rioters.

May 6. Judge Spencer relocates the Lozano trial from Orlando to Tallahassee.

May 12. Antoine Miller, Henry Watson, and Damian Williams are arrested in connection with the Reginald Denny beating.

May 16. Tens of thousands of protesters rally in Washington, D.C., demanding billions in federal aid for the rebuilding of Los Angeles and other inner cities.

May 21. Antoine Miller, Henry Watson, and Damian Williams are indicted on 33 charges for assaults against 13 people, including Reginald Denny, at the intersection of Florence and Normandy.

August 4. A federal grand jury returns an indictment against the four acquitted LAPD officers for violating Rodney King's civil rights.

October 29. The jury acquits Lemrick Nelson of all charges in connection with the death of Yankel Rosenbaum. Over 1,000 Hasidim assemble in protest.

December 7. A Los Angeles County grand jury indicts the Menendez brothers on murder and conspiracy charges. The grand jury also finds the special circumstances that would allow prosecutors to ask for the death penalty if Erik and Lyle are convicted.

1993

February 3. The federal civil-rights trial begins against Koon, Powell, Briseno, and Wind.

February 15. Alan Dershowitz argues Mike Tyson's appeal before a three-member panel of the Indiana Court of Appeals.

February 26. A massive bomb explodes in an underground parking garage beneath the World Trade Center in New York City killing six and injuring over 1,000.

March 5. Judge Spencer rules that Lozano's retrial will remain in Tallahassee despite agreement between the prosecution and the defense that the trial should be moved again.

March 10. The appellate court orders the Lozano trial back to Orlando.

April 17. The jury finds Powell and Koon guilty of violating Rodney King's civil rights; Briseno and Wind are acquitted.

April 19. Ending a 51-day standoff, the FBI, under orders from the Justice Department, raids and burns down David Koresh's compound in Waco, Texas. Koresh and 80 of his followers die.

April 20. Judge Spencer rejects the plea from a member of the victim's family to return the Lozano trial to Miami.

April 23. The Florida Supreme Court rejects a motion to move the Lozano trial back to Tallahassee.

April 28. Reginald Denny files an $80 million lawsuit against the City of Los Angeles for damages allegedly resulting from the LAPD's decision to withdraw its forces from the area of the riots.

May 28. After deliberating about six hours, a jury of three whites, two Hispanics, and one black acquits Officer Lozano on both counts of manslaughter. The National Guard is mobilized.

June 23. Lorena Bobbitt cuts off her husband John's penis with a 12-inch kitchen knife.

July 20. The trial of Erik and Lyle Menendez, with two juries, begins in Van Nuys Superior Court.

August 2. A Prince William County, Virginia, grand jury indicts John Wayne Bobbitt for marital sexual abuse.

August 6. The Indiana Court of Appeals votes two to one to uphold Mike Tyson's conviction.

August 19. The trial of the three accused of violence against Reginald Denny and 12 other motorists begins.

August 25. A federal grand jury indicts Sheik Omar Abdel Rahman for orchestrating the World Trade Center bombing, for plotting to blow up the United Nations building, the Lincoln and Holland tunnels, and the Manhattan FBI office, as well as for the assassination of Rabbi Meir Kahane. The grand jury also indicts 14 others, including El Sayyid Nosair, for the two bomb plots as well as for the murder of Rabbi Kahane under a federal racketeering statute.

September 30. The Senate unanimously passes a resolution urging the Justice Department to investigate the murder of Yankel Rosenbaum.

October 15. Defense expert Ann Burgess testifies that Erik Menendez's fear of his parents had "rewired" his brain.

October 18. The jury acquits Damian Williams and Henry Watson on the most serious charges, including aggravated mayhem and attempted murder. Williams is found guilty on one charge of felony mayhem for his attack on Denny and on four counts of misdemeanor assault on the other motorists. Watson is found guilty of one count of misdemeanor assault; the jury deadlocked on a felony assault charge.

November 2. Rudy Giuliani defeats David Dinkins in the New York City mayoralty election.

November 8. In Manassas, Virginia, the trial of John Wayne Bobbitt for marital sexual abuse begins.

November 9. Antoine Miller pleads guilty to felonious assault and receives 27 months probation.

November 10. After deliberating four hours, the jury of nine women and three men finds John Bobbitt not guilty of the charge of sexual marital abuse.

November 12. In Cincinnati, Steven Cook files a federal lawsuit against Cardinal Bernadin for sexual abuse that allegedly occurred some 17 years previously. Cook claims recent discovery of the incident with the aid of a psychotherapist.

December 7. In a plea-bargain arrangement, Henry Watson pleads guilty to the felony assault charge on which the jury had been deadlocked.

December 7. Colin Ferguson, with notes in his pockets detailing racial prejudice he suffered from whites, Asians, and other blacks, boards a Long Island Railroad commuter train and guns down six passengers and wounds 19.

1994

January 10. In Manassas, Virginia, Lorena Bobbitt's trial begins for the malicious wounding of her husband John.

January 13. The jury of six men and six women in the Erik Menendez trial deadlocks and Judge Stanley Weisberg declares a mistrial.

January 17. Because of the Los Angeles earthquake, deliberations by Lyle Menendez's jury are postponed until January 24, when the jurors resume deliberations in a trailer.

January 21. A Prince William County jury composed of seven women and five men deliberates seven hours over two days to find Lorena Bobbitt not guilty of malicious wounding of her husband by reason of insanity. Lorena Bobbitt is ordered to submit to psychiatric observation at Central State Hospital.

January 25. Attorney General Janet Reno announces that the United States Justice Department will conduct an investigation into possible civil-rights violations in the killing of Yankel Rosenbaum.

January 29. The jury of five men and seven women in the Lyle Menendez trial deadlocks and Judge Stanley Weisberg declares a mistrial.

February 25. Dr. Baruch Goldstein, a follower of Rabbi Kahane, massacres at least 29 Muslim worshipers in a mosque in Hebron.

February 28. Judge Herman Whisenant orders Lorena Bobbitt's conditional release from Central State Hospital. She is directed to seek counseling for up to six months.

February 28. Steven Cook withdraws his charges against Cardinal Bernadin.

March 4. The four defendants charged in the bombing of the World Trade Center are found guilty.

March 7. The Indiana Supreme Court decides not to accept Mike Tyson's petition to have the court review his rape conviction. Tyson is scheduled to be released in May 1995.

April 19. In Federal District Court in Los Angeles, Judge John Davies presiding, a jury awards Rodney King $3.8 million in compensatory damages from the City of Los Angeles for violating his civil rights in connection with the beating King sustained on March 3, 1991.

May 2. Oral argument takes place in the appeal from the federal conviction of Officer Koon and Sergeant Powell.

May 24. Judge Kevin T. Duffy sentences each of the four defendants convicted on a range of charges connected to the World Trade Center bombing to a total of 240 years of imprisonment. The calculation is based on the deceased victims' life expectancies.

June 1. After prolonged deliberations, a nine-person federal jury in Los Angeles, including one African-American, decides against imposing punitive damages against six police officers implicated in the beating of Rodney King.

June 12. Sometime between 10:00 P.M. and midnight, Nicole Brown Simpson, the former wife of O.J. Simpson, and Ronald Goldman are stabbed to death outside Nicole's home in Brentwood, California.

June 13. From a little after 2:00 A.M. to 5:30 A.M., LAPD detectives search the grounds of O.J. Simpson's estate. Officer Mark Fuhrman finds a bloody glove behind the room where a guest, Brian Kaelin, is staying. At 5:30 A.M. the officers request a warrant to search O.J.'s house. At noon, officers question O.J. for three and a half hours and then release him.

June 14. Judge Patricia Gifford denies Mike Tyson's motion for early release from prison. She cites his lack of genuine remorse and insufficient progress in his efforts to gain a high school diploma in prison.

June 17. At 9:00 A.M., police inform Robert Shapiro, Simpson's lawyer, that Simpson should submit to arrest at 11:00 A.M. for having murdered his wife and Goldman. Simpson disappears with his friend Al Cowlings. By 6:00 P.M., the police locate him moving in a car on the freeway.

June 22. The LAPD releases tapes of Nicole calling the police begging for protection from her ex-husband, O.J. On the tapes, O.J. can be heard ranting and screaming obscenities.

June 24. A California grand jury investigates whether O.J. Simpson should be indicted for the double murder, but Superior Court Judge Cecil J. Mills dismisses the grand jury after it becomes clear that the jurors are aware of prejudicial evidence against O.J. reported in the media but not officially presented by the District Attorney. The case proceeds directly to a preliminary hearing without a grand jury indictment.

June 26. Domestic-violence hotlines report substantial increases in the number of calls since Simpson's arrest on June 17: 27% in New York, 35% in Denver, 50–80% in Houston, 20–30% in Chicago, and 80% in Los Angeles.

June 28. LAPD Chief Daryl Gates's successor, Willie Williams, dismisses Officer Timothy Wind from the LAPD for unnecessarily kicking King during the beating.

June 30. Simpson's preliminary hearing begins. Simpson's lawyers file a motion before Municipal Court Judge Kathleen Ann Kennedy-Powell to suppress any evidence collected by police officers at O.J.'s home on the ground that Officer Mark Fuhrman's initial entry onto the property violated the Fourth Amendment.

July 7. Judge Kennedy-Powell rules that the search of O.J. Simpson's home was constitutionally valid.

July 8. Judge Kennedy-Powell rules that there is sufficient evidence to bring O.J. Simpson to trial for the murders of Nicole Simpson and Ronald Goldman. Simpson is held without bail.

July 22. Simpson pleads "absolutely, 100% not guilty" to charges of murder.

August 11. A federal grand jury indicts Lemrick Nelson, Jr., for having violated Yankel Rosenbaum's federal civil rights—namely by stabbing him to death on August 19, 1991.

August 17. Lemrick Nelson pleads not guilty in Federal District Court in Brooklyn to charges that he violated Yankel Rosenbaum's federal civil rights.

August 18. In Federal District Court in Brooklyn, John Anderson, a key defense witness in the Lemrick Nelson trial, pleads guilty to charges of giving false testimony to federal officials.

August 19. A three-judge panel of the Federal Court of Appeals for the Ninth Circuit in San Francisco unanimously affirms the convictions of Sgt. Stacey Koon and Officer Laurence Powell for violating Rodney King's civil rights. The panel also rules that Koon's and Powell's sentences, imposed by Judge John Davies of Federal District Court in Los Angeles are too lenient and remands the case for resentencing in line with the Federal Sentencing Guidelines.

September 6. In U.S. District Court in Indianapolis, Judge Sarah Evans Barker rules that a writ of habeas corpus brought by Mike Tyson be "dismissed with prejudice."

September 8. In a pre-trial hearing before Judge David Trager of Federal District Court in Brooklyn, Lemrick Nelson's attorneys, Trevor Headley and Michael Warren, petition Judge Trager to recuse himself on the ground that Judah Gribetz, head of the committee that recommended him for judicial appointment, was also head of the Jewish Community Relations Council which was active in the campaign to bring about federal civil rights charges against Nelson. Postponing his decision on recusal, Judge Trager directed Nelson's attorneys to make the motion in writing.

September 9. Los Angeles District Attorney Gil Garcetti decides not to pursue the death penalty, but will seek a sentence of life imprisonment without parole, in the trial of O.J. Simpson.

September 26. Jury selection begins in the trial of O.J. Simpson.

NOTES

INTRODUCTION

   1. Shakespeare, *The Merchant of Venice*, Act III, Scene 1.

   2. Genesis 4:10.

   3. American Bar Association Task Force on Minorities and the Justice System, *Achieving Justice in a Diverse America* (July 1992).

CHAPTER ONE

   1. Warren Hinckle, "The Ten Days that Shook San Francisco," *Image Magazine, San Francisco Examiner*, November 6, 1988, 28, as quoted in Kenneth Salter, *The Trial of Dan White* 404 (1991). [Hereafter cited as Salter].

   2. *The Times of Harvey Milk* (film by Robert Epstein and Richard Schmiechen, 1984).

   3. Id.

   4. Id.

   5. The transcript is edited and reproduced in Salter at 12.

   6. Id.

   7. Marc Reidel, *Stranger Violence: A Theoretical Inquiry* 49–50 (1993).

   8. 4 William Blackstone, *Commentaries on the Laws of England* 201 (1765–69).

   9. California Penal Code § 189.

   10. California Penal Code § 188.

11. The new language came from the pen of Justice Roger Traynor. See *People v. Thomas*, 41 Cal.2d 470, 261 P.2d 1 (1953) (concurring opinion); *People v. Washington*, 62 Cal.2d 777, 402 P.2d 130, 44 Cal.Rptr. 442 (1965).

12. Telephone interview with Thomas Norman, May 5, 1994.

13. M'Naghten's Case, 8 Eng. Rep. 718 (H.L. 1843).

14. Id. at 722–23.

15. Id.

16. *Parson v. State*, 81 Ala. 577, 2 So. 854 (1887); *People v. Cantrell*, 8 Cal.3d 672, 105 P.2d 1256, 105 Cal.Rptr. 792 (1973) (adopting the test in California).

17. *Durham v. United States*, 214 F.2d 862 (D.C. Cir. 1954).

18. Model Penal Code § 4.01.

19. See *California Jury Instructions: Criminal* § 4.00 (Third Ed. 1970); *People v. Glover*, 257 Cal.App.2d 502, 65 Cal.Rptr. 219 (1967).

20. *People v. Drew*, 22 Cal.3d 333, 583 P.2d 1318 (1978).

21. *People v. Wells*, 33 Cal.2d 330, 202 P.2d 53 (1949).

22. Salter at 397. A slightly revised version of this instruction is now found in *California Jury Instructions: Criminal* § 8.11 (Fifth Ed. 1988).

23. Italics in this portion of the instruction have been added to indicate phrases that will be discussed later. The deleted portion refers to the doctrine of felony murder.

24. Model Penal Code § 210.3(1)(b).

25. Id.

26. Salter at 146.

27. Id. at 151.

28. Id. at 135.

29. Id. at 316.

30. Id. at 192.

31. Id. at 188.

32. Id. at 191.

33. Id.

34. Id.

35. Telephone conversation with Douglas Schmidt, October 11, 1993.

36. Salter at 86.

37. This observation was confirmed by defense counsel Douglas Schmidt, telephone conversation, October 11, 1993.

38. *People v. Saille*, 54 Cal. 3d 1103, 820 P.2d 588, 2 Cal. Rptr. 2d 364 (1991).

CHAPTER TWO

1. *USA Today*, April 30, 1992. See also Linda Feldmann, "Bush Wins Points for Speech on L.A. Riots," *Christian Science Monitor*, May 4, 1992, at 1 ("according to one opinion poll, 89% of the public disagrees with jury's acquittals").

2. *The New York Times*, April 14, 1994, A24.

3. In addition to the four indicted, there were 17 other LAPD officers, two CHP officers, and two school district security agents. *The New York Times*, May 11, 1991, A9. Anna Deavere Smith counts 19 police bystanders, presumably excluding the school security agents. Anna Deavere Smith, *Twilight: Los Angeles 1992* at 258 (1994).

4. California Vehicle Code § 2800.2. Federal prosecutor Steven Clymer said in oral argument that "Mr. King was stopped because he was committing the crime of felony evasion." Closing Argument by Steven Clymer in the federal trial, April 8, 1993.

5. Closing Argument of Michael Stone in the state trial, April 21, 1992.

6. Stacey Koon, with Robert Deitz, *Presumed Guilty: The Tragedy of the Rodney King Affair* 35 (1992).

7. See *Briseno v. Superior Court of Los Angeles County*, 233 Cal.App.3d 607, 284 Cal.Rptr. 640 (August 21, 1991).

8. *Powell v. Superior Court of Los Angeles County*, 232 Cal.App.3d 785, 283 Cal.Rptr. 777 (July 23, 1991).

9. Id. at 802, 283 Cal.Rptr. at 788.

10. On the notion of a fair trial, see Chapter Five.

11. *People v. Wheeler*, 22 Cal. 3d 258, 282 n. 29, 583 P.2d 748, 765 n. 29 (1978).

12. Testimony of Laurence Powell in the state trial, March 31, 1992.

13. Closing argument of Michael Stone in the state trial, April 21, 1992.

14. See generally George P. Fletcher, *A Crime of Self-Defense: Bernhard Goetz and the Law on Trial* (1988).

15. Koon, supra note 6, at 87–90.

16. See *Report of the Independent Commission on the Los Angeles Police Department* (The "Christopher Report") 70–80 (1991).

17. Testimony of Sergeant Charles Duke in the federal trial, March 22, 1993.

18. See note 4 supra.

19. This analysis is based on an informal and speculative telephone conversation with prosecutor Steven Clymer in May 1994.

20. *Powell v. Alabama*, 287 U.S. 45 (1932).

21. *Brown v. Mississippi*, 297 U.S. 278 (1936).

22. E.g., *Mapp v. Ohio*, 367 U.S. 643 (1961) (Fourth Amendment exclusionary rule applied to the states); *Gideon v. Wainwright*, 372 U.S. 335 (1963) (in a case originating in Florida, the Supreme Court held the Sixth Amendment right-to-counsel provision applicable to the states); *Malloy v. Hogan*, 378 U.S. 1 (1964) (in a case arising in Connecticut, the Supreme Court held Fifth Amendment privilege against self-incrimination applicable to the states).

23. For discussion of these issues, see *Screws v. United States*, 325 U.S. 91 (1945).

24. *Georgia v. McCollum*, 112 S.Ct. 2348 (1992).

25. *Tennessee v. Garner*, 471 U.S. 1 (1985).

26. *California Jury Instructions: Criminal* § 9.26 (Fifth Ed. 1988).

27. Testimony of Sergeant Charles Duke in the federal trial, March 22, 1993.

28. Testimony of Sergeant Charles Duke in the federal trial, March 19, 1993 (adopting the language of Counsel Ira Salzman).

29. Testimony of Sergeant Charles Duke in the federal trial, March 22, 1993.

30. Id.

31. Id.

32. Smith, supra note 3, at 64.

33. Testimony of Sergeant Charles Duke in the federal trial, March 22, 1993.

34. Id.

35. Id.

36. Id.

37. See George P. Fletcher, *Rethinking Criminal Law* 555–62, 689 (1978).

38. Testimony of Rodney King in the federal trial, March 10, 1993.

39. As told to Anna Deavere Smith. See Smith, supra note 3, at 243.

40. *Los Angeles Times*, May 12, 1991, M5.

41. Testimony of Officer Melanie Singer in the state trial, March 6, 1992. Compare her testimony in the federal trial, March 26, 1993 ("it looked as if he had split the cheek from this portion here to the chin").

42. Id.

43. Koon, supra note 6, at 33–34.

44. *Los Angeles Times*, March 5, 1993, B1.

45. Testimony of Rodney King in the federal trial, March 9, 1993.

CHAPTER THREE

1. As quoted in Carole Agus, "Verdict's Familiar Injustice," *Newsday*, November 1, 1992, 3.

2. *Jerusalem Post*, November 4, 1993. (The Israeli term used in the cartoon is *Haredi*.)

3. See *Forward*, January 28, 1994, 7.

4. *Wisconsin v. Yoder*, 406 U.S. 205 (1972).

5. Richard Goldstein, "The New Anti-Semitism: A Geschrei," *Village Voice*, October 1, 1991, 33.

6. Stephen L. Carter, *The Culture of Disbelief* 60 (1993).

7. Philip Gourevitch, "The Crown Heights Riot and Its Aftermath," 95(1) *Commentary*, 29 (1993).

8. Kunstler initially thought that Nosair should rely on a plea of insanity. But Nosair insisted he was innocent. See *The New York Times*, December 23, 1991, B8.

9. *Washington Post*, December 23, 1991, A4.

10. *The New York Times*, November 13, 1991, B2.

11. *People v. Kern*, 149 App.Div.2d 187, 545 N.Y.S.2d 4 (1989) (decision based on state constitution).

12. *Jerusalem Post*, December 19, 1991.

13. *The New York Times*, February 1, 1994, A18.

14. See the reference to the lone hold-out labeled a "jackass" by the other jurors. *Jerusalem Post*, December 23, 1991.

15. The remark is attributed to a Miami lawyer, Ellis Rubin. *Washington Post*, December 23, 1991, A4.

16. Some people criticized the jury for its failure to convict Nosair of attempted murder against Carlos Acosta. The jurors responded, plausibly, that the state had not proven to their satisfaction that Nosair had shot with the intent to kill. *The New York Times*, December 23, 1991, B1.

17. National Public Radio, Morning Show, February 2, 1992.

18. Howard Jacobson, *Roots Schmoots: Journey Among Jews* 373 (1993).

19. *The New York Times*, December 1, 1991, A45.

20. *The New York Times*, December 23, 1992, A19.

21. See Richard Girgenti, *A Report to the Governor on the Disturbances in Crown Heights* Vol. I, 45 (1993). [Volume II hereafter cited as Girgenti Report (II).] The percentage of Jews living in Crown Heights is uncertain. The official figures show "White Nonhispanic" population to be 8.3%. Id. at 39. The percentage of Jews living in Brooklyn as a whole is about twice as high.

22. Id. at 56.

23. Id. at 57.

24. Girgenti Report (II) at 29.

25. The police later released Cleon Taylor because he was too young to book. The arrest was voided "for insufficient evidence." Trial testimony of Richard Sanossian, September 23, 1992.

26. Trial testimony of Officer Mark Hoppe, September 24, 1992.

27. Trial testimony of Detective Steven Litwin, September 30, 1992.

28. The last sentence is a response to Litwin's question, "What did he do?" Id.

29. Trial testimony of Sergeant Brian Wilson, October 1, 1992.

30. Trial testimony of Transit Officer Robert Lewis, October 2, 1992.

31. Girgenti Report (II) at 23–25.

32. This is based on an informal identification of 6 out of 120 names as Jewish. *The New York Times*, November 30, 1992, B3.

33. This is the composition at the start of the trial. See Girgenti Report (II) at 25. By the time of the verdict, a Hispanic had replaced one white juror.

34. Opening Statement by Arthur Lewis, September 23, 1992.

35. Id.

36. Id.

37. Id.

38. See Chapter Two at p. 44.

39. Trial proceedings, September 30, 1992.

40. Id.

41. Id.

42. Id.

43. Trial proceedings, October 2, 1992.

44. Id.

45. Id.

46. Girgenti Report (II) at 96.

47. Trial proceedings, October 15, 1992.

48. This analysis of the jury's behavior is based on extensive interviews of the jurors conducted by the researchers for the Girgenti Report (II) at 85–144.

49. Girgenti Report (II) at 92.

50. Trial proceedings, October 2, 1992.

51. Id.

52. *Wall Street Journal*, October 27, 1993, A23.

53. Girgenti Report (II) at 114.

54. *The New York Times*, November 13, 1992, B3.

55. 8 U.S.C. § 241.

56. 8 U.S.C. § 245(2)(B).

57. *The New York Times*, January 26, 1994, A1.

CHAPTER FOUR

1. E. Hale, *The History of the Pleas of the Crown 635 (1778 ed.)*.

2. Susan Brownmiller, *Against Our Will: Men, Women and Rape*, 244 (1957).

3. William Congreve, "The Morning Bride" (1697).

4. Brownmiller identifies Helene Deutsch, writing in the mid-1940s, as the leader of this movement. See Brownmiller, supra note 2, at 350–56.

5. John H. Wigmore, *Evidence in Trials at Common Law* § 924a (Chadbourn Ed., 1970).

6. *People v. Hernandez*, 61 Cal.2d 529, 393 P.2d 673, 39 Cal.Rptr. 361 (1964).

7. *State v. Snow*, 252 S.W. 629, 632 (Mo. 1923).

8. 61 Cal.2d at 531 n.1.

9. *Government of the Virgin Islands v. John*, 447 F.2d 69, 72 (3rd Cir. 1971).

10. Id. at 73.

11. *Wynne v. Commonwealth*, 216 Va. 355, 218 S.E.2d 445 (1975).

12. 410 U.S. 113 (1973).

13. California Penal Code § 1127d.

14. California Penal Code § 1127e.

15. Indiana Code § 35–37–4–4.

16. Susan Estrich, "Rape," 95 *Yale Law Journal* 1087 (1986).

17. See G. Gregory Garrison and Randy Roberts, *Heavy Justice: The State of Indiana v. Michael G. Tyson* 254–55 (1994) (prosecutor's recollections of the trial).

18. Id. at 255.

19. *The New York Times*, April 17, 1991, A17.

20. *Los Angeles Times*, December 12, 1991. A24.

21. Estrich, "Palm Beach Stories," 11 *Journal of Law and Philosophy* 5, 12–13 (1992).

22. *Tyson v. State of Indiana*, 619 N.E.2d 276, 286 (August 6, 1993).

23. Andrew Marvell, "To His Coy Mistress" (1650–52):

Had we but world enough and time,
This coyness, lady, would be no crime.

24. Lord Byron, "Don Juan" (1818).

25. Of course, the approach of the rational better might prove too much. A rational better might rely on other probative but prejudicial matters, such as William Kennedy Smith's record of sexual assaults against other women.

26. *People v. Olsen*, 36 Cal.3d 638, 685 P.2d 52 (1984) (reasonable mistake as to age of girl under 14 no defense).

27. See G. Gregory Garrison and Randy Roberts, supra note 17, at 245.

28. See id. at 245–47.

29. As quoted, id. at 245.

30. *Director of Pub. Prosecutions v. Morgan*, 1976 A.C. 182, 2 All E.R. 347, [1975] 2 W.L.R. 913 (H.L.). See also the later case, *Regina v. Cogan*, 2 All E.R. 1059, [1975] 3 W.L.R. 316 (C.A.).

31. 176 A.C. at 214, [1975] 2 All E.R. at 361.

32. Id.

33. I have criticized the decision at length in *Rethinking Criminal Law* 699–707 (1978).

34. *The Times*, May 7, 1975 (J. C. Smith); May 8, 1975 (Glanville Williams).

35. *Papajohn v. the Queen*, [1980] 2 Supreme Court Reports 120.

36. Brief for Appellant Michael Tyson, *Tyson v. State of Indiana*, at 41.

37. *Tyson v. State of Indiana*, 619 N.E.2d 276, 295–297 (August 6, 1993). Of course, Tyson himself could have generated an account of Washington's "equivocal behavior" and thus undermined his claim of actual consent. He would have had to testify that she said maybe instead of yes.

38. Id. at 305.

39. This usage is endorsed by the students of the *Harvard Law Review*. See "Developments in the Law—Legal Responses to Domestic Violence," 106 *Harvard Law Review* 1498 (1993).

40. Speech to the American Medical Association, March 10, 1994.

41. *Compare* " 'Til Death Do Us Part," *Time*, January 18, 1993, 38 (giving the figure as 22–35%) *with* Christina Hoff Sommers, *Who Stole Feminism? How Women Have Betrayed Women* 201–203 (1994) (debunking conventional statistics).

42. Id.

43. *State v. Norman*, 378 S.E.2d 8 (1989).

44. Id. at 9.

45. California Evidence Code § 1107(a).

46. California Evidence Code § 1107(b).

47. For a good argument, see Sharon Byrd, "Till Death Do Us Part: A Comparative Law Approach to Justifying Lethal Self-Defense by Battered Women," 1991 *Duke Journal of Comparative and International Law* 169.

48. See Richard Rosen, "On Self-Defense, Imminence, and Women Who Kill Their Batterers," 71 *North Carolina Law Review* 371 (1993).

49. *State v. Norman* at 18.

50. David Faigman, "The Battered Woman Syndrome and Self-Defense: A Legal and Empirical Dissent," 72 *Virginia Law Review* 619 (1986). For the foundations of this research, see Seligman, Maier, and Geer, "Alleviation of Learned Helplessness in the Dog," 73 *Journal of Abnormal Psychology* 246 (1968).

51. 72 *Virginia Law Review* at 641.

52. Anne Coughlin, "Excusing Women," 82 *California Law Review* 1 (1994).

53. Id. at 81.

54. Id. at 83.

55. Id.

56. Mira Mihajlovich, "Does Plight Make Right: The Battered Women Syndrome, Expert Testimony and the Law of Self-Defense," 62 *Indiana Law Review* 1253, 1274–75 (1987) (citing jury studies in the early 1980s).

57. *Los Angeles Times*, April 16, 1992, A3.

58. *Time*, September 27, 1993, 32.

59. *The New York Times*, January 29, 1994, A1.

60. See, in particular, "Menendez Justice," *Vanity Fair*, March 1994, 108.

61. See *The Orlando Sentinel*, January 29, 1994, A1; *Star Tribune*, January 29, 1994, A7.

62. The guiding jury instruction, *California Jury Instructions: Criminal* § 5.17 (Fifth Ed. 1988), reads as follows:

> A person, who kills another person in the honest but unreasonable belief in the necessity to defend against imminent peril to life or great bodily injury kills unlawfully, but does not harbor malice aforethought and is not guilty of murder.

Nothing in this language suggests that the defendants' perceptions should be controlling on the question of imminence. The leading case is *People v. Flannel*, 25 Cal.3d 668, 160 Cal.Rptr. 84, 603 P.2d 1 (1979). This opinion is also ambiguous on the same question.

63. *State v. Norman* at 18.

CHAPTER FIVE

1. Walter Schaeffer, "Federalism and State Criminal Procedure," 70 *Harvard Law Review* 1, 26 (1956).

2. European Convention on Human Rights Article 6, paragraph 1, sentence 1:

> In the determination of his civil rights and obligations or of any criminal charge against him, everyone is entitled to a fair and public hearing within a reasonable time by an independent and impartial tribunal established by law.

3. The full text of Article 11 (d) reads:

> Any person charged with an offence has the right . . . (d) to be presumed innocent until proven guilty according to law in a fair and public hearing by an independent and impartial tribunal.

4. *In re Murchison*, 349 U.S. 133, 136 (1955).

5. *Tyson v. State of Indiana*, 619 N.E.2d 276, 301 (1993) (Court of Appeals, Sullivan, J., dissenting) (emphasis added).

6. *Hayes v. Missouri*, 120 U.S. 68, 70 (1887).

7. 4 William Blackstone, *Commentaries on the Law of England* 358 (1765–69).

8. This was supposedly the view of Frederick the Great in Germany. See 1 Loewe-Rosenberg, *Die Strafprozessordnung* 623 (1963).

9. *Tyson v. State of Indiana*, 622 N.E. 2d 457 (1993).

10. Indiana Code of Judicial Conduct, Canon 3(C)(1).

11. *Tyson v. State of Indiana*, 619 N.E.2d 276, 300 n. 33 (1993).

12. G. Gregory Garrison and Randy Roberts, *Heavy Justice: The State of Indiana v. Michael G. Tyson* 240 (1994).

13. Id.

14. *Tyson v. State of Indiana*, 619 N.E.2d 276, 302 (1993) (dissenting opinion).

15. *Heavy Justice*, supra note 12, at 241–42.

16. Brief for Appellant at 53, citing Vivian Berger, "Man's Trial, Women's Tribulation: Rape Cases in the Courtroom," 77 *Columbia Law Review* 1, 67 (1977).

17. *Heavy Justice*, supra note 12, Acknowledgments at x.

18. United States Constitution, Fifth Amendment. According to the language of the Amendment, the charge may be made in a "presentment or indictment," and the requirement is applicable only in cases of "capital or otherwise infamous crime." And it does not apply in "cases arising in the land or naval forces, or in the Militia, when in actual service in time of War or public danger."

19. Id. The Fifth Amendment reads: ". . . nor shall any person be subject for the same offense to be twice put in jeopardy of life or limb."

20. Id. The Fifth Amendment reads: "nor shall any person be compelled in any criminal case to be a witness against himself."

21. *Hurtado v. California*, 110 U.S. 516 (1884).

22. *The New York Times*, April 5, 1993, A10.

23. *The New York Times*, March 1, 1993, A15.

24. See quote in Chapter Three at note 40.

25. United States Constitution, Article III, Section 3.

26. *Rogers v. Richmond*, 365 U.S. 534 (1961).

27. *Garrity v. New Jersey*, 385 U.S. 493 (1967).

28. *United States v. North*, 920 F.2d 786 (D.C. Cir. 1990), certiorari denied 111 S.Ct. 2235 (1991).

29. *Singer v. United States*, 380 U.S. 24 (1965) (a defendant does not have a constitutional right to insist on a bench trial).

30. *The New York Times*, May 29, 1993, A1.

31. *Richmond Newspapers, Inc. v. Virginia*, 448 U.S. 555, 571 (1980).

32. Id. at 572.

33. Id. at 573.

34. *Irvin v. Dowd*, 366 U.S. 717 (1961).

35. For examples of outrageous press coverage, see *Sheppard v. Maxwell*, 384 U.S. 333 (1966); *Estes v. Texas*, 381 U.S. 532 (1965).

36. *The New York Times*, April 22, 1994, B1.

CHAPTER SIX

1. See the comment of Jim Elliot, supra Chapter One, at p. 15.

2. For a similar proposal, see Paul Robinson, "Rules of Conduct and Principles of Adjudication," 57 *University of Chicago Law Review* 729, 766–67 (1990).

3. *The New York Times*, January 29, 1994, A1.

4. *Time*, February 4, 1985, 64.

5. This report is based on a report in *The New York Times*, April 14, 1994, B2.

6. Uniform Victims of Crime Act § 203.

7. Id., Comment. (Comments approved by ABA, February 9, 1993).

8. Id.

9. See *The New York Times*, April 14, 1994, B2.

10. StPO [German Code of Criminal Procedure] § 385, 395.

11. StPO [German Code of Criminal Procedure] § 185(3).

12. StPO [German Code of Criminal Procedure] § 390.

13. Uniform Victims of Crime Act § 216.

14. 501 U.S. 808, 111 S.Ct. 2597, 115 L.Ed.2d 720 (1991).

15. 115 L.Ed.2d at 729.

16. *Booth v. Maryland*, 482 U.S. 496 (1987).

17. 115 L.Ed.2d at 735.

18. Id. at 744.

19. *Booth v. Maryland*, 482 U.S. 496 (1987).

20. Immanuel Kant, *The Metaphysics of Morals* 140–45 (M. Gregor trans. 1991).

21. Exodus 21:22.

22. Kant, supra note 20, at 142.

23. See David Daube, *Studies in Biblical Law* 122–23 (1947).

24. Leviticus 19:16.

25. Jaime Malamud-Goti, "Human Rights Abuses in Fledgling Democracies: The Role of Discretion," in *Transition to Democracy in Latin America: The Role of the Judiciary* 225 (Irwin Stotzky ed. 1993).

CHAPTER SEVEN

1. Alexis de Tocqueville, *Democracy in America* 296 (Vintage ed. 1945).

2. "Jury Acquits Jack Kevorkian," *The New York Times*, May 3, 1994, A1.

3. Alexis de Tocqueville, supra note 1, at 297.

4. Harry Kalven, Jr., and Hans Zeisel, *The American Jury* 56 (1966).

5. Jon Van Dyke, *Jury Selection Procedures: Our Uncertain Commitment to Representative Panels* 3 (1977). 1 W. Holdsworth, *A History of English Law* 325 (1927); Charles Wells, "The Origin of the Petty Jury," 27 *Law Quarterly Review* 347, 357 (1911). For a general survey of the history, as understood by the Supreme Court, see *William v. Florida*, 399 U.S. 78, 88 n. 20 (1970).

6. *Williams v. Florida*, 399 U.S. 78, 100 (1970).

7. Id.

8. Id. at 100–101.

9. Peter Sperlich, ". . . And then there were six: the decline of the American Jury," 63 *Judicature* 262 (1980).

10. *Ballew v. Georgia*, 435 U.S. 223 (1978).

11. Stuart Nagel and Marian Neef, "Deductive Modeling to Determine an Optimum Jury Size and Fraction Required to Convict," 1975 *Washington University Law Quarterly* 933.

12. *Ballew v. Georgia*, 435 U.S. 223, 234 (1978).

13. Nagel and Neef, supra note 11, at 946–48, 956, 975.

14. *Johnson v. Louisiana*, 406 U.S. 356 (1972).

15. *Apodaca v. Oregon*, 406 U.S. 404 (1972).

16. *Burch v. Louisiana*, 47 L.W. 4393 (1979).

17. *Batson v. Kentucky*, 476 U.S. 79, 97 (1986).

18. Id. at 85. The principle dates to *Strauder v. West Virginia*, 100 U.S. 303, 305 (1880).

19. Id. at 102.

20. The dissenters were Justices Burger and Rehnquist.

21. *Batson v. Kentucky*, 476 U.S. at 107 (concurring opinion), citing *Hayes v. Missouri*, 120 U.S. 68, 70 (1887).

22. There are exceptions. In *People v. Wheeler*, 22 Cal.3d 258, 583 P.2d 748 (1978), the California Supreme Court wrote: "[T]he People no less than individual defendants are entitled to a trial by an impartial jury drawn from a representative cross-section of the community."

23. *Powers v. Ohio*, 499 U.S. 400, 407 (1991).

24. *Georgia v. McCollum*, 112 S.Ct. 2348 (1992).

25. This is the argument used by Justices O'Connor and Scalia in their dissenting opinions in *Georgia v. McCollum*, 112 S.Ct. 2348 (1992).

26. *Strauder v. West Virginia*, 100 U.S. at 308.

27. *Georgia v. McCollum*, 112 S.Ct. at [44].

28. Id. at [9].

29. *J.E.B. v. Alabama ex rel. T.B.*, 114 S.Ct. 1419 (1994).

30. Id. at [25].

31. Id.

32. Carol Gilligan, *In a Different Voice: Psychological Theory and Women's Development* (1982).

33. J. Gregory Garrison and Randy Roberts, *Heavy Justice: The State of Indiana v. Michael G. Tyson* 193–94 (1994).

34. Reid Haster, Steven Penrod, and Nancy Pennington, *Inside the Jury* 141 (1983).

35. *State v. Davis*, 504 N.W.2d 767 (1993), certiorari denied May 23, 1994.

36. For a survey, see Van Dyke, supra note 5, at 45–83.

37. *Twilight: Los Angeles 1992*, as performed at the Cort Theatre in New York, April 1994. The interview with "Maria" (last name not given) is not included in the published version of the play. The quotations are based on my recollections of the performance.

38. See Van Dyke, supra note 5, at 167–69.

39. See James P. Levine, *Juries and Politics* 36–37 (1992).

40. For these and other proposals, see *The New York Times*, April 7, 1994, B1.

41. Alexis de Tocqueville, supra note 1, at 295–96.

42. George P. Fletcher, *A Crime of Self-Defense: Bernhard Goetz and the Law on Trial* 243, n. 9 (1988).

43. James Fyfe, "Enforcement Workshop: The Expert Witness in Suits Against Police (Part 2)," 21 *Criminal Law Bulletin* 515, 518–20 (1985).

44. See Chapter Two at 48–50.

45. *Los Angeles Times*, October 24, 1993, A1.

46. *Los Angeles Times*, October 21, 1993, B1.

47. *Los Angeles Times*, October 20, 1993, B1.

48. *The New York Times*, May 3, 1994, A20.

49. Id.

50. See note 37 supra.

51. Jerome Frank, *Law and the Modern Mind* 181 (1930).

52. See note 1 supra.

CHAPTER EIGHT

1. See the *Timeline* beginning at p. 259 for details.

2. See the *Timeline* for the amusing effort to locate the trial in the "right" Florida community.

3. *Newsweek*, January 24, 1994, 52.

4. See the discussion of *Payne v. Tennessee*, 111 S.Ct. 2597 (1991) in Chapter Six at p. 198–201.

5. *Wiedergutmachung: Alternativ Entwurf* (1992) (draft statute prepared by a group of 18 German professors).

6. *Batson v. Kentucky*, 476 U.S. 79, 108 (Marshall, J., concurring).

7. Jon Van Dyke, *Jury Selection Procedures: Our Uncertain Commitment to Representative Panels* 7 (1977).

8. I am indebted to Akhil Amar for this analogy.

9. *Groppi v. Wisconsin*, 400 U.S. 404 (1971).

10. See George P. Fletcher, *A Crime of Self-Defense: Bernhard Goetz and the Law on Trial* 186–188 (1988).

ACKNOWLEDGMENTS

Many of my colleagues read portions or all of the manuscript, agreed with parts of it, and criticized other parts. Particularly worthy of mention are Vivian Berger, Harold Edgar, Kent Greenawalt, Henry Monaghan, Richard Uviller, Bruce Ackerman, Akhil Amar, Saul Berman, Anne Coughlin, and Jaime Malamud-Goti. I also received valuable support and advice from my student research assistants, Pamela Csewska, Jack Kint, and Seth Kalvert. My associate Russell Christopher contributed greatly. I appreciate the occasional enthusiasm of colleagues and co-workers about the project, but some, no doubt, would insist that I add the usual caveat: I alone am responsible for my arguments and for my ten reform proposals.

I am grateful to the management and staff at Court TV, particularly to Fred Graham and Vicki Stivala, who graciously enabled me to view tapes of the entire Yankel Rosenbaum trial in their New York newsroom.

I am indebted to my teacher Herbert Morris for helping me, at the last minute, to formulate the subtitle of this book.

Daniela Lupas helped me in innumerable ways and more than anyone else curbed my excesses and boosted my spirits at times when both were necessary.

INDEX

A

Abraham, Nemesio, 90

Abramson, Leslie, 141, 143, 145, 238

abuse. *See also* battered women; Menendez case; Simpson, O.J., case
claims as defense tactic, 140–147
as homicide justification, 137
recalled, 140, 263
by victims, 141–147, 243–245, 255

accidental killings, 19, 20, 22, 139

Accused, The, 102

Acosta, Carlos, 76, 80, 81, 84, 262, 264

acquittals
appeal of, 96, 162, 224–225
Bobbitt case, 268, 269
clarification of grounds for, 180
Denny case, 268
jury's power of, 229
Kahane case, 72, 84–86, 185, 226, 264
King case, 103, 245–246
Lozano case, 267
odds in favor of, 152
Rosenbaum case, 5, 72, 103, 266
Smith case, 115, 118, 264
Tyson case, 125

African-Americans
anti-Semitism and, 73–74, 75, 77, 83
on juries, 41–43, 67–68, 213–217, 250
on King case juries, 41–43, 67–68
response to King case, 1–2, 3, 51, 66–67, 186
in Rosenbaum case, 91, 92

Against Our Will: Men, Women and Rape, 108–113

Allen, Bryant, 39

American Bar Association, 5, 190–193, 194, 198, 248

American Civil Liberties Union, 161

American Jewish Committee, 74

American Law Institute, 24, 26

Anderson, John, 89, 97, 271

Anti-Defamation League, 72–74

anti-Semitism, 70–77, 81–84, 86, 92–94

appeals
King case. *See* King, Rodney, federal case
Norman case, 135–136, 146
by prosecutors, 96, 162, 224–225
rape cases, 111–112
Tyson case. *See* Tyson, Mike, case

Argentina, 204

King, Rodney, case (*continued*)
   change of venue, 41–43, 169–
      170, 252, 253, 263, 264
   expert testimony in, 35, 46–50,
      55–61, 231–233, 235, 255–
      256
   grand jury, 160
   indictments, 38, 160, 262
   judge's contact with
      prosecution, 41–42, 153
   jury selection in, 251, 257–
      258
   Los Angeles police internal
      investigation, 165, 175
   PCP use as factor in, 41, 44,
      45, 107
   race as issue in, 226. *See also*
      African-Americans
King, Rodney, federal case, 48–
   49, 51–61, 165–166, 266
   appeal, 67–68, 175, 205–206,
      270, 272
   double jeopardy issue in, 161–
      162
   jury, 221, 226, 238, 253
   King's testimony at, 62, 65–67,
      249
   prosecutor's ethnic group, 118
   sentencing, 68, 175–176, 205,
      272
Kolatch, Sari, 90, 96, 98, 118
Kollek, Teddy, 69–70
Koon, Stacey C., 41, 44–46, 61–
   64, 161, 162, 186
   appeal by, 67–68, 175, 205–
      206, 270, 272
   indictment of, 38, 262
   internal investigation
      testimony, 165, 175
   at King arrest, 40
   sentencing of, 37, 175–176,
      205, 272
Koresh, David, 267

Kowalski, Barry, 56, 66, 118–119
Kuby, Ronald, 77, 105
Kunstler, William, 77, 78, 79, 81–
   83, 105, 153, 228

L

Lansing, Jill, 145
Lasch, Moira, 118–119
Latinos, 51, 241
Lau, Gordon, 13, 14
"learned helplessness," 135, 138,
   140
Leeper, James, 96
Levy, Roland, 30, 33
Lewis, Arthur, 91–98, 100, 102,
   103, 106, 197, 228
Lewis, Robert, 89, 91, 95, 96, 99–
   100
Lifsh, Yosef, 87, 263
Litwin, Sergeant, 95, 96
Lloyd, Clement, 261
Los Angeles, City of
   Denny suit against, 267
   King suit against, 269
Los Angeles District Attorney, 45
Los Angeles Police Department
   (LAPD)
   defendants. *See* King, Rodney,
      case
   effect of King case on internal
      loyalty, 62–65
   image in King case of, 44–46
   internal King case
      investigation, 165, 175
   policy of, 48–50, 58–61, 232–
      233, 255–256
Los Angeles riots, 1992, 1, 37–38,
   265
Lozano, William, case, 170, 242,
   261, 262, 265, 267
Lubavitch sect, 71, 87